Sisters in Time

SISTERS IN TIME

Imagining Gender in Nineteenth-Century British Fiction

SUSAN MORGAN

New York Oxford
OXFORD UNIVERSITY PRESS
1989

Oxford University Press

Oxford New York Toronto
Delhi Bombay Calcutta Madras Karachi
Petaling Jaya Singapore Hong Kong Tokyo
Nairobi Dar es Salaam Cape Town
Melbourne Auckland

and associated companies in
Berlin Ibadan

Published by Oxford University Press, Inc.,
200 Madison Avenue, New York, New York 10016

Oxford is a registered trademark of Oxford University Press

Library of Congress Cataloging-in-Publication Data
Morgan, Susan, 1943–
Sisters in time: imagining gender in nineteenth-century
British fiction/Susan Morgan.
p. cm. Includes index. ISBN 0-19-505822-4
1. English fiction—19th century—History and criticism.
2. Heroines in literature. 3. Sex role in literature.
4. Women in literature. I. Title.
PR868.H4M67 1989 823′.8′09352042—dc 19 88-30285 CIP

9 8 7 6 5 4 3 2 1

Printed in the United States of America
on acid-free paper

To Eric, for the circus and the bridge

Acknowledgments

I am grateful to many people for their help with this book: to Jerome McGann for his consistent intellectual generosity in caring about, and expanding, my ideas; to the ACLS and Vassar College for helping to pay for the time to write down those ideas; to Stuart Tave, who has not read this particular project, for generally inspiring my thinking about fiction; to Charles Pierce for lending me his clarity in shaping my thoughts; to Susan Kneedler for the richness of her vision of Austen's fiction; to Barbara Page and Beth Darlington for reading, and improving, parts of the manuscript; to the anonymous readers, whose suggestions were so extraordinarily helpful as to leave me regretting that I have no way to thank them personally; to my beloved students at Stanford and Vassar for animating so vividly my one constant arena of discourse about ficton; to Eric Goodman for, at the least, his editorial brilliance; and, finally, to Ethan and Seneca Goodman for always reminding me that the life of the mind is, by itself, a wicked lie.

Contents

Sisters in Time

1

Imagining Gender in Nineteenth-Century British Fiction

The best fiction is truer than history.

THOMAS HARDY

The best fiction is history.

SUSAN MORGAN

Elizabeth Bennet, Emma Woodhouse, Jeanie and Effie Deans, Lucy Snowe, Catherine Earnshaw, Becky Sharp, Mary Barton, Lily Dale, Dorothea Brooke, Gwendolen Harleth, Clara Middleton, Diana Warwick, Esther Waters, Tess Durbeyfield, Sue Bridehead, Kate Croy, and, of course, those traveling Americans, Isabel Archer, Maggie Verver, and Milly Theale—for many of us these names echo powerfully, invoking the great stories told about them and, more generally, invoking one of the most impressive periods of sustained productivity in a genre, British fiction in the nineteenth century. There are other names as well, too many to mention, some the inventions of the same writers who created these characters and some the inventions of writers less presently familiar. What must strike us about these creations is that they are all women.

I begin with these women, with the phenomenon itself, the fact of them, the sheer weight of their collective existence. And that weight is more than mere quantity of numbers. In their novels these women play a major, usually the major, role. They are not a Daisy Buchanan or even a Hester Prynne, significant, yes, perhaps even central, but as some combination of myth and pawn. Nor are they a Sophia Western, too naturalistically luscious to be mythic but hardly the main event. They don't exist as an other, however dynamic, outside the central consciousness of the narrative. And they cannot be summed up as one of those convenient siblings, the light and dark heroine. They are not the reward or the beings about whom or for whom others undergo struggles of conscience. They undergo those struggles, make their choices, and live out, or perhaps die of, the consequences of their actions. Like everyone else, they pays their money and takes their chances. So often in literature, that everyone else has been male. But in Britain, in the nineteenth century, in novel after novel, there these women are.

Of course, the men are there as well. I need only mention Edward Waverley, Heathcliff, Henry Esmond, Adam Bede, Willoughby Patterne, and Michael Henshard. But their collective literary existence is hardly surprising, and this book, though it will take them up, is not about them. It begins with the fact that in a culture where women, both in life and in art, have continually been conceived of as less central to human concerns than men, one of the major periods of fiction should be so rich in novels that locate their center of consciousness in a woman. The nineteenth century, the great age of the British novel, is also the age of the great heroines. I began writing this book to examine why.

The subject matter is hardly new. Among many critical studies that consider British heroines, Nancy K. Miller and Roy Roussel have looked at the heroine in eighteenth-century fiction, and have considered communities of women and men portrayed in novels written by both men and women.[1] Lee Edwards considered heroines in two centuries of English and American novels.[2] Tony Tanner examined heroines in three French and German fictions to discuss adultery in the novel; John Lucas considered the question of women in a few nineteenth-century novels in *The Literature of Change*; and Jenni Calder analyzed women and marriage in Victorian fiction.[3] Studies more focused on the nineteenth-century British heroine include Rachel Brownstein's recent *Becoming a Heroine*.[4] And the book that most strongly influenced my own work is Carolyn Heilbrun's *Toward a Recognition of Androgyny*.[5]

What distinguishes my approach from many others may initially be no more than its emphasis on the very quantity of these heroines. I begin by insisting on precisely the wholeness of the phenomenon, the point that the creation of an Isabel Archer is linked to the creation of a

Diana Warwick, a Gwendolen Harleth, a Becky Sharp, and a Lucy Snowe. The very extensiveness of the heroines in nineteenth-century British novels is significant, is worth trying to explain. Indeed, to borrow James's famous phrase about Isabel Archer, I want positively to make an ado about it.

Immediately, difficult questions of interpretation arise. How do these heroines function, and how does their function express their being women? Or does it? Why, when authors could choose men or women leads, did they so often choose women? This question is particularly interesting with writers such as Sir Walter Scott, George Eliot, and Henry James, who in different books use protagonists of different sexes, and with varying degrees of success.[6] Perhaps the current, most prominent questions concern women writers, women writing about women. What did their choices of heroines have to do with their own place in the culture, their values, their class, their possibilities in relation to men's, their sense of themselves as artists and as women? And how are those issues manifested and/or transformed in the content and the form of their work? These last two questions probably direct most feminist studies of nineteenth-century British literature that have been undertaken in this decade. They have definitely been the issues of the moment. But they are not mine.

These specific questions of focus and interpretation are framed by even more difficult theoretical questions that continue to trouble me. Have not the past fifteen years of criticism labeled it a suspect, if not an absolutely reactionary, procedure to try to talk at all about such an old humanist concept as heroines? First, there is no such thing as a literary phenomenon separated from questions of language, of class, of culture, of life. Connected to this insight is a second: that the very notion of character, with its implicit idea of a separate or contained self, is false. I want particularly to address this second insight.

It was exhilarating to learn that the author/subject is dead. But the news was also, in its frequently aggressive language and its structure of "down with the old order, up with the new," tiresomely familiar, another turn in what William Blake called the Orc cycle, another critical event with a disquietingly masculine timbre. Many feminists have suggested that rejecting the subject may be theoretically radical but can also be reactionary, a way of eliminating any real political change. As Paul Smith argues in his useful discussion of the subject, current conceptions "have tended to produce a purely *theoretical* subject, removed almost entirely from the political and ethical realities in which human agents actually live." Such conceptions "tend to foreclose upon the possibility of resistance."[7] More specifically, Andreas Huyssen asks, "doesn't post-structuralism, where it simply denies the subject altogether, jettison the chance of challenging the ideology of the subject (as male, white, and middle class) by developing alternative and different notions of subjectivity?"[8]

The question may be what, and who, we mean by the term *subject*. Masculine critics, long dominating the field of nineteenth-century British fiction in both writing and publishing, generally did not present the phenomenon of the nineteenth-century British heroine as significant. They simply overlooked it in validating more apparently substantial topics. This is not to say that heroines weren't analyzed and evaluated. They were, but as forms of the traditional "subject" (effectively male). Moreover, the heroines and their novels (and the heroes as well) were frequently evaluated in terms of how well they fulfilled the readers' unexamined notions of the "subject." It is certainly true that current critical theorists along with feminist theorists and practical critics have made critical blindness and sexism posing as "humanism" untenable. As Jane Flax points out in her helpful article, "Postmodernism and Gender Relations in Feminist Theory," "the single most important advance in feminist theory is that the existence of gender relations has been problematized. Gender can no longer be treated as a simple, natural fact."[9]

The answer, then, to privileging the traditional "subject" is not to do away with the notion of the "subject" in our approaches to literature. Instead, we need to historicize the subject, to recognize it as a matter of culture, rather than of nature, and as having particular, and changing, clusters of attributes. As George Eliot told us long ago, character is character in the making. Our interpretative task must therefore include seeking to render explicit which definitions of the "subject" both the text and the reader sustain.

This obligation seems to me not only generally true but also particularly crucial when the field of study is nineteenth-century British novels. To approach them with a notion of the "subject" as a fixed or essential self is to misinterpret completely the temporal nature of their enterprise. But to approach them without aiming to develop a flexible notion of the "subject" as some sort of human agency is also to deny their political force. Either position seems to me to preclude appreciating their achievement. Indeed, I would argue that when Paul Smith calls for a responsible criticism that includes "recognition of both the specificity of any 'subject's' history and also of the necessary negotiation with other 'subjects'," and when Nancy K. Miller calls for

"Changing the Subject," they are describing the project not only of current twentieth-century criticism but also of much nineteenth-century British fiction.[10] And that project, like the current revolution in criticism, is tied up with questions of gender.

One of the most important ways in which recent critical theory took up the insight that a text, as well as a subject, does not stand alone has been to insist on the cultural, psychological, and social significance of the sex of its creator.[11] With the explosion of feminist criticism in the 1970s, perhaps the simplest approach, suddenly illuminating but less popular now in the 1980s was to point out how literature has reflected, examined, and sometimes propagated women's inferior status in the culture.[12] With this basis of woman-as-victim, a more complex critical approach developed. It may well have started with Virginia Woolf's observation that sometimes women writers, having trouble finding a voice in a male culture, turn for relief and resuscitation to the works of other women writers.[13] Feminist readers, from Mary Ellmann to Kate Millett to Ellen Moers to Elaine Showalter to Sandra Gilbert and Susan Gubar, have recovered and explored an entire network of connections and influences among women writers.

To consider women authors as a connected group has proved a rich critical standpoint.[14] The strategies have ranged from the mythic to the linguistic to the historical, while the underlying perspective is most often psychological. This approach looks to the heretofore hidden sources of women's power. Its presumption, cultural rather than biological, is that "because the female subject has been excluded from the polis, and hence decentered, 'disoriginated,' deinstitutionalized, etc., her relation to integrity and textuality, desire and authority, is structurally different."[15]

The critical notion of a separate women's tradition, while properly insisting on the political and social dimensions of our literary inheritance, has some practical and theoretical problems. One practical problem is that many of the nineteenth-century heroines of British novels, heroines whom I read as positive forces, are inscribed by the voice of a man. Some current feminist criticism is moving away from the vision of a separate women's tradition and turning to the ways both men and women participate in similar traditions. In this study I argue implicitly against the notion of a woman's voice in fiction. I admire and, by implication at least, defend many fictional images of women created by men. This is not to say that the heroines in men's and women's books are identical, or indistinguishable according to the sex of their authors. It is to say that many nineteenth-century novels written by women are deeply and positively intertwined with many written by men, just as many written by men are deeply and positively intertwined with many written by women. And it is also to say that a positing of any particular narrative tradition in that century seems to me dangerously inaccurate if it ignores those deep connections between the work of male and female novelists.[16]

Between them, the works of Scott and Austen shaped the appropriate topics of novels for the following fifty or more years. Of course, Eliot was deeply influenced by Austen and Elizabeth Gaskell, much more deeply than readers have acknowledged or have critically explored. And part of my purpose here is to present some of the facets of that influence. But the same must be said of Scott's neglected influence. It wasn't just that everyone read Scott's novels. Everyone loved them. The popularity of his work in the first half of the nineteenth century was enormous. I view as a serious compliment Eliot's extravagant claim that "I worship Scott so devoutly" that "it is a personal grief, a heart-wound to me when I hear a depreciating or slighting word about him."[17] He was certainly the favorite novelist of the Brontë children. And who is to say, for example, that when Gaskell wrote her novels the claims and griefs of her own motherhood or the sights of working-class Manchester loomed larger as an imaginative influence than her extensive childhood reading of Scott.[18] All these influences, surely, had their day.

Why, then, should we as feminist critics work to delineate a major set of relationships among the fictions of a group of early and mid-nineteenth-century novelists and just count Scott out of our consideration, a writer the women novelists themselves strongly counted in? To borrow part of Nancy Armstrong's account of her own critical enterprise, I focus on "the extent to which the gender of literary language is not in fact bound to the sex of the writer but to the rules of the genre."[19] I consider gender not literally but literarily, in terms of the definitions of gender imagined by, imaged in, the text.[20] My focus on character, on the phenomenon of the heroine, and my belief that the significance of the "subject" is connected in essential ways to the novel's treatment of time in the nineteenth century place this study outside considerations of the sex of the authors and hinge almost everything on the gender of the characters.

But does such an approach simply revert to another isolation of, depoliticization of, and glorification of the sacred "text?" Does it create some pure realm of literary history? The reason I believe it doesn't has partly to do with some of the problems created by the focus on the sex of the author. The political problem has been captured in Lillian Robinson's critique of much earlier feminist criticism, that "women's literature and the female tradition tend to be evoked as an autonomous cultural experience, not impinging on the rest of cultural history."[21] The tendency to approach novels by women as separate from, as "not impinging on," novels written by men is an example of Robinson's point.

Recent feminist readers whose critical enterprise has included placing women's literature in relation to the rest of cultural history have pointed to a related, theoretical problem. As Armstrong warns, "what we have implicitly done by making a separate tradition of such relatively homebound authors as Anne Radcliffe, Austen, the Brontës, Mrs. Gaskell, Elizabeth Barrett Browning, George Eliot, and Virginia Woolf is to make men the participants and engineers of history, the creators of ideology and forgers of political conscience."[22] In other words, even when we grant that to select works by the sex of the author means to acknowledge the forms of culture rather than of biology, to recognize the radically different cultural messages that have shaped women and men in our society, and also to recognize the intertwining of literature with issues of class, race, and culture, we are still in serious critical difficulty. To read works by women in relation to a dominant cultural ideology that would silence women binds the texts necessarily, and thus ahistorically, by their definition as responses to an encompassing context. Rebels or victims, the authors, and their books remain caught in a cycle they have not made and, most crucially, are not defined as having the power to remake. Aiming to place them within their cultural frame, we may actually have placed them outside time.

Many postmodern critics from Fredric Jameson and Michel Foucault to Gayatri Spivak and Edward Said have taught us to understand that literature is complicitous in culture, is not a matter of eternal verities but of temporal ideologies. One special revelation that feminist criticism, particularly understanding the dominance of the patriarchy, has stressed is that literature's complicity need not reduce it to some sort of party organ. Literature is not, on the one hand, the voice of the dominant masculine ideology (with, possibly, if female authored, another rebellious voice within it). It is not, on the other hand, always powerless to make policy itself, a tool of, rather than a participant in, shaping culture.[23]

But the response that privileges works by women may ultimately depower them as shapers of both literary and cultural ideology. An essential critical enterprise must be to locate the political power of women's fiction. The pitfall seems to be that—either by generically reading women-authored texts in terms of a repressed or conventional surface with strategies of self-expression and innovation underneath or by discounting the major cultural influences of literature and thus of the women and the men who wrote it—we may ourselves participate in promoting an ideology that insists on women's powerlessness, in their lives and in their words.[24]

As we have begun to place the works of women in relation to the culture, we have run the risk of offering a partial insight for a whole truth—for example, the popular critical dichotomy of proper lady versus woman writer.[25] While ample evidence exists that the ideology of the lady flourished in Victorian England, we have too easily generalized it as the major public definition of womanhood that real women had to face. Yet no convincing historical argument exists to support the conclusion that the ideology of the angel in the house had the status of a dominant ideology. Nor does evidence exist to refute the suggestion, as in my later discussion of Gaskell's *Ruth*, that the ideology was transformed, and even inverted, into a call for the public role of women. Such evidence as the novels themselves argues that women did have a strong voice in shaping Victorian culture.[26] Given the many public voices of nineteenth-century British women, the accurate question may be, what in the culture enabled them to speak?

Novels can, and many novels do, create their own definitions of masculine and feminine values, definitions that may or may not subscribe to the external definitions of their culture or their readers. That is surely part of their charm. And it is also part of their significant power within a culture to function as one of the major modes of modifying and reinventing ideologies as well as disseminating them.[27] Culture, after all, consists of changing structures, and surely a literary criticism that sees literature as a pawn of the forces of culture is as suspect as one that sees literature as culturally untouched. One of the substantive and fascinating patterns in British fiction develops through the diverse and related ways different novels define and explore the notion of gender. This study attempts to trace a particular pattern in some nineteenth-century novels.

These novels represent gender in terms of its usefulness as a tool for social progress, a means of changing, and thereby improving, the ways we can choose to live in time. Whatever the practical social purposes novelists such as Gaskell, Eliot, or George Meredith had in writing their novels, there were also more fluid, less defined, and more tentative qualities to their work. I assume generally that the novels I discuss represent voices in what was a continuing and unresolved debate about the future of England, voices that should be interpreted more as exploratory and suggestive inventions than as reflections of an already established ideology or as calls to specific reforms. Whether these voices were heard, whether they had a political and social influence in reshaping cultural as well as literary ideologies, and what particularly that influence might have been are all questions this study does not begin to address. Its effort does not go beyond suggesting why such questions need to be asked. But they remain, nonetheless, of crucial critical importance.

This study, then, focuses primarily on gender as a category of analysis and concentrates narrowly on writers' words rather than on both their words and their lives and on the public effects of their words. Certainly the latter is the more encompassing, the truer, vision. Yet literary history is a part of, not apart from, real history. Literature is a part of culture, and however often it may be just an expression of culture, it is also often a real power within it. That power, that voice, can be raised to create or support or subvert many ideologies. What for me justifies the incomplete vision of this book is the effort to describe and trace a particular strain of belief in nineteenth-century England articulated and explored in novels. Its power is yet to be evaluated in our understanding of Victorian political, cultural, and literary history.

In *Toward a Recognition of Androgyny*, Carolyn Heilbrun suggested that "in the novel as a whole, and especially the English novel, women characters and the embodied 'feminine' impulse have occupied an especially important place."[28] Heilbrun's nonliteral commitment to the feminine impulse exists in the context of her book's more extensive commitment to androgyny. Heilbrun locates the literary existence of the woman as hero as a "modern historical phenomenon," appearing in novels from around 1880 to 1920.[29] I attempt to extend Heilbrun's argument by suggesting that the phenomenon of the feminine heroic occurs in British fiction throughout the nineteenth century. Beginning with Austen's novels, I turn back to some of our traditional heroines, to the characters engaged in the pervasive activities of nineteenth-century British fiction, the sagas of courtship and marriage, as well as to heroines with a different tale to tell. These stories offer some of the most positive images of women that our literature has produced. To borrow W. M. Thackeray's subtitle for *Vanity Fair*, these are novels without a hero because they are novels with a heroine. "Woman as hero was born, not from feminism, but from the author's realization that women at that moment best symbolized the human condition."[30]

An answer to the ontological question of this glittering constellation of nineteenth-century heroines must expand to a perspective that can link the idea of the feminine to many other historical issues. Austen's heroines embody radical alternatives to the classic Pygmalion and Galatea pattern of roles for women in eighteenth-century fiction. In the process of creating and understanding themselves and other characters, these heroines dramatize the connections between imagination and time. Scott's great contribution, the first peasant heroine in British fiction, Jeanie Deans, embodies a definition of a new kind of hero, one available both to men and to women. Consciously or not, the new heroinism carries a sense of history that can take us out of repeating the past. The work of both Scott and Austen is infused with social optimism, including a prophetic sense of the power of fictions to offer a way to a better future, to be portraits of a world that could be (even when, as with Scott, these take the literal form of portraits of a world that has been).

The essential argument of this book, an argument that will gain depth and carry conviction only through particular analyses of the novels themselves, is that the great march of British heroines in the nineteenth century exists in part because it was through women leads that writers, both male and female, could successfully dramatize their pervasive concerns about history and community progress. The novels I take up have a social purpose in the sense that they contain visions of how life, and I mean life outside novels, could be better, not only for individuals but centrally for the communities, the villages, and cities of England, for the nation itself. The answers the novels suggest are, of course, varied. But they share the historical consciousness that the future must not repeat the past. And basic to that consciousness is the idea that to continue traditional definitions of gender does mean to be trapped in a cycle of repetition, and, therefore, to remain outside history. To change must mean to change what we mean by masculine and feminine, male and female. Gender, then, must be an issue in any account of Victorian notions of progress. Indeed, an idea of feminization is at the center of nineteenth-century fiction's ideas of historical process.

From the beginning of this study, with the chapter on Scott and, perhaps less obviously, on Austen, the category of heroine is critically inadequate. Such specifics as the relations between Scott's young heroes and his peasant heroine; the links for Gaskell between the private and public spheres; the changing choices for lead characters in Meredith's and James's work; and such constant topics as the descriptions of and relations between characters; what writers borrowed from previous writers and transformed; and the identification of a writer with his as well as her heroine all point to a narrative commitment not merely to female leading characters. A better way to describe the shared interest of these novelists and the shared issues in their novels is the question of how to define feminine, and masculine, qualities. And the further question these novels play with is how rearranging these definitions can also rearrange relations between characters and, both inside and outside fiction, can change the relations between private and public events.

This book thus investigates the significance of gender in some influential nineteenth-century fictions. Its materials include books by men and women, with the principle of selection not being a writer's sex but rather a writer's interest in issues of progress and gender. Its subject is how, in certain nineteenth-century novels, living in time, in history, is understood as a matter of becoming feminized.[31] Its concern, initially with female leading characters, is more accurately with gender as an imaginative category, with the meaning of feminine and masculine as these terms may be dramatized through female and male characters. Like the novels it examines, it assumes that gender differences are a matter of culture, deeply absorbed. And also like the novels, it views those culturally imposed differences—whether their cause be evolutionary, psycholinguistic, reproductive, or merely unknown—as open to change.[32] Gender differences are, of course, real. But they are nonetheless artificial. Recognizing this does not mean replacing the inevitabilities of biology with the inevitabilities of culture. As Jane Flax warns, "Gender can become a metaphor for biology just as biology can become a metaphor for gender."[33]

Thinking about gender critically requires that we become constantly attentive to three continuing but still historical truths: our culture's hostility to what it calls the feminine, indeed, its use of the label *feminine* to function precisely as a catch-all for qualities and values it would devalue; the cultural pressure to cloak coercion in inevitability—and thereby to deny the possibility of choice—by identifying culture with nature, feminine and masculine with actual women and men; and every reader's complex and partly unexamined notions about gender.

Gender definitions are, finally, the products of human imagination. They therefore can be reimagined. That is part of the activity of many nineteenth-century British novels. I argue that the appropriate feminist critical approach to nineteenth-century British fiction is to discuss not simply women, whether as authors or as characters, but masculine and feminine, whether appearing as men or as women, as authors or as characters. I would claim that the material of this book is what Nancy Miller calls feminocentric novels, but in a significant rather than a literal sense.[34] Its subject is heroines as leading characters in their stories. And the last of its heroines is Lambert Strether, a man.

The topic of gender is hardly new in the history of literary criticism. Long before the writings of recent feminist writers illuminated for many readers, including me, the value of considering gender in interpreting British fiction, it had been recognized as a significant element in eighteenth-century novels and used in interpreting them. *Tom Jones* and *Tristram Shandy*, both much admired and much credited as formative influences on the development of the novel, though strikingly different from each other in story, style, and point of view, share a fundamental quality. That quality is intimately connected to the kind of strong critical appreciation the two novels have received. They are both about a man, and not just in the literal sense that the title character is the hero. They are both specifically concerned with male virility, with, of course, the penis. Handsome Tom Jones sports the easy, assured confidence and enjoys the adventures that come of having a reliable and virtually irresistible best friend, while Tristram Shandy probes with alluringly obsessive virtuosity the anxieties arising from a possibly defective piece. To paraphrase Churchill, never has so much been so gloriously made from so little.[35]

Among traditional readings of eighteenth-century British novels, the virility of Henry Fielding's fiction and the comic longing for virility of Laurence Sterne's (brilliantly revealing, I was taught, man's confrontation with his mortality) were gracefully counterpointed by the supposedly feminine charms of Samuel Richardson's fiction, its insights into the subtleties of the female mind.[36] If Tom Jones has long sparkled brightly among critics as the quintessential action hero of eighteenth-century fiction, with Tristram Shandy the intellectual hero, Clarissa Harlowe has reigned as their dark queen, the quintessential heroine. This early instance of critical attention to gender in novels significantly affected interpretations of Fielding's and Richardson's fiction. First, such attention generated a rich collection of supposedly descriptive qualities that have amounted to virtually a definition of masculine and feminine in the work of these novelists. *Tom Jones* and

Joseph Andrews offer external realism, panorama, event, action, a breath of fresh air, the great outdoors, sophistication, everything that stands up to be counted, the outer world. *Clarissa Harlowe* offers psychology, motive, obsessions, attention to minutiae, passions, intensity, all that circles in on itself, the inner world. Thus art reproduces biology, or, rather, our literary criticism about art reproduced our culture's clichés about biology.

Along with inducing a predictable set of metaphoric attributes that we were to believe were deduced from the text, this critical application of gender extended to our understanding of the authors. Descriptions of the lively style of *Tom Jones* shifted easily to assumptions about the manly heartiness of its author, and to a biographical selectivity that stressed his active public career. Richardson, literally also a man, had to be endowed with a feminine sensibility, and we were offered a portrait that tended to stress his personal life rather than his successful business and his professional activities. The standard portrait is of someone who didn't often go out, was a bit of a prude, and made the apparently bizarre choice to spend much of his time talking and writing to women friends.[37]

The unspoken premise that men write masculine and women write feminine literature, when it did not fit the literal truth, could simply be turned into a psychological truth. Like Richardson, James has long been painted a sissy. The importance of that premise might be measured by the tenacity, despite available facts, of the critical legend that James as a young man may have been emasculated or at least sexually damaged in some mysterious accident.[38] And on the other hand, we were offered George Eliot, too ugly to be feminine, too smart to be a woman, living the masculine life of the mind. Her illicit situation was diluted by the general, polite sense that, of course, she didn't have sex with George Lewes, was too old when she took up with him anyway, and was never really a physically passionate woman, despite the suggestive evidence of her previous affairs, despite such interesting moments as living in John Chapman's house as his new lover, along with his mistress and his wife. Weren't we all taught to view the alliance of Lewes and Eliot as a meeting of two minds, a sort of intellectual fraternity, thus the true importance of their both knowing German and writing for the same journal?

In the history of criticism the defined masculinity of Fielding's fiction and femininity of Richardson's fiction exemplify ways in which readers traditionally described gender as operating in many fictions. Masculine and feminine were generic terms, multiple qualities that everyone already understood, clustering around the obelisk and the box. Apart from such drawbacks as inaccuracy and injustice, the critical weakness of these approaches, and the lesson they offer to later critics, is that an externally imposed understanding of gender in texts covers up the important fact that many texts do treat gender, but as a changeable rather than immutable group of qualities, culturally given but not culturally fixed.

The psychological account of Richardson's feminine sensibility and of both his and, therefore, his heroine's sexual repressions continues an oppressive cultural stereotype about women, even though its object is a man. But more important, it assumes a fixity about the meanings of masculine and feminine that precludes our noticing how those meanings are reinvented in the novel. We miss how gender does function in *Clarissa* and thus also miss a major aspect of Richardson's contribution to the literary possibilities open to the novelists who came after him. By way of her numerous daughters in late eighteenth-century gothic and sentimental fiction, Clarissa Harlowe is the model that will appall and inspire the great early nineteenth-century innovators, Austen and Scott. Challenging and rejecting the powerful heritage of this virgin mother, their own portraits of heroines and their creative revisions of masculine and feminine revolutionized the British novel and marked its future.[39]

I have taken up six nineteenth-century novelists whose works I admire and believe to have been publicly visible and influential in their own time. Austen, Scott, Gaskell, Eliot, Meredith, and James all created great heroines. All of them used their creations to explore questions other than those of women's social and psychological roles, particularly questions about a character's possibilities for gender definition and what turns out to be very much the same issue, a character's power in time. Most of these writers, in their novels at least, cared little for the actual dilemma of growing up female in nineteenth-century England. And even those who did care, such as George Meredith, connected that social concern to other themes.

I have looked at how these writers' heroines function within their stories and at what the novels seem to be concerned with: how gender functions, first in terms of the implications for character of developing masculine and feminine qualities. I have looked at how gender functions more pervasively, in order to trace larger patterns and interests, particularly those concerned with the redemptive possibilities of a temporal and historical perspective. Within each of the chapters I have attempted to demonstrate how attending to the question of gender can solve, and often dissolve, some long-familiar critical problems and can bring enlarged understandings of particular works. My effort is, most immediately, practical criticism. Secondarily, I see this book as a small part of a greater task: that of suggesting the role of literary ideas about gender in the development and fate of nineteenth-century British culture.

Finally I do think there is a more than individual explanation of the presence of so many powerful leading women in nineteenth-century British fiction. These heroines represented the fictional transformation of religious values into secular values, of Christianity into femininity, of eternity into history, of fixity into change. The novels argue that a sense of history is the precondition for any social or individual progress. That sense of history, including the sense that character means character in process, self is self in time, celebrates qualities of connectedness the culture has traditionally undervalued and labeled as feminine. Thus the qualities of mercy and forgiveness consistently appear in these novels as progressive models of human relations. These qualities take from a divine model not so much the notion of omniscience as the notion of the falseness of an atomistic identity. In the work of Scott, Gaskell, or Eliot, mercy is not about great power but about great fluidity, an acute sensitivity to one's own potential for becoming different. The power to influence is intertwined with the recognition of one's own, culturally feminine, potential for being influenced. And both are inevitable articulations of what it means to understand that we live in time.

One measure of Blake's real prophetic power about the century to come is his poetic representation of the move into time and into love through troubled feminine figures, as the lamentations of Oothoon and the terrified longings of that perennial virgin, Thel. Oothoon understood that, however much divinity may live within herself, she cannot be emancipated alone. One's identity is not shaped, nor can the self be fulfilled, outside a connection to others. This is not a matter of weakness or dependency, of femininity understood as an incompletely developed self. It is a matter of having historical vision. As many nineteenth-century novelists, male and female, wrote about how individuals and, by implication, societies develop, as they wrote about progress, about a new sense of history, about time passing and to come, they represented the changing awareness, the all-too-human sense of increased vision along with loss, as a feminine attribute.

Wordsworth, of course, writing poetry as autobiography, represented that increased vision along with loss as male. And his, not Blake's, was the prophetic voice that was heard. Even when Wordsworth's figures of loss are dramatized as female as well as male, that loss is his own. Nonetheless, his definition of that male loss, much like Percy Shelley's or Scott's or like James's a century later, turns out to mean those attributes culturally labeled feminine. Nineteenth-century novelists such as Eliot and nonfiction writers such as John Stuart Mill recognized that, and so heard his prophecy correctly, in ways that should put many more elaborate and more sexist twentieth-century readings of Wordsworth and romanticism to shame.

Many nineteenth-century British novels, because of their sense of time and history, because of their prophetic function as visions of what we have to hope for or to dread from the future, inevitably explore the question of what qualities we need to help us along or what will sink us. It is not just that there are novels about men and women or that many of them highlight women. Gender, not merely the actual sex of a character but, more precisely, the cultural traits used to define and to value (or devalue) a person of either sex, the moral significance of gender, is at the center of the subject of many novels. To ask with what are we to face and hopefully direct the future leads directly to questions of what have been defined as masculine and feminine values, attitudes, roles. Should we see ourselves as separate or together? Are we brave? In what way? Are we aggressive? Tolerant? Aspiring? Self-renunciatory? In other words, do we, and should we, act as what we call masculine or feminine? Must it be either–or? How do we discriminate between the two? Who has defined, who now defines, which is which? Which qualities have the best chance? And what kind of survival do we mean when we talk of the best chance, of fitness for the future. What does progress mean?

Well before Darwin, new theories of geological time and evolution were part of the intellectual climate within which many mid- and late nineteenth-century novels were written. Whatever novelists might actually have known or not known about these new sciences, many agreed with Meredith's view that when we drove to science the other day all we got was a new tail. Meredith, and Eliot, as Gillian Beer has so impressively argued, believed that fact needed the help of imagination if there were to be real social progress.[40] But in spite of their criticism of evolutionary theory in the sciences, for these two novelists, as for many others, the idea of evolution had "extraordinary hermeneutic potential."[41] It was an inspiring part of a general sense of the power and the inevitable obligation to make history in novels and in life. This sense predated the public dissemination of evolutionary theory, in Austen's innovations with character as a human agent responsible for making her own history and in Scott's and Gaskell's views of the heroic qualities that can lead us as a community to a better future.

Many British novelists of the past century demonstrate a sophisticated sense of the interplay of traditionally labeled masculine and feminine values, certainly beyond what we have so far granted them and perhaps beyond our own. Our culture's masculine, and ultimately repetitive rather than progressive, view of progress as a matter of self-definition and aggression, of winning over someone or somewhere else, has traditionally controlled literary criticism. Predictably, that criticism has chosen to be deaf to these prophetic voices from the last century. These British novels also implicitly defend the power of art and argue not only for its power but also for its imaginative, social, and political responsibility to offer guidelines for how England should progress. To understand the alternatives between masculine and feminine values, to understand cultural pressures, "so as to choose," in Isabel Archer's words, was crucial to the enterprise of imagining a future that could both rescue and abandon the past. Readers cannot look comprehensively at ideas of time, of history, of progress, in nineteenth-century British novels without also taking up ideas of gender. The two are intertwined.

My argument has a presumption: the belief that the values that our culture and much of British literature have labeled feminine—the values of gentleness, flexibility, openness to others, friendship, love—are preferable, morally and practically, for both men and women, to values conventionally labeled masculine—those of fixity, justice, rigor, and aggression. I believe, of course, that I share this perspective with the works I discuss, that it is not a question of my interpreting it into them but perhaps even of them interpreting it into me. The influence of these novels on my own political thinking has been at least as great as has the current revolution in criticism, including feminist criticism and theory. That possibility grants a cultural and political power to fiction, a power that many recent literary theorists have been conspicuously reluctant to grant to literature but that the works themselves, in their assertions of prophetic voice, would lay claim to.

The gender categories of masculine and feminine, like the literal categories of male and female, turn out almost immediately to be inadequate to this critical enterprise. The specific meaning attached to these terms can range from positive to negative for feminists as well as for misogynists. What I examine in these books is not simply masculine-labeled values as opposed to feminine-labeled values. More accurately, I look at masculine values understood as heroic in opposition to feminine values understood as heroic.[42] In order to suggest that these values, whether typed as masculine or feminine, are defined in terms of their possible power to create change, to make history, and to empower the people who accept and express them, I have turned to calling them masculine heroic or feminine heroic.

What I hope to suggest by such terms is that these novels about gender are also about heroism, about what it means to be heroic, particularly, though not exclusively, if you are a heroine. The feminine-labeled values of flexibility and mercy are not denigrated as feminine in these novels as they so often are in the culture, including in other novels. To call mercy or flexibility feminine is not a way of labeling them as powerless, as ineffectually idealistic or naive. They do not, as feminine, carry the implication of being passive, as Scott's groundbreaking exploration of the meaning of heroism shows, and as we see in Harry Mortimer and Jeanie Deans and later in the equally heroic efforts of Lucy Snowe and Dorothea Brooke. Nor do feminine values as dramatized in these novels imply being self-effacing, as we see in Austen's persuadable Anne Elliot, "only Anne," or in Gaskell's gentle and assertive phoenix, Ruth Denbigh.[43] And of course, men can, and should, embody feminine heroic values, as we see in Scott's reputedly passive young heroes, in Austen's education of the dashing Captain Wentworth, in Gaskell's Thurston Benson, and in James's Lambert Strether. Moreover, women can remain fixed in masculine heroic terms, often those established by their fathers, as do Gaskell's Sylvia Robson and James's invisible Mrs. Newsome and Kate Croy.

A feminine heroic tradition in nineteenth-century British fiction includes books written by men and women. It was one of the most prominent lines of influence through which the genre that in so many senses belonged to women developed in the nineteenth century. The feminine heroic tradition in the novel was concerned with depicting the relations between what we invent and what will come true, both privately in defining ourselves and publicly in shaping our culture. Narrative art can be prophetic of a better future in which notions of masculine and feminine might change. This feminine literary tradition linked notions of history, gender, and the novel. It may well have been the most influential tradition of nineteenth-century British fiction.

Finally, I want to note the celebratory quality of the claims for a feminine heroic vision, the kind of empowerment it promises. We see it in the energy of Emma Woodhouse's self-love or the exuberance of Molly Gibson's reply to her lover in *Wives and Daughters* that she won't be happy living "only in trying to do, and to be, as other people like."[44] The world of perception, of persuasion, of love, of forgiveness, is imperfect. And it is also the only place lush enough to provide Emma's "perfect happiness." It is Jeanie Deans's isle of Roseneath, Elizabeth Bennet's Pemberley, and Cathy and Hareton's Thrushcross Grange. It is the earthly paradise, that world of loss and self-fulfillment under the limited but not dividing sky—at least until mid-century, when Eliot begins to envision that heaven on earth as dominated by men.

Feminine heroism in both male and female characters pervades nineteenth-century British fiction as a personal but emphatically not an individualistic answer to the public problems of how not only to face the future but to create a better future in a changing and confused world. Firmness, stoicism, and assertiveness are to be exchanged for perceptiveness, adaptability, and openness. Yet the fictional portraits of the empowering possibilities of feminine heroism are modified as the century goes on to portraits of decreasing power, at least in the public realm. These novels progressively follow through to conclude that this new answer is limited, as in Dorothea Brooke's fate as a wife or Lambert Strether's return to Woollett; is morally ambivalent rather than clear, as in Clara Middleton's increased egoism or Milly Theale's beneficent and deadly forgiveness of Merton Densher and Kate Croy; and won't save us anyway, as in Tess Durbeyfield's destruction not simply by the modern masculine perspectives of Alec D'Urberfield and Angel Clare but by the combined forces of the past and the future.

When, near the end of the century, Tess lies down at Stonehenge, the nineteenth-century literary dreams of cultural progress, the novels of a better future born of, yet transcending, the past, are nearly over. So too is the ascendancy of the great heroines. And the two endings are intimately linked. We are left with a shrunken and defeated vision of what can be, as Angel, the sadder but wiser man of the future, holds hands with Liza-Lu, "half girl-half woman, a spiritualized," disembodied, and disempowered "form of Tess."

The social promise envisioned in the relations between fact and fiction, between history and story, that had been revealed when Scott turned the true account of Helen Walker's journey of sisterly mercy into his great novel about making history through feminine heroism, has metamorphosed into pessimism about any sort of progress by late in the century. Well before Thomas Hardy's *Tess*, with its regressive concluding image of the childlike Liza-Lu, another factual story of another woman's confrontation with masculine justice and her desperate choice to kill her illegitimate child had been encapsulated in another historical account. The public source this time was a brief report in a newspaper, concluding with the phrase, "Wragg is in custody."

With unforgettable power, Matthew Arnold recalls that factual history and that phrase for us in "The Function of Criticism at the Present Time." As Arnold so eloquently reveals, that crude and cryptic line, defeminizing and thereby dehumanizing its subject, also encapsulates the Victorian response, both social and linguistic, to actual events. Our power to see, to understand personal and social history, and, in Shelley's hopeful exhortation at the beginning of the century, to imagine what we know, has shrunk to this: a desexed single syllable, a dead child, a four-word tragedy. And with all his eloquence, Arnold cannot transform that tragedy, for a woman and a culture, into a hope for the future. His eloquence is directed instead at prophesying the mockery to which the masculine idea of cultural progress will lead.

"Wragg is in custody" speaks volumes in its brief way of what has already happened by 1864 to the hopes of so many nineteenth-century writers for real social progress away from the cycle of moral uprightness and cruelty of the Satan of Blake's Milton. The old masculine structures of justice and aggression have triumphed, while the Christian/feminine values of forgiveness and renewal are losing their imaginative force. The bleak prophecy of Gaskell's *Sylvia's Lovers* will come true. In the sad words of Blake's mental traveler, England remains a land of men, of men and women too. And no more than that. All will be caught up in an unimagined future, both historical and literary, that will bring a world war, a different understanding of gender, and a different imaginative use of it in a new art.

2

Why There's No Sex in Jane Austen's Fiction

> Embraces are Cominglings from the head even to the Feet.
> And not a pompous High Priest entering by a Secret Place.
>
> WILLIAM BLAKE

> The sky will be much friendlier then than now, . . .
> Not this dividing and indifferent blue.
>
> WALLACE STEVENS

At the beginning of the nineteenth century the work of two novelists, Jane Austen and Sir Walter Scott, moved beyond the structures of the sexual novels of eighteenth-century fiction. As I will discuss in Chapter 3, Scott took up the definition of the hero as a figure of masculine power, a creator and seducer, a gothic hero-villain, and showed the fictionality, the destructiveness, of that representation. So, of course, had Samuel Richardson, and with a fulsomeness that Scott's hero-villains cannot match. But Richardson, who was not "in love with the productions of time," did not move outside the form. Scott and Austen did. What masculine power, presented as natural and sexual, did not allow for was that a heroine could be a creator. Scott offered a new definition of the heroic shaper, one that both men and women could be. And Austen metamorphosed the idea of the virgin heroine and, with it, the whole understanding of what the relations between character and plot could be.

This is not to claim that, apart from Scott's Jeanie Deans, Austen's novels were alone in offering new portraits of heroines.[1] In Susan Ferrier's 1818 *Marriage*, the long-suffering heroine, Mary Douglas, is threatened by an unattractive marriage prospect rather than by a rake, and her main opponent is not a man but her ambitious and selfish mother. Like Fanny Burney's work, Ferrier's novel used and also devalued sentimental conventions, with their sexual definitions of worth. In slightly earlier novels, Maria Edgeworth also used sentimental conventions that defined most of her heroines in predictable sexual terms.[2] When she created heroines with innovative possibilities the plots remained conventional. They placed the favored heroine, Belinda Portman in *Belinda*, Helen Stanley in *Helen*, at a distance from the center of the action.[3] That center offers a traditional sexual ingenue caught in her traditional plot. The lead heroine stands to the side, as visitor, as observer, and finally as repairer of other people's lives. Edgeworth did not tell a major story of how that new heroine would work out her own life. So the heroine, Belinda or Helen, never really comes to life as a memorable creation. It is as if Edgeworth could create her, and could empower her, but not over her own plot, only over someone else's. Edgeworth did not give her the issues that would empower her to generate a story of her own making. Austen did.

Austen's first novel, *Northanger Abbey*, parodies the convention of the heroine as it had appeared in gothic and sentimental fiction.[4] The plot turns on the relations between Catherine Morland and Henry Tilney, she the familiar seventeen-year-old ingenue, he the experienced man of the world. Through the manipulations of the wicked Isabella Thorpe but also through the guidance of the benevolent Henry, the plot depicts the limitations of unequal relations and, by implication, condemns their inequality regardless of their particular moral hue. Austen's challenge casts the shadow of ego on even the whiteness of Lord Orville's soul. Evelina is endowed with such extreme ignorance that she fears, and quite correctly, that she has appeared in society as literally an idiot. This quality actually charms Lord Orville as a proof of her utter inexperience, which equals purity, once, that is, he has assured himself that she is not literally damaged in the head.

Can any reader imagine that Austen defines a reasonable and well-informed hero as one who likes his heroines merely ignorant rather than all the way to imbecilic? Does ignorance only mean sexual ignorance, and sexual ignorance mean purity of heart? It is Lord Orville and possibly that sister author, not Austen, who find it reasonable to desire ignorance in a woman. Catherine Morland is ignorant. But that is hardly to be admired. It is to be laughed at and, more important, to be represented as a condition of youth that needs to be gotten over. The story the novel tells is precisely the story of how to get over the state of innocence, when innocence means not purity and ignorance but mere ignorance. In Austen's first novel, as in all her novels, the bond between innocence and purity and the bond between experience and corruption have been severed. That may well be the most liberating cut in British fiction. The male urge to guide, to guard, and above all, to shape, along with, on the female side, a natural propensity to worship and be shaped, will not give us the parameters of an Austen love affair.[5]

The subject of power and personal relations, of influence, using, and shaping, is the explicit subject of Austen's last completed novel, *Persuasion.* The Pygmalion dynamic had provided the basic plot situation of her first novel. It is not a matter of chance or simply of personal psychology but of sensitivity to literary tradition that Henry James will also begin as a novelist by borrowing a classic narrative version of the Pygmalion pattern, in Roger Lawrence's bringing up of Nora Lambert in *Watch and Ward.*

In his belief in the intimate connection between inner and outer, between self and "the whole envelope of circumstances," James simply follows Austen, Scott, and most nineteenth-century novelists in between.[6] He also follows their insistence that such a connection is dynamic rather than static, relative rather than absolute, a matter of place and time. This dynamic connection can function as positive or negative, for good or for evil, a point that could be called the basic structural premise activating nineteenth-century novel plots. Which is to say that what happens matters, and that it matters is good, though in what way it matters becomes the question and often the problem.

The relation between inner and outer is most evil, the self is most dangerously susceptible, either when the outer is seen as totally shaping the inner or when its influence can simply be denied. Chameleon poets may be fine as authors, but they are not honored as characters in nineteenth-century novels, any more than are their opposites, the recalcitrant virgins from the previous century, the shrieking Thels. Instead, nineteenth-century novelists prefer their characters to live the Wordsworthian premise of half perceive and half create. Along with some romantic poems, the great celebration in English fiction of the benign possibilities of relations between self and the world outside self is probably an Austen novel, perhaps *Northanger Abbey* or *Persua-*

sion. But by the end of the century the possibilities had darkened. And no one would explore their darker forms more elaborately than James.[7] In his novels "you must betray or, more fortunately perhaps, you must be betrayed."[8]

The general theme of manipulation appears in James's novels as what Tony Tanner calls value versus worth and what William Gass terms William James's pragmatism versus Kant's categorical imperative.[9] More concretely, James's novels identify creativity with control and desire with destruction. This is the subject of *The Portrait of a Lady*, which Gass calls "James's first fully explored case of human manipulation . . . of what it means to be a consumer of persons, and what it means to be a person consumed."[10] The ambiguity in Madame Merle's notorious remark, "I don't pretend to know what people are meant for. . . . I only know what I can do with them" (207), captures this double meaning of value, as using people and making or shaping them.

James's characters often don't limit themselves to using people; they go so far as to shape people in whatever image they desire. Indeed, many of his best manipulators are purists, not caring to use others unless that use means virtually making a new identity. I think of Olive Chancellor and Basil Ransom in their struggle over Verena Tarrant in *The Bostonians*, or the recurrent Jamesian focus on relations between adults and children, such as those between Gilbert Osmond and Pansy. The user in these various plots is engaged in a creative, even a divine or godly act. One of the most troubling and fruitful obsessions of James's fiction is the simple point that to be a creator, whether artist or god, is not inherently to be bad or good. Thus his fascination with the circumstances, the subtleties, that might make a creator into one or the other. And so the odd moral interchangability of such apparently morally opposite shapers as Madame Merle and Mme. de Vionnet.

The idea of the links between creativity, power, and sexual desire is a major part of James's literary inheritance. This idea goes back to eighteenth-century fictional structures, to the would-be soul stealers, the rakes of sentimental fiction and the aspiring hero-villains of gothic fiction. It goes back to the classic eighteenth-century role of heroines as would-be victims, as matter to be made, as art in the making. And it also goes back to the revolutionary innovations of Austen's novels. In spite of their deep optimism and James's competitive reduction of that optimism to a view of them as songs of an arrested spring, Austen's novels first rewrite the conventions about character in British fiction in ways that were to open its possibilities for nineteenth-century British novelists and for James.

Writing from a perspective that does not suspect life of being soul-destroying or approve of an idea of character as fixed, Austen substitutes her own fictional pattern of romantic encounters for the pattern of male dominance as it appeared in many eighteenth-century novels. Gone is the scope and power of Richardson's Lovelace or Lord Orville or even Anne Radcliffe's Montoni. Can we imagine Lord Orville making jokes about the price of a true Indian muslin as Henry Tilney does, or Evelina teaching him how to laugh at himself as Elizabeth Bennet will with Mr. Darcy?[11] The relation between inner and outer is still conceived as a matter of influence and change, but change conceived as slow growth, as a matter of choice and self-responsibility, as mutual creativity between inner and outer, and as cause for joy. On this subject of the joy of fresh perceptions, it is time we recognized that, between Catherine Morland and Henry Tilney, it is Henry who has more to learn. That cynically wise young bachelor who mocks the banal conventionality of responses to Bath in his early conversations with Catherine will undergo his own education through knowing her. He will learn the power of circumstance to enlighten and to refresh the soul.[12]

To see Catherine's resistance to being educated by the presumably superior Henry Tilney as mere stupidity, to believe that whatever she does learn she learns from him, and to judge that whatever she learns from him must be worth knowing, is simply to read the old pattern back into the novel. It hardly matters whether one approves of Henry representing the rational male world or disapproves of Catherine being such a portrait of female silliness and inferiority.[13] Both political perspectives ignore the literary inheritance Austen addresses in *Northanger Abbey*, the convention that the narrator explicitly mocks and that the story self-consciously transforms.

The originality of this early Austen novel is that its heroine is given the task of molding herself rather than selecting the right man to do the molding, keeping still (or keeping busy) until he comes along. Catherine is a slow learner in large part because, for all her ignorance, she has a healthy sense of self. She can shape her own impressions, and this, after all, is the substance of what Henry teaches her. Catherine learns to "consult your own understanding, your own sense of the probable, your own observation of what is passing around you" (197). She is an active participant in, an active creator of, her own education, her own changing self. In Henry's telling phrase about understanding others, "if it is to be guess-work, let us all guess for ourselves" (151–52). It is to be guesswork, and Catherine Morland begins the wonderful guessing game that will animate many a character and generate many a plot in nineteenth-century British fiction.

Austen's literary inheritance was a landscape littered with endangered virgins.[14] As Nancy K. Miller, in her study of some eighteenth-century British and French novels, puts it, "the heroine's text is the text of an ideology that codes femininity in the paradigms of sexual vulnerability."[15] Eighteenth-century British novels are also full of instances where one character takes up and transforms, or tries to transform, another, with the transformation usually including sex.[16] As early as 1683–87 a long and mutually gratifying seduction process, between Philander and his younger, less powerful sister-in-law, Sylvia, animates Aphra Behn's *Love Letters Between a Nobleman and His Sister*.[17] In Daniel Defoe's great 1722 novel, Moll Flanders begins her story as a child who wants to make herself into a gentlewoman. Instead, the gentleman who takes her up turns her into an incestuous whore—which may be Defoe's definition of an English gentlewoman. Many of Henry Fielding's comic scenes turn on the question of who will make whom, sexual pun intended. In Fielding's 1742 novel, Lady Booby wants Joseph Andrews, but her desire entails metamorphosing a farm boy into an urban page. And in the suggestively incestuous plot of Eliza Haywood's 1744 *The Fortunate Foundlings*, a socially powerful gentleman becomes the guardian of an ingenue and is so pleased with his own shaping as to find Louisa irresistible and to attempt her seduction. Haywood's own career conveniently marks the general change from the risqúe novels of the 1720s to the moral fictions of the 1740s. But the change in morality doesn't change plot possibilities for heroines. Both kinds of novels define their heroines sexually, as virgins and whores. Sexuality is a matter of identity, and identity a matter of sex.

Late century gothic novels drip with sex of the aggressive sort, often in the form of blood, often the more titillating by being repressed, symbolic, and grotesque.[18] I think of Horace Walpole's Manfred of Otranto, spurned by the fair Isabella, reaching from behind to thrust his dagger into the breast of his own fair daughter. Or J. Sheridan Le Fanu's vampire, Carmilla, herself long ago the innocent victim of male appetite, brushing her lips softly against the cheeks of the unwitting Laura. Or the imprisoned and starving young lover in Charles Maturin's *Melmoth, the Wanderer*, who begins literally to gnaw on his sweetheart's arm.

Late century and early nineteenth-century sentimental and domestic novels seem to have fallen hopelessly in love with the mid-century narrative vision of the heroine as vulnerable virgin. Burney consistently places her heroines between the illicit advances of the bad man and the saving hand of the hero. Even novels that offer a critical perspective on the sexual definition of character rely on it. Charlotte Lennox's famous 1754 *The Female Quixote* features a heroine whose sexual fears are fantastic. Yet she is taught to understand that fact by a more powerful male. Tobias Smollett, while creating some educable characters, nevertheless offers as his young heroine in *The Expedition of Humphry Clinker* that familiar figure, the possibly endangered virgin. Lydia may travel all over England and Scotland, but all she really does is wait demurely for her man. Mary Wollstonecraft's *Maria, or the Wrongs of Woman* is directly in this sentimental tradition.[19] And among Mary Shelley's novels, *Mathilda* uses a father's incestuous love for his ingenue daughter, while *Falkner* uses the convention of an older man adopting a young girl, who grows up "to epitomize feminine virtue."[20] Gothic or sentimental, imitative or innovative, conservative or radical, supportive or critical of the convention, eighteenth-century novels constantly invoke the dynamic of male sexual aggression and female sexual powerlessness.

The recurrent pattern of sexual violation in eighteenth-century novels speaks to us of what I would call depressingly patriarchal social and psychological relations between the sexes in eighteenth-century England. Ruth Perry has shown in fascinating detail how the educational training of and social expectations for women led them to live lives of enforced leisure filled, and justified, by sexual and romantic fantasies.[21] Mary Poovey's analysis of eighteenth-century conduct books underlines the extent to which the social concern with propriety was based on the pervasive and oppressive assumption that "women are fundamentally sexual," and thus need to be kept under control.[22] Sexual dominance, at least in the invented stories in novels, would obviously be a satisfying way of portraying that control.

But I want to argue that the prevalence of sex and seduction in eighteenth-century novels also speaks in a less ominous voice, a voice that has less to do with the injustices of society and more to do with the equalities of art. This recurring pattern in eighteenth-century novels also addresses what was the relatively new narrative problem of a relatively new genre: the possible relations between character and plot created by the novel form itself. And along with this aesthetic problem, it addresses the real problem of a general, and probably

Christian, sense, that life is a danger to self.[23] It is neither a literary nor a social accident that the century that gave rise to the novel is notable for its fictional virgins and rakes, its literary rapists and seducers and whores. These literary conventions, while partly reflecting the oppressive social situation of women in eighteenth-century Britain, often carry quite a different significance as well.

In the first place, the novels tend to side with the vulnerable heroine, at least until 1764, when the gothic hero-villain begins to sing his own siren song. The good in these sexual novels means to be untouched by events, to remain as we were born, innocent and pure. Character is, or should be, fixed. Stasis is virtue. Therefore action, event, and plot are attacks on character. What better image for this state of affairs, this encounter between plot and characters, than insidious seduction or aggressive rape. Experience and plots can only violate characters by changing their identity, the very essence of themselves as "subject." What Moll Flanders, with all her energy for life and sense of independence, loses in her trek toward material substance is precisely herself, the self she wanted to be and might have been. Judith Lowder Newton says of Burney's *Evelina*, that "to read this history of a young lady's entrance into the world is to read a chronicle of assault."[24] This is as true of the aggressive and fallen Moll as of the gentle and pure Evelina. If coming to life, coming of age, is imaged as a sexual violation, what better representation of the self who must stand against the transforming and thereby corrupting power of experience than as a woman and a virgin?

But once we admit that there is a positive view of all those sexually vulnerable heroines in eighteenth-century novels, that they represent the good in human nature, the evil and injustice in life, we must go on to see the negative implications of this representation of human innocence. There are distinctive narrative consequences of imaging life as assault and humanity as female. The generative point, for both heroines and plots, is that heroines can move from being good to being corrupt, or they can stay good. That is all they can do. What characters like Richardson's Clarissa Harlowe, Fielding's Sophia Western, and Burney's Evelina cannot do, except by mere willingness, is to initiate changes in themselves.

To represent character change as sexual violation means that it must be accomplished by a man. Perhaps the most significant critical point about eighteenth-century sexual novels is that the plot cannot be initiated by the heroine but only by a fallen woman or a man. Male and female figures do not and, given their biological definitions, cannot have the same plot possibilities in eighteenth-century novels. As Patricia Meyer Spacks has noted, "denial of likeness, then, lies at the heart of the matter."[25] Once narrative action is dramatized in the form of sexual action, then female characters, who cannot force the matter, can only try to charm the men into initiating that action. Heroines are inherently defined as reactive. They are necessarily relegated to being the material out of which life and fiction will be made. As J. M. S. Tompkins long ago noted, "in many books the heroine is entirely passive."[26] The line between virgin and whore, as John Cleland and Fielding and so many others represented it, is the line between has not and has, a line drawn—in writing and in life—by men.[27]

If Lady Booby appears to initiate the action between herself and Joseph Andrews, she, like Moll, can make such a move only because at some point a man made such a move on her. Her identity was long ago shaped by another than herself. Just as important, what she initiates she does not complete. Lady Booby cannot change Joseph's identity along with his clothes. Whatever the woman's experience or the man's lack of it, whatever her precedence in age and class, whatever her economic power over him, realizing the action, having the sexual power to force the change of identity can only be accomplished by a man.

The other side of the exclusively male sexual power to change someone totally is to change them not at all. No one is a bit of a virgin. If women can make nothing happen, this has a double sense. For what they can do is to make *nothing* happen. Yet even that passive resistance, that dramatic role as immovable object, can be undermined. Heroines, at the last resort, can always be raped. It doesn't matter so much whether they actually are. It only matters that they, and the reader, are always aware of the possibility, and thus are always aware of the ultimate fragility of their identity. Of all the eighteenth-century heroines I recall, only Clarissa Harlowe is grand enough really to make nothing happen, no matter what a man can make happen. And the effort kills her.

Given the physical basis of this eighteenth-century convention of plot and character, a specific given is the greater physical strength of men. Always lurking in these novels is the fact that a man can literally dominate a woman—if he cares to, if he chooses. Therefore, there must always be a limit to how much a heroine, a virginal heroine, can like the physical world. As Clarissa so grandly taught us, to counter the man's physical superiority by granting the women spiritual superiority can ultimately be done only at the price of denying the value of the whole physical world, of physical life itself. If the vessel is frail, like the rest of mere matter it can be declared to be without intrinsic worth. Finally, the only option left to the permanently vanquished is to deny the validity of the game.

Less radically, when heroines in eighteenth-century fiction begin as good and are not violated, they can still be transformed. But that transformation is a change in style rather than in essential character. With Burney's ingenues, being good turns out to be a matter of learning how to be good gracefully. Lord Orville shapes the unformed Evelina on her entrance into the world. He must protect her from the villain she could not herself physically withstand. Her virginity is in his hands. But since her purity is a given, his pedagogic and creative power does not take the form of changing her identity but rather of maintaining it and making it visible, of giving it external form. In an essential sense he does not change her at all. Nothing happens. For Pamela or Evelina or Belinda, being brought to life means getting to be Audrey Hepburn, dressed beautifully, behaving decorously, and dancing with a prince at the ball.

Before we post-Freudians explain the eighteenth-century parade of frosty ingenues as repressed projections of their authors' prudery or secret desires, we might ask why a heroine should love sex at all, given that it signifies the measure of a hero's physical, social, and economic power over her, his potential to transform her very identity. That point will surely take the bloom off the rose. Rape isn't fun. Neither is a romantic seductivity that demands a heroine's consenting gratitude for the implicit fact that it is kind enough, restrained enough, not be be rape. Passion does mean the loss of self. Rejecting passion means embracing an unchanging self. All good eighteenth-century fictional virgins prefer death to dishonor, stasis to change—or ought to. The ones who don't, Roxana and Moll, Fanny Hill, will go on to live immersed in the substantial pleasures of a material universe. But pure or fallen, for all of them biology (which is to say, literary convention) has determined fate.

The passage from innocence to experience, which will become the richest metaphor in nineteenth-century fiction for exploring the interaction of character and plot, for representing the dynamic relations between self and world through which a subject develops identity, is suspect in eighteenth-century fiction. It means one thing for heroines: the loss of virginity, a loss of self. It is a fall into the endless abyss of corruption, marked by the "Blast of Heaven" that tortures Defoe's guilty Roxana, ended by the intolerable screams that bring death to Richardson's hideous Mrs. Sinclair.

If Elizabeth Gaskell's *Ruth* is the nineteenth-century novel that finally rewrites the conventions of the sexual novel for heroines, the eighteenth-century novel that marks the full parameters of the genre and offers the fullest attack on it, is Richardson's *Clarissa Harlowe.* Clarissa is one of the greatest heroines in British fiction. She is also its most famous victim of rape. As the history of its criticism shows, and as many of its recent critics say, there are quite a few ways to read *Clarissa.*[28] The very point that there are various ways to read it has itself become the suject of recent deconstructive interpretations of the novel, most notably William Warner's *Reading Clarissa: The Struggles of Interpretation* and Terry Castle's *Clarissa's Ciphers.*[29] The new criticism has asked readers to recall that Richardson's text engages in its own strategies for creating interpretations, for making up the meaning of the text, both for its characters and for its readers. I propose that our awareness of those strategies extend to the recognition that this text, and the characters within it, both played with and were trapped in a framework of conventions that were literary as well as linguistic, sociohistorical, religious, mythic, and psychological. Much of the intensity of this novel lies in the lushness with which it explores it narrow literary trap.

Clarissa explores the full entrapment created for a heroine, (and, ultimately, a hero) within a narrative tradition that defines character in sexual terms. Richardson's great novel describes a heroine's rite of passage in terms that make clear that she can never cross over to experience without the loss of self. The novel examines with apparently infinite richness what that might mean and why it should be. Castle and others are convincing in their claims that we don't need to pick the what and the why, don't have to prefer the Christian or the Freudian or the Marxist explanation, may indeed be blind if we do. But whatever our critical frame, we must recognize the gender basis of Richardson's work. It matters that Clarissa is a woman, that she cannot find a heaven on earth because she is a heroine rather than a hero. Clarissa is the object of Lovelace's unrelentingly destructive desire because she is "Woman," because Lovelace is a man. Whatever else the conflict between these two means, that something else cannot simply absorb, and thereby transcend, its identification with biological identity. What happens to Clarissa is both the logical climax of and the nadir of the fate of the ingenue heroine in the sexual novels of eighteenth-century British fiction.

Part of the brilliance of *Clarissa*, then, is that it takes as its subject—and explicitly debates and rejects—the very definitions of human nature that, as unspoken and implicit assumptions, defined the characters and animated the plots of so many other eighteenth-century novels. *Clarissa* does not challenge the notion of human nature as initially and admirably virginal, or the notion of experience as a danger to self. In its suspicion of life in time it remains of its age. But it does challenge the physical basis of defining women's characters, the physical justification for male superiority and female vulnerability. It does tear away the protective and false veil of naturalness and reveal as a wicked fiction the eighteenth-century literary definition of human sexuality.

Is sexual passion natural? And is Clarissa unnatural in her denial of sexual passion? Is she repressed? So say many modern critics. And so, in his fashion, said Lovelace. But nature and sexuality, as Richardson's presentation of Lovelace so brilliantly reveals, are both human constructs. The proper question, then, is how does culture define nature in a particular novel—what does sex mean? In eighteenth-century sexual novels it is a masculine construct that would give men control over women's lives and heroines' plots. In *Clarissa* sex means, of course, Lovelace's power, Clarissa's loss of it. This is not nature. This is culture. This, as Richardson so ingeniously exposed, is Lovelace, and all he represents, endlessly making it up. Yet even within a culture that refuses to allow her to do so, Clarissa chooses her own fate.

But the fate she chooses is death. No wonder that near the end of the century Blake was so impatient with the limitations of imaging a woman's life as the pale virgin shrouded in snow and so insistent that the beginnings of new visions had to be located in images that were less binding of our joys and desires, less restrictive of our potential for change. No wonder that he foresaw a better future for both masculine and feminine precisely by ejecting from imagination the idea of purity, and thus also the idea of violation, for the Thels and Ololons and Oothoons and Spectres of Milton, as well as the Bromions and Theotormons (and Milton himself), who litter the pages of Blake's poetry. And as Austen's fiction was so soon and so brilliantly to demonstrate, Blake was both accurate and prophetic in terms of the history of the novel.

Clarissa stands as the novel that made possible the innovations of its inheritors. It offers both the richest representation and the most damning critique of the convention of the pure heroine in the British novel. In exploring the meaning of the convention, in revealing it *as* a convention with political, social, and economic functions, Richardson's novel offers what remains to this day the most profound analysis in British fiction of the human and literary consequences of, and the human and literary motives for, defining a woman in essentially sexual terms. What *Clarissa* illuminates is that those consequences, those motives, are evil. After reading *Clarissa* and the equally limiting alternative offered in *Sir Charles Grandison*, we can surely see why new life for the novel would next lie in a fiction that would look to define character, particularly female character, in other than sexual ways. The sexual novel continued after *Clarissa*, was certainly inspired by it, and continues even now. But *Clarissa*'s significance in literary history must include its power to decry the very genre of which it is the most sublime representative.

If character change in eighteenth-century novels cannot be imaged as gradual growth but only as a crude and sudden metamorphosis, and if it can only be recounted as a chronicle of victorious assault, it still is change. Virgin ingenues, in fiction at least, may seem a little static by age thirty or thirty-five. More relevant to the development of British fiction are novels about the moment of growing up, about a young lady's entrance into the world, though these are restricted in their inventiveness by a convention that evaluates a successful rite of passage as undesirable. Marriage, after all, is just a less dramatic form than rape of terminating a heroine's original identity. There is life outside virginity. There is even life for heroes outside their obsessions with someone else's virginity. But how does one write stories about it?

At the beginning of the new century, in a move still viewed by many liberated modern readers as an obstacle to claims for her high seriousness, Austen got rid of the sex.[30] And I don't mean only those endless rapes, seductions, threats of seductions, rumors of seductions, rencontres, suspected rencontres, or just extremely unlikely rencontres that must, nonetheless, be guarded against. While most of the sexual energies in eighteenth-century novels are energies of aggression, there are a few heartbeats of less violent desires. Along with Joseph Andrews's blushing admiration of Fanny's cleavage, some familiar instances might be Tom Jones eating oysters, the Widow Wadman's interest in Uncle Toby Shandy's spot, Tabitha Bramble's shocked focus on Humphry Clinker's bare posterior, and even a page or two of *Clarissa*.

But Austen has none of this, and readers have not been slow to decide why. Austen was, after all, unmarried and respectable. How utterly familiar to us all is the assumption that because there was no sex in Austen's life, there is no sex in her books. But this biological principle limits art to the experiences of life. It has to ignore the apparently virginal biographies of those undeniably passionate writers, John Keats and Emily Brontë. The supposedly more sophisticated critical version that argues that Austen, unlike Keats or Brontë, didn't like sex, and was more rational and detached, is cheap psychology.[31]

Moreover, no one literally means that there's no sex in Austen's novels. That she had heard of, and even dared refer to, sex outside marriage we infer from the bastard status of Harriet Smith in *Emma*. Austen frequently found sex to be a useful plot device. Four out of the six completed novels conveniently dispatch the heroine's undesirable beau by involving him in an illicit affair. After Willoughby's past seduction of Eliza Williams in *Sense and Sensibility*, these costly interludes move to within the time of the story itself. In *Pride and Prejudice* Mr. Wickham and Lydia Bennet run off together and will be stuck with each other, while in *Mansfield Park* Henry Crawford thoughtlessly talks himself into an affair with Maria Bertram Rushworth and loses Fanny Price. In *Persuasion* the device becomes explicitly comic, when Mr. Elliot, another smooth talking hero to be hoisted on his own petard, ends by running off with that freckle-faced widow, Mrs. Clay. And the last we are told of them is that "it is now a doubtful point whether his cunning, or hers, may finally carry the day" (250).

Such language and plot arrangements are hardly the work of a rigid morality. When Lydia Bennet and Mr. Wickham run off, they are considered shallow and immoral, but also better off married and accepted back into the family. This practical approach contrasts with Mr. Collins's hypocritical Christianity, in his suggestion that the family forgive the sinners but never receive them again. Given this attitude in the novel written immediately before *Mansfield Park*, we ought to be willing to consider that Edmund Bertram's horror in *Mansfield Park* at Mary Crawford's suggesting "an acquiescence, in the continuance of the sin, on the chance of a marriage" (458) is his own moral attitude rather than his author's.[32] Henry and Maria's adulterous affair is worse than Lydia and Wickham's. But to have a principled eye is not necessarily to look only with the earnest eye of righteousness. I must wonder at the reader who assumes that Austen would have more in common with the moral perspective of Edmund and Sir Thomas Bertram than with that of Fitzwilliam Darcy and Mr. Bennet. When Austen writes of a different family, she writes of a different response, one fitting the characters of the two Bertram men.

Once we grant, as I think we must, that the evidence in the novels speaks against being able to tell whether the novelist was herself a prude, or was repelled by sexuality, we have only gotten so far as to clear away a confusion. The distinctive point is not what Austen's own sexual attitudes might have been. The point is what kind of sex is missing from her novels. For it is not SEX, whatever that may be, that is missing, but rather sex defined in a particular way. For 150 years readers have been looking at Austen's work and claiming with Charlotte Brontë that "the Passions are perfectly unknown to her."[33] Where, they have in some form or another asked, is the sex? Where, in George Moore's grander phrase, is the "burning human heart in English prose narrative?"[34] Instead of Wilson's "Clarissa, Lovelace, and passion," all we get are evasions like the infamous proposal scene in *Emma* that outrageously announces that "what did she say?—Just what she ought, of course. A lady always does" (431). The general conclusion has been that Austen's fiction, without sex, without the symbols of sex, is without passion. And that is the great limitation of the work and the author.

Yet surely we can see that replacing a love scene that has become so established as to be considered de rigueur in domestic fiction with a joke about its predictability is a beautifully simple way to make the point that such a scene is merely a convention. Honoring such a convention would violate the values of this novel. The proposal is not worth dramatizing for the very reason that it is not—indeed, explicitly is not allowed to be—the climax of Emma's story. Readers who want more of the love story between Emma and Mr. Knightley, more of his declarations of passion for her and her silence or modest protestations, perhaps really want less of, and a lesser, Emma.

My purpose here is not to defend the presence of passion and sex in Austen's novels. Indeed, I want to be absolutely clear about insisting that her novels do have sex and passion. For Austen, as for the romantic poets, particularly Percy Shelley and Blake, sexuality is a part of full humanity. Susan Kneedler has observed that in Austen's novels "new emblems of sexuality are created which serve to remove the violence from ideas of the erotic."[35] The feelings between such characters as Elizabeth Bennet and Fitzwilliam Darcy or Elinor Dashwood and Edward Ferrars do unite a range of emotions including what we call the sexual. There are other ways to love a man than within the traditional pattern of male dominance and female submission that the culture, and much of eighteenth-century British fiction, has passed off on so many men and women as a truth of nature. And there are other passions besides the sexual, and other loves a woman can have besides the love for a man. Surely, Elinor Dashwood's deep affection for her sister, Emma's divine imagination at work to make Highbury interesting, Elizabeth Bennet's intense intelligence at play in the environs of Netherfield, all qualify as forms of passion. Offering forms of passion other than what tradition has defined as natural and sexual is at the heart of what Austen brings to portrayals of women in British fiction. Austen's fiction "fuses the physical with the emotional and the intellectual to create a sense of total human relationships."[36] It is not something distinct that can be broken off from one's other feelings like a leg from a torso.[37]

If sex is not a leg that can stand on its own, it is also not the heart of the matter, the essential human desire and act, of which all other desires and acts are somehow symbols, sublimations, or denials. It is sexuality as a phallic leg, and sexuality as a vaginal heart, the kernel of Captain Wentworth's "beautiful glossy nut" (88) of character, that Austen banishes from her fiction. When I argue that Austen has gotten rid of the sex I refer specifically to a literary sexuality, the notion of sexuality in so much of eighteenth-century fiction that could define character, and plot, in sociobiological terms. That notion does, of course, occur outside novels and outside the eighteenth century, a dark fact that brightens the continuing radicalism of Austen's work.

The romantic encounters between Austen's leading characters are not literally sexual and, more significantly, do not embody traditional conventions of sexuality. The landscape around Hartfield or Netherfield contains no such projections as Penistone Crags in *Wuthering Heights*; the rooms are littered with nothing so evocative as the "woman's little pink silk neckerchief" in *Adam Bede*. Moreover, there is sex after Austen. The familiar sexual conventions are there all along in the gothic novels of the first two decades of the nineteenth-century. I don't deny the effectiveness of the burning human heart, "high-sorrowful and cloyed," Cathy's rides to Penistone Crags, Hetty's pink handkerchief and Tess's red ribbon, and various characters forgetting themselves in a boat. All I claim for Austen is that its absence, its temporary and localized absence, was a great boon for British fiction, and should be understood as a great achievement. This sexuality is absent not because Austen's novels or their author are unnatural (which they are), but because *it* is. And the great novels after Austen that depict this sexuality paint it for the artifice it is, for what Austen's exclusions revealed it to be.

Many Austen readers, themselves committed both to sex and progress, seem relieved to assert that in her last novel, *Persuasion*, passion at least, though not, of course, actual sex, does appear.[38] We have frequently been assured by readers who wish Austen well that she, like her own Anne Elliot, "learned romance as she grew older" (30). Well, perhaps so. And perhaps she knew about romance all along. I don't want to argue here the psychology of Austen's sexual attitudes. I do want to insist that culture has created our definitions of what is natural, particularly what is natural in our heterosexual relations. And what it has created, as we all know, is a hierarchy, an imbalance of power grounded in and justified, and often maintained, by the greater physical strength of men. Austen's fiction simply leaves out the whole politics of domination and submission that we have been so carefully taught to confuse with a natural passion.

There are crucial literary as well as cultural and psychological reasons for the banishment of sex from Austen's fiction. These are positive and liberating reasons that have to do with Austen's innovative achievement in redefining the possibilities of the novel form. These reasons point to her enormous and still uncredited influence over the issues and structures of nineteenth-century British novels. And they speak to a primary critical question of this study: why are there so many women leads in nineteenth-century British fiction?

All Austen's heroines, from Catherine Morland to the one aged twenty-seven, are sexual virgins. But the enormous difference, the difference that will transform ideas of character and suddenly and immeasurably enrich the novel form, is that Austen does not define Catherine's innocence in sexual terms. With one stroke of that vaginal, virginal, pen, Austen renders irrelevant what in previous English novels had enjoyed the position of central relevance, that the heroine is a virgin. Perhaps Austen's own virginity, her status as a spinster, so long held to be a measure of her limitations as a writer, should instead be regarded as the catalyst for one of her profoundest achievements. Perhaps it required a virgin woman novelist to introduce into British fiction the simple point that women can grow, can be educated, can mature, without the guiding catalyst of a penis. Austen merely conceives the inconceivable. She erases the physical basis of character. She abandons the fiction of nature for the fiction of art. And the remarkable result is that she can hold a heroine responsible for herself. Even Clarissa, that most fully responsible of eighteenth-century heroines, found herself hemmed round, and pierced, by a man.

What did female sexuality mean in British fiction before Austen? It meant male sexual power. And that power was justified on the grounds of biological inevitability. I understand, therefore, why traditional critics, normatively masculine and defending the Pygmalion pattern as natural, condescended to Austen for doing away with the sexual, and thereby physical, definition of heroism, why they emphasized the critical portrait of Austen as a spinster writer, inexperienced and cold and repressed. They knew their enemy and, as it were, attacked her work in ad hominem terms. But feminist critics should be wary of engaging, in the name of modernism or feminism or the sexual revolution, in the same old phallacy. One way to describe Austen's historical importance, her place in British literary history, is to say that her work introduces an entire canon of brilliantly individual, highly visible, imaginatively influential women characters for all of whom it is effectively insignificant that they have never been laid.

A more modern way to say this, borrowing the language as well as the insights of Adrienne Rich, is that Austen's work discloses the institutional character of our fictional portrayals of heterosexuality.[39] Her novels replace the conventions of difference and dominance with the conventions of similarity and equality. To shift the center of female (and male) identity from the physical plane reveals the biological basis for determining the possibilities of character and event in British fiction for what it really always was, a narrative construct rather than an imitation of nature. The difference between male and female nature evaporates, as does any inherent difference in plot possibilities for heroes and heroines. To perceive that the determination of identity and fate by biology in fiction is itself a fiction might lead to the perception that it is also a fiction in life. It certainly means that in nineteenth-century British novels the operative fiction about gender is no longer that it is a truth but that it is a fiction. In liberating the roles possible for women and men in British fiction, Austen's novels also liberate the idea of gender from its false grounding in biology, its false claims to inevitability, its self-definition as truth. It stands forth as an imaginative category, carrying all the usual baggage of human inventions, both the oppressions and the freedom.

The radical premise of Austen's novels that distinguishes them so essentially from previous novels and makes them the original ances-

Austen's characters encounter experience in non-sexual terms,

Locke

Only are rewarded a hero when they have lost their "innocence"

tors of so many later novels is that plot is not a threat to character, life not an assault on self. On the contrary, character and plot can be intertwined in a dynamic and positive relation, and part of the subject of the novels is how that relation can most positively be created and sustained. The notable absence of sexual definitions of character in Austen's novels is inextricable from their equally notable premise that experience is good. Austen's heroines are morally free to love the actual world. It's a wonderful life, full of the sights and sounds of the Musgrove's hotel room in Bath, full of Mrs. Jennings's earthy friendship and Miss Bates's love of Mr. Knightley's apples, full of the randomness of robbers in a turkey coop that can precipitate the "perfect happiness" of Emma's union. In fact, the novels positively argue that their heroines ought to love the world, that to do so need not mean to be worldly or materialistic or corrupt, to be Mrs. Selwyn or Moll Flanders or Lady Booby. What it might be instead, what the encounter with experience and the loss of innocence means when it is not defined in sexual terms, is the previously unexplored question that Austen's novels introduce into British fiction.

To become experienced is a delightful and morally desirable activity, occurring perhaps in one crucial scene of illumination but also continuing the rest of one's life. Austen's heroines usually do lose their innocence, and the point is that they should. Indeed, they only earn the reward of the hero, often only know enough to want the hero, when they have successfully completed their passage. Colonel Brandon's eighteenth-century masculine defense of Marianne Dashwood's charming innocence, that "there is something so amiable in the prejudices of a young mind" (56), should be rebutted for all of us tempted to agree by Elinor's reply that such innocence is a way of Marianne remaining less than she can become.[40] In spite of Brandon's sentimental taste for pure ingenues and his fondness for the superior role of benevolent hero, he can save no one from her own mistakes. As the history of his involvement with the two Elizas suggests, he never could. And it is precisely her innocence that Marianne must outgrow before she is capable of loving Brandon.

In essential Blakean, and Austenian, fashion, not to move from innocence is the true fall, into an Ulro of self-absorption. Why we must finally condemn both Charlotte Lucas and Mary Crawford is that both have refused to learn from experience, have chosen to view events in that old, literal way.[41] Their eyes are closed to life's imagined futures and their possibilities for emotional fulfillment. What links these frozen Thel figures is not their literal sexual condition, for Mary is a virgin while Charlotte is about to produce that Collins olive branch, but rather their shared materialism. This closed and self-protective vision is built on a cynicism that shares with the cult of virginity the refusal to believe that life's possibilities may be richer than one's preconceptions.

Mary and Charlotte, for all their worldly realism, for all that one is pregnant and the other raised with sailors and given to dirty jokes, are variations on the virgin figures in sentimental fiction.[42] They are essentially passive as well, seeing character as fixed and plot as potential violation, though of their mental rather than their physical structures. The brilliant difference is that these Austen characters are depicted as being themselves responsible for having chosen the idea of an unchanging self as a philosophic position, rather than the idea being assumed in the narrative as a biological given, a natural incapacity to generate change from within. The determinism of biology has become the willfulness of personality. "At my time of life, opinions are tolerably fixed" (93), says Marianne Dashwood. Marianne is just seventeen. But then, at what time of life would that remark be good? "I'm not romantic you know. I never was" (125), says Charlotte Lucas at twenty-seven, as if one cannot become what one never was.

Many eighteenth-century novels implicitly affirm rape through forcing a choice between death and rape, because rape equals experience, which equals character change, which equals life and plot development. This dilemma dissolves once a heroine's physical vulnerability and inviolateness are not placed at the center of her identity. She does not have to reject the experiences of life in order to affirm her self. One can hardly blame a heroine for remaining a virgin. But in eighteenth-century British novels that too often turns out to mean that one cannot oblige her to be responsible for her own development. One can blame a heroine for what Austen presented as the narrative consequences of defining her identity on the basis of an inviolate state. That inviolateness can no longer be justified as virginity. One can blame a heroine for insisting on the desirable fixity of life, on the irrelevance and the danger of experience, on the ineffectiveness of time and the meaninglessness of history. One can blame a heroine for refusing to make a future different from the past.

The new sense of narrative possibility in developing character implies a new dimension to the narrative artist, as a creator, rather than a mimic of the given patterns of human nature and society. Both definitions are, of course, artificial, a matter of art rather than of nature. The artist drops the fiction of being a copyist for the fiction of being the inventor. He or she, in Meyer Abrams's classic symbol for the changes in poetry, exchanges the mirror for the lamp.

In fiction that acknowledgment of creativity, of making character, applies not only to the writer but to the characters themselves. For what else are they engaged in but the making of their characters? We know from the opening moments of *Northanger Abbey*, when we are told that Catherine Morland is "in training for a heroine" (15), that the narrative question is what she will make of herself, and the narrative problem is that she begins by choosing the wrong thing. That question and that problem are radically different from those confronted by Clarissa or Evelina. But the startling point is that even an eager, ignorant, seventeen-year-old like Catherine has some creative power to make herself into something. And the question she must answer, of how to use that power, is very much the question her author must answer as well. *Northanger Abbey* is the kind of manifesto for Austen's imagination of what fiction can do and be. Thus the formal possibility that Austen and then Scott (following Austen) introduce so lavishly into British fiction becomes a matter of content, becomes, indeed, the major content of many of the great British novels of the century.

One way in which that content appears is through discrediting the old sexual modes of judging character and event. The subject of a late nineteenth-century novel, Hardy's *Tess of the D'Urbervilles*, is a woman being sexually defined. Those familiar Pygmalion figures—Alex D'Urberville and Angel Clare—along with the men at the threshing fields, Tess's mother, the red ribbon in her hair; all mark Tess as a lush bit of nature, a sexual being, a passive but vital object awaiting her destiny at another's hand. Tess's story, explicitly about a woman who is being sexually defined, is only possible as the inheritance of nineteenth-century novels in which a woman is not sexually defined. The power of Hardy's book partly depends on our sense, as experienced readers of British fiction rather than as socially liberated men and women (what novelist could count on that?), that there is something evil, something tragic and destructive, and especially something culturally invented about the apparently natural process of defining a woman sexually. We know better. And one reason we know better is the whole background of nineteenth-century heroines, beginning with those of Austen, who stand silently yet evocatively behind this latest, lost dairymaid. Hardy, and Eliot and Meredith and many others, could explore the evils of a woman being sexually defined by her culture a good deal because Austen had banished from fiction, and thereby revealed as fiction, the fiction of a woman being by nature sexually defined.

Austen juxtaposed the old and new heroine, in her portrait of the Dashwood sisters in *Sense and Sensibility*. In that story, both sisters are charming, attractive, and concerned about the intentions of a man. But all that means something far different than it would have meant in previous novels. Elinor Dashwood is sensible and loving and in control of her own life. Marianne Dashwood plays the traditional eighteenth-century ingenue, the beautiful seventeen-year-old who is seduced by a cad, though seduced emotionally and imaginatively rather than sexually. And to the regret of some readers even now, this sentimental heroine chooses to throw away both her true love for her untrue lover and her old conventions.[43] She chooses a new kind of lover and new kinds of conventions that will give her a new and wider ranging future role. Heroines, even beautiful, charming heroines like the Dashwood sisters, Emma Woodhouse, and Elizabeth Bennet, or later, Gaskell's Ruth Denbigh, Eliot's Gwendolen Harleth, or Meredith's Clara Middleton, do not have to be sexually defined. All their stories form the background of meaning that illuminates Hardy's insight that what happens to Tess is a tragedy not of universals but of history, not of nature but of nature created by culture; a tragedy of time and class, of place, and of gender.

Women in Austen's novels don't need rescuing because they are not put in an inherently physical relation to a man. Austen's heroes and her villains are not depicted as physically able to protect her heroines or, on the other hand, physically able to overpower them. They all, heroes as well as heroines, have to find something else to do. And we must measure their value in terms of what they find. In the first two decades of the new century Scott and Austen are the two novelists who will be most continuously interested in the subject of heroism. When conventional masculine heroics appear in Austen's work, as when in *Emma* Frank Churchill rides up on horseback to rescue Harriet Smith from the gypsies, the encounter is offered precisely as a red herring. It merely distracts Emma from recognizing the significant heroism toward Harriet that occurs when Mr. Knightley notices at the Crown ball that Mr. Elton has snubbed Harriet and asks her himself to dance.

Austen's novels frequently do invoke the conventions of the dangerous villain or the rescuing hero only to debunk them. In *Sense and Sensibility* we know from the way Willoughby meets Marianne Dashwood, by rescuing her from a fall in the rain, that this hero is no hero at all. "Marianne's preserver" (46), as her younger sister calls him, is a narrative joke. And contrary to what readers of eighteenth-century fiction might expect, Willoughby's not being a hero does not mean that he is really the villain. Though Willoughby does come right out of the tradition of villainous seducer, that is exactly not the point of his relations with Marianne. Willoughby betrays Marianne, but not sexually. He betrays her by being self-indulgent and passive, by preferring the easy sporting life to having to struggle with financial difficulties in order to be with the woman he loves. As his final scene with Elinor at Cleveland establishes, we are not finally allowed to think of Willoughby as a seducer. We cannot categorize him as a villain or a hero, just as a badly educated young man with a certain charm.

By *Persuasion* the threatening villain convention is explicitly invoked as a joke. Mr. Elliot's designs on Anne Elliot are, absurdly, honorable. And as for Anne hurrying to reveal Mr. Elliot's past black character, she is busy with her social and romantic interests in Bath, and his false character, "like the Sultaness Scheherazade's head, must live another day" (229). Villains, it turns out, don't matter much at all in Austen's fiction. They are certainly not given power over women. Anne was never charmed by Mr. Elliot, even in her ignorance. And Mr. Wickham, who is also never a sexual threat, could fool Elizabeth Bennet about his black character only because she was so intent on being blind. Even Henry Crawford is never depicted as a sexual threat to anyone including the heroine, though that heroine is the physically weak, timid, little creepmouse, Fanny Price. Austen's heroines choose their relations to men.

Yet Henry does run off with that paragon of health and good horsemanship, Maria Bertram Rushworth. Maria's story is an important moment in Austen's treatment of sex and heroines. The fate of the "unfortunate Maria," being banished to an establishment "in another country—remote and private" (465) with the grotesque Mrs. Norris as duenna, may well be the coldest and most seriously unforgiving moment in Austen's fiction. Why should her most punitive conclusion be reserved for the woman who has committed adultery? The treatment of Maria has seemed to many readers to be an example of Austen's horrified righteousness at the idea of a woman's sexual appetite, particularly an appetite gratified, and at the expense of social order. They have read it in biographical and/or negative terms.[44] My own claims for a literary and positive explanation of Austen's treatment of sex can stand on the meaning of the resolution to this difficult novel.

We must be wary of seeing Maria as an example of individual sexual freedom being vanquished by social or authorial oppression. *Mansfield Park* does offer an extended critique of social oppression through its presentation of the upbringing of children in both the Bertram and the Price households and its representation of how, for both sets of parents, material issues and personal comfort take priority over their responsibilities to raise their daughters and their sons. The novel specifically attacks the superficial education of the Bertram girls, the emptiness of their lives, and the economic pressures on Maria to marry a man she cannot love. Moreover, the previous generation of sisters, Mrs. Bertram and Mrs. Price, have become lazy and giddy mothers because they too were raised as foolish heroines, valuing the equally false tales of romantic love or luxury, both of which require finding the appropriate hero, more than the requirement to find ways themselves to live productive lives.

Maria moves from her mother's preference to her aunt's, from a man who can provide luxury to a man who can provide romance. For it is important to remember that Henry Crawford is a seducer because Maria Bertram Rushworth actively chooses to be a seducer herself. The barrenness of both her options marks the social constriction within which young women were supposed to live their lives. Why then her cruel punishment, so clearly affirmed by the author as well as by the society that author creates?

We cannot account for Maria as a victim of an unhappy marriage who, her creative energies necessarily channeled into the narrow role of flirt, is vulnerable to being seduced by a cad. Whatever our modern sympathies with the socially imposed plights of unhappy wives allowed no acceptable form of fulfillment of their own, that is not an interpretation that actually fits the particular story Austen tells in *Mansfield Park*.[45] Instead of concluding that it is the story Austen should have told, and that she didn't tell it is another example of her social conservatism and failed feminism, we need to look more fully at the meaning of Maria's awful fate.

Like Kate Chopin's Edna Pontellier in *The Awakening*, Maria is an unhappy wife in a culture that oppresses women. Both heroines, confronted with the limitations of their socially allowed lives, choose to escape through what is effectively a suicide. Edna's choice is presented ambivalently, as a gesture of defeat and also a gesture of self-assertion and adventurousness. It is, in other words, a suicide that is granted some dignity. Exactly what Austen's text does not allow us is any sympathetic understanding of, any admiration for, Maria's gesture of escape from the dreariness of life as Mrs. Rushworth. Indeed, we are required to condemn it perhaps more fully than any other violation in Austen's fiction, more than Willoughby's seduction and abandonment of the young, pregnant, poverty-stricken Eliza Williams, more than Mr. Elliot's refusal to help the desperately ill Mrs. Smith, and, of course, more than Henry Crawford's own part in the adultery with Maria. Is this the double standard, just Austen siding with the boys, or, at least, giving the practical warning that we'd better side with the boys if we don't want to be destroyed?

What Maria Bertram wants from Henry Crawford is not sexual. Nor is Austen's condemnation made on the grounds of Maria's sexuality.[46] Austen's negative view of a sexuality that is really asexuality has a significantly different basis from the negative views of sexuality in novels like *Clarissa* or Laclos' *Les liaisons dangereuses*. From the time of the couple acting together in *Lovers' Vows*, theirs was a game of power and self-assertion on Henry's part and the self-preening of an adored object on Maria's. Maria's feelings for Henry have everything to do with her desire to be first in society, her competitiveness with her sister and with Fanny, and a love of conquest that at least matches Henry's own. She needs the light from his eyes to brighten her dull sense of her own value.

But that is not all. Maria's artificial passion for Henry is fueled not only by her fragile ego but also by the intensity of her real desire not to have to take her life into her own hands. She puts it instead in Henry's, wishing he will solve her future more satisfactorily than her father and her husband solved her past and her present. Maria turns to a romantic and sexual fantasy for quite the right reason. Because of its promise that a hero will fix her life for her, will give it vitality, that as a romance heroine she will get to lead an exciting life that nourishes her ego and at the same time get to keep her passive role. With brilliant inconsistency, Maria willfully insists on getting to play Galatea to Henry's Pygmalion.

We may like to claim that Maria had no choice, that it's not her fault but rather society's and Austen's. But that is a conscious and reductive misreading. *Mansfield Park* insists that women, given all the forms of social and familial oppression that constrict them, given their personal forms of physical and emotional weakness, can yet make positive choices within those forms, can and must make their own lives.[47] Edna Pontellier chooses in a novel that does not believe anymore in women's power of choice, that, indeed, obtains most of its power from its brilliant analysis of how women have been denied that very power.[48] Maria chooses not to choose in a novel that insists that she, and even women much less powerful than she, can have real control over their lives. The difference between the two works may finally be one of emphasis, with Chopin stressing the need for a fuller consciousness of oppression and its destructive effects and Austen arguing for the positive possibilities of an individual woman's response, no matter what the level of oppression.

If some modern readers find Austen's fiction naively individualistic and optimistic, or less correctly feminist than a literature focusing on the presumably larger issue of culture's pervasive oppressiveness of women and how it erodes their abilities, I suggest that all of us struggle, and Austen's fiction unsentimentally insists that we should. Moreover, her fiction insists that sex is never just a matter of nature, of something outside of, and somehow free of, the meanings and hierarchies of culture. Picking Henry Crawford, that most socially acceptable and humanly unacceptable of bachelors, as your romantic fantasy is not a natural nor an unconventional nor a passionate act. And running off with him, while certainly a social violation, is hardly a physical fulfillment. But it is the logical fulfillment of social values that violate women. Is Henry sexy? Only if a woman is a masochist, which is to say, totally imbued with patriarchal values. As Susan Kneedler has commented, "we can measure how lost our sense of liberation has become if sex in any form is interpreted as liberation for women, and restraint in any form is maligned as conservative prudery."[49]

Austen's portrait of Maria is not about sexual passion, though it is about a woman starved for a sense of self. Through Maria, and also through Mary Crawford, *Mansfield Park* analyzes with subtlety and great moral force the social roles women fit into, and the narrative conventions heroines play out, that choke their potential for developing themselves.[50] Yet through Fanny the novel insists that the least powerful among us can still have the power to reject those oppressive roles and to refuse their false rewards. The novel's promise is that in our culture there are roles within which women can realize their possibilities and find passionate fulfillment. To find Henry Crawford sexier than Edmund Bertram, Mary Crawford freer than Fanny, is to prefer the charm of conquering and giving in as "the only heterosexual relations available," to the charm of "long-loved and intimately known people, . . . the charm of sisterhood, of brotherhood, and of love with equality."[51]

When, as modern liberated readers, we view as emotionally stunted a fiction that removes a heroine's meaning from the level of sexual vulnerability, we are not as liberal, nor Austen as repressed, as we may think. The passivity inherent in so many late nineteenth- and early twentieth-century socially conscious portraits of heroines, stressing their oppressive situation as victims while acknowledging their own sexual appetites, overleaps many nineteenth-century portraits of women in British fiction to return to the simpler categories of the eighteenth. The virgin ingenue, the would-be victim of the bad man, saved or fulfilled by the good, is really a kind of twin to many a sexually experienced twentieth-century heroine who, while already a victim of the bad man and knowing that the bad man is the same as the good, still cannot save herself except by exile and seclusion.

I turn back to Richardson's prophetic literary claim that no writer who follows nature and tries to keep the Christian system in his eye can make a heaven in this world for his favorites. What makes that heaven on earth impossible, as Richardson's own great novel attests, is male sexual desire, understood as the will to create and control. Another way to say that is that the male will to create, when represented in fiction naturalistically as sexual desire, means destruction for the woman. It means a denial of her possibility to create her own life and her own art. The problem with a heaven in this world for a woman is that the man who would play lover would also get to play artist and god. In such a context, female sexuality is just another way to serve the patriarchy.

Not only in *The Awakening* but in many modern and early modern novels, male characters are still attempting to define female characters, still offering them a form of rape. And the fact that this rape is now sophisticatedly social and psychological rather than literal, and that the heroine now knows or comes to know that the white knight is probably more dangerous than the black, must surely invoke the nineteenth-century insights of Eliot's *Mill on the Floss* and also move back to the insights of *Clarissa.* But these novels also invoke the limiting point about *Clarissa*, that finally the woman is a victim, however charming, however heroic, however sublime. Whatever we may decide that Clarissa wins, and I believe she wins a great deal, we all also know that she loses everything.

There are many great victimized heroines. I think not only of Maggie Tulliver but of Hardy's sublimely painful versions, Tess of the D'Urbervilles and Sue Bridehead.[52] The twentieth century offers us the heroines of Jean Rhys. Granted the eloquence of many such portraits in three centuries of British and American fiction, there is yet no critical or moral ground to claim them as somehow more radical or more politically acceptable than Austen's insistent visions of female responsibilities and power. Neither position is really the more progressive, either socially or historically. And if I defend Austen here it is only to right what I see as an imbalance.

It may be that many feminist critics' questioning of Austen's work is simply an offshoot of the particular emphasis on political consciousness in the last two decades. Our own coming to consciousness as feminists and resultant sense of victimization and horror at our male-dominated culture has directed our literary values as well. The revitalization of the women's movement in the 1960s meant that *The Mill on the Floss* or *The Awakening* or *The Yellow Wallpaper* spoke to many of us more powerfully than *Mansfield Park* or the sparkling *Pride and Prejudice*. Yet the proper outrage of many modern women writers and readers about the situation of women in our culture should not damage our ability to admit and enjoy the powerful images of women's potential and fulfillment in nineteenth-century British fiction written by both men and women. Nor should it obscure our recognition of the extent of Austen's achievement in her portrayals of women characters. Suddenly, overwhelmingly, in English fiction, women are not viewed in physical terms. And they are also not excused on account of those terms. They are expected to have high expectations. They are, in fact, morally required to do so. Failing to believe in their own abilities to make a future, falling back on the old fictional modes of defining heroines in terms of their own weakness and the external measures of materiality or male admiration, are treated virtually as crimes. Let us not confuse that with prudery.

If, as in the case of Maria Bertram, the novel is rigorous in its condemnation of her failures and is utterly unsympathetic to her choices for gaining personal happiness, that is itself the measure of the extent, and the value, of what Maria's fate might have been. Maria Bertram, in the common phrase, threw herself away. And that, for a heroine in an Austen novel, no matter what her social and familial provocations, no matter what her personal limitations, is the ultimate sin. I can think of no novelist who has believed more in women's own power, who has demanded more of her heroines, and thus has granted more to them, than Austen.[53]

The absence of sex in Austen's work represents neither a moral absolutism nor an historical conservatism nor a psychological limitation. Instead, as Austen stresses so explicitly in *Northanger Abbey*, it represents a literary innovation. And, as I have been stressing, it also represents a political innovation. The change from previous fiction is more accurately a matter of replacement than of loss. It redefines the nature of power and the power of nature in British fiction, by turning away from their physical, and therefore masculine-dominated, base. It is an original narrative response to the meaning of sex in eighteenth-century novels, a liberating absence relative to what had become a limiting presence, a matter of tradition and the feminine talent, a brilliant breakthrough in ideas of character and plot, a cause for celebration, a grand literary and historical event. For what it liberates is the role of women in British fiction. After Austen, heroines, and heroes and novels, could never be quite the same.

Austen's great revision of the pattern of male dominance and female vulnerability is *Emma*. Its heroine is herself the great manipulator, the shaper of the young, virgin soul. Yet, as Wayne Booth put it, we travel with Emma, all our focus is on this varied heroine.[54] In what I can only call conventional eighteenth-century fashion, Emma initiates the action of her story when she notices the raw potential of that most archetypal of virgin ingenues, that pretty, blonde, blue-eyed, artless seventeen-year-old of curious circumstances and unknown birth, Harriet Smith. Like generations of readers before her, Emma finds Harriet's beauty of a sort she particularly admires. She is struck by "those soft blue eyes and all those natural graces" (23), particularly the grace of being "so artlessly impressed" by Emma. She decides, as an "interesting" and "certainly a very kind undertaking" (24), that she "would notice her," she "would educate her," she "would form" that receptive mind and heart. To this artless creature, Emma will add the art. Emma thus enters the usually male ranks of experienced creators in novels who benevolently reach out to guide and train those virgin ingenues, inevitably fair, artless, and seventeen, with whom the heroes, in this ego-nourishing process, will fall in love. Emma is one of the boys .

There is, of course, a conventional critical explanation for this violation of literary convention, and readers over the years have offered parts of or variations on it. The bare lines of the standard argument are more or less that *Emma* is a moral tale, that Emma adopts the Pygmalion role of creator toward Harriet, the dominant role, because she has too much ego—or more excitingly, because she wants to play at being a man.[55] Is this penis envy? Whenever, wherever, that question is asked, the answer seems to be yes. But Emma is not going to be allowed to get away with these overreaching hero-villain antics (or this socially unconventional behavior, or this attempted sex change), because if Emma doesn't know her place, Austen does. And that's why she writes her story, that's what she writes it about. The plot is precisely Emma learning her place, taught by that most appropriate of teachers, the mature and wise man. Mr. Knightley, by this account, turns out to be the true Pygmalion of this novel, the real man, the natural penis, the artist figure, the guide. And Emma, enfin, is put in her place.

There are two kinds of problems with readings that emphasize Emma's development as one of learning her limits relative to someone else's masculine superiority, an emphasis that in the published criticism of this novel seems to mean that the father figure knows best.[56] First, there is the textual evidence. On the simplest plot level, at the end of the novel it is the husband who must move in with the wife. More substantively, at the end of the novel Emma is still sublimely vital, still enacting her own desire to be first, and explicitly claiming that "I always deserve the best treatment, because I never put up with any other" (474). This is not the language of humility, or dependency. Emma is still laughing at Harriet's malleability and, in general, dominating and enlivening the pages, while Mr. Knightley continues his usual, manly, lovable, virtually invisible self. Some proponents of the above interpretation do notice Emma's final exuberance and merely conclude that the ending mood is inappropriate, too upbeat, or Emma still too flawed to deserve what they would read as an unconvincing claim for "perfect happiness."[57] These readers can only be bent on writing their own version of how and what heroines learn.

Beyond the textual evidence, there is a formal problem. To interpret Emma as a false Pygmalion figure is to reestablish the very literary tradition the novel overturns. It is to attempt to deradicalize the novel yet again. It is to ignore the literary history behind Austen's work. It is to ignore that *Emma* was written in relation to a well-established tradition of the roles possible for heroines and that this novel, like all Austen's novels, explicitly laughs at, rejects, and replaces the all-too-familiar presentation of eighteenth-century fictional heroines. The archetype has been unveiled as a cultural convenience and a literary cliché.

That unveiling is the point of the story of Harriet Smith. Harriet offers an extended comic attack on the narrative conventions of the ingenue. Harriet's unknown father and mystery benefactor turns out to be a tradesman. As for her fate, when Harriet switches her affections back to her farmer after only one sociable evening in London, we can hardly take seriously that the proper power relations of the traditional pattern are being reestablished, that Farmer Martin at last has shaped his ingenue. Emma's closing jokes about her protege, her finding it "too much to hope even of Harriet, that she could be in love with more than *three* men in one year" (450), and wondering whether Farmer Martin was referring to Harriet's hand or "the dimensions of some famous ox" (473), are about Harriet being so malleable as to be mere matter. The joke is on the entire naturalistic convention of the heroine as Galatea. The joke is also on the convention of Pygmalion.

Emma Woodhouse, handsome, clever, and rich, with her joyous egoism and her demanding imagination, is one of the earliest and grandest of nineteenth-century fictional creators. Emma decides to take up Harriet because Emma is bored and vain and manipulative, but also because she is creative. In the language of little Bilham about Mamie Pocock's turning away from the new Chad Newsome in *The Ambassadors*, the difference between using and shaping is that "she doesn't want to 'profit,' in that flat way . . . she wants the miracle to have been her own miracle."[58] Emma's purpose, like Henry and Mary Crawford's, is to structure human relations in terms of conquering and giving in. Readers can surely do better for Austen than to imagine that she created Emma just to have a hero supplant her as the real conqueror. It is not the characters but the roles themselves that the novel chastises.

Emma is Highbury, is the vitality of Highbury, is the life of her novel, is the one reason we ever turn a page. She illuminates everything in Highbury, including Mr. Knightley. However much traditional readers may have wanted to posit a real world somewhere else, where John Knightley lives, where Mr. Knightley and Robert Martin have their rational business conversations, that masculine and superior world Gaskell so sublimely named Drumble; that world does not exist in *Emma*. What does exist, as in *Cranford*, is the mind of the heroine and the feminine world of the country town she inhabits. It is a social world of visiting, a few dinners, parties, and outings, and a secret engagement. It is a world where both men and women live and thrive, which may be why Mr. Knightley must move to Hartfield to have his happiness.

Lionel Trilling long ago gave us the two isolated insights that Emma is special in that she has a life as a man has a moral life, and in that her desire to shape her world is, "in its essence, a poet's demand."[59] And he was lucidly accurate. Yet those insights need an appropriate historical context, that of the relation of Austen's novel to eighteenth-century conventions about heroes and heroines.[60] Moll, Clarissa, and Evelina also have moral lives. But they were all similarly different from, and in the same vulnerable relation to, men. Not Emma. She has a moral life that is neither different from nor endangered by anyone else's, including the hero's. As Trilling noted, "she doesn't have it as a special instance, as an example of a new kind of woman, . . . but quite as a matter of course."

Emma's desire to shape the lives of others is both morally flawed and fundamentally imaginative. Yet we need not conclude that her imagination is immoral. The full implications of Catherine Morland's obligation to make herself are developed in Austen's portrait of Emma. The character becomes the creator, the artist figure. The epistemological and the moral dilemma of the story is where to direct that creativity, how to use one's imagination, what it means to have the power to shape a life.

Similar questions were being posed for the gothic hero-villains. Why isn't Emma like Mary Shelley's Victor Frankenstein? Well, in many ways she is. Emma was making an unnatural monster out of Harriet, as an alternative to turning her creative powers toward developing a committed and responsible life for herself. To steal Shelley's implied terms in her critique of Frankenstein's indifference and cruelty to his creature, Emma was turning to masculine rather than feminine forms of creativity.[61] Shelley's lead character is a man, and she casts his crimes and his powers in a gothic mode. Austen rejects the conventions of both gothic and sentimental fiction for their masculine bias. While Shelley's novel critiques that bias through her revised vision of gothic convention, Austen's work turns instead to making a new convention that presents in positive forms a vision of feminine creativity. And more radically than in Shelley's vision, that creativity does not originate, even by implication, from the biological fact of the uniquely female ability to procreate.

Emma's manipulation of Harriet is a moral crime of both ignorance and ego. But it is also, to modify Trilling's words, a novelist's demand. All Austen requires is that Emma be a better novelist, better morally and, I want to stress, imaginatively, than her use of eighteenth-century aesthetic conventions would allow her to be. What those conventions precisely would not allow for is herself, her own powers to create. Emma's stories about Harriet, like her stories about Jane Fairfax, are notable for their sentimental, and sexist, clichés. Pygmalion's proper object is not an external Galatea. It is Pygmalion.

Emma never lacked imagination. Like her creator, she had lacked an established narrative paradigm that could contain her own story. But unlike her creator, she fell back on retelling the old stories, with their twin roles of masculine power and feminine dependency. And she picked for herself the role of power. The novel's answer is not to pick for her instead the role of dependency. The answer is to reject both. Even the presumably empowering masculine role is unacceptable, as immoral for the hero as for the heroine.

Emma's crime, as much a failure of invention as of morals, will in the end fade into invisibility against the brilliance of Emma's "dancing, singing, exclaiming spirits" (475) lighting up herself and her world. She makes life interesting for us and finally for herself. Our last views are of Emma refusing to call Mr. Knightley by his first name because she had done it in one of her "amiable fits" (462) ten years ago, laughing at the responses of his brother and her father to the question of whether he or she is the luckier in their match, and assuring her father that the marriage is a good idea because who but Mr. Knightley "is so ready to write his letters" (466). Emma is a flawed character who deserves perfect happiness.

When Austen deconstructs the convention of the traditional hero through her lively heroine, she also redefines creativity. It is no longer a matter of natural talent, a matter of power radiating from the physical to the economic and social and artistic spheres, at its worst, Henry Crawford's acting ability or, at its best, Mr. Knightley's quiet perceptiveness. The masculine hero is unmasked for what he always was, a figure of dominion and its inevitable companion, destruction, a cultural and literary myth posing as a physical fact. Creativity is always a matter of invention, not of natural fact. And true creative power, the power to create one's own life, not somebody else's, neither dominates nor excludes. It is not masculine but feminine. And it is available to whomever would choose it, to men and to women, to Emma Woodhouse and to Harriet Smith, to Henry Crawford and to little Fanny Price.

Austen's fiction establishes a link between, indeed an interfusion of, women and creativity—not as inspirations but as creators. As Trilling surmised, in Austen's work women characters move from the roles of muse or artistic material to the role of poet, to "maker of the song she sang." The merging of the artist and woman enters British fiction with Austen's heroines. It recurs in novels throughout the nineteenth century, in the continuing identification of artists as women, the continuing identification of novelists with their heroines, and, most significantly, in the continuing vision in nineteenth-century fiction of creativity as a feminine value.[62]

3

Old Heroes and a New Heroine in the Waverley Novels

For fiction, read Scott alone; all novels after his are worthless.

CHARLOTTE BRONTË

Sisterhood is Powerful.

ROBIN MORGAN

Scott was long ago claimed by the men. While Thomas Carlyle attacked his fellow Scot's lack of passion and his career of "writing impromptu novels to buy farms with," Leslie Stephen met these charges by pointing out Scott's similarities to Carlyle and asserting Scott's work to be a "manly companion."[1] In an important 1858 review that praised Scott's vigorous realism, Walter Bagehot noted that it is "more difficult for him to give a representation of women than of men," and suggested that this is because Scott lacks delicacy, a "certain unworldiness of *imagination.*" Bagehot concluded (wrongly) that Scott compensates by not adopting that habit of lady novelists, of inventing "the atrocious species of *plain* heroines."[2] Critics of this century, from Georg Lukacs and David Daiches to Francis Hart, Avrom Fleishman, and David Brown, have discussed Scott's contribution to the novel in such terms as the intersection of public and private history, the nature of the hero, theories of law and justice, the evolution of society—all terms we recognize culturally as masculine.[3]

These readers and many others are right. Scott's novels are about such subjects. They are historical novels, and history, not as it is lived but as it has been recorded and publicly recalled, has been male. Scott's novels are also about that most masculine of men's activities, armed combat: duels, battles, war. Even Mark Twain, himself an aggressive representative in the congress of American male novelists, chastised Scott for going too far, for romanticizing chivalry and thus causing the American Civil War.[4] When writers and readers present or discuss the big picture, women know they have at best a seat in the gallery. This is the time for preparing care packages for the front, like Louisa May Alcott's little women, or for praying a lot, like Scott's own Flora McIvor and Lilias Redgauntlet. While Scott and his heroes and his male critics are out in the highlands and the lowlands, recreating the fate of nations and the meaning of history with their swords and their pens, attacking here, defending there, the smell of world-historical ink in the air, women must wait.

But the subject of Scott does not end there. In spite of the impressive intellectual assault that has been made on the Waverley novels, particularly on those difficult topics of the nature of history or the complex relations in the novels between morality, justice, and the law, most readers would admit to dissatisfaction in our understanding of Scott's work. He is the "Great Unread" and, to some extent even now, the great undiscussed. Although there has been some attempt to place the novels in the context of European literature, there remains as an open issue the question of their relation to the fiction of Scott's own time and place.

We might recall here that Scott himself often asserted that he was influenced by the fiction of Maria Edgeworth, that Scott saw himself as among the writers offering a new kind of fiction, and that he considered Jane Austen's work, in spite of its differences from his, to be produced by a kindred practitioner of that new fiction. Further, when we think of the great British novelists of the generation following Scott's—Dickens, the Brontës, and Gaskell—it is the Brontës whose appreciation of his work seems most strong. And it is the work of the Brontës and Gaskell, more than that of Dickens, that takes up and transforms Scott's methods and concerns.

In other words, the roughly contemporaneous literary context within which to consider the Waverley novels is composed primarily of novels written by women. Perhaps our appreciation of Scott's fiction, and our understanding of its place and its influence, have been limited in part because of our blindess to the centrality of the work of Austen, the Brontës, and Gaskell in shaping nineteenth-century fiction. And our blindness, both about their importance and about Scott's, is part of our traditional neglect of the subject of women and gender in fiction. It is time for readers interested in women and in gender to stop waiting and to reconsider Scott.

Despite Bagehot's praise, despite the masculine timbre of Scott's work, despite his own description of it as "the Big Bow-wow strain," as opposed to Austen's domestic refinement, the wizard of the North is the creator of a great heroine, Jeanie Deans in *The Heart of Midlothian*.[5] Jeanie Deans is the first peasant heroine in British fiction, the beginning of a line of rural women that includes Catherine Earnshaw, Sylvia Robson, and Hetty Sorrel, and culminates at the end of the century in Tess Durbeyfield. Of all these heroines, Jeanie is the plainest, the plumpest, the oldest, and, with the possible exception of Catherine Earnshaw, the most empowered to make changes in her world. What Jeanie wants to happen and tries to make happen, does happen. Her efforts are realized, her dreams come true.

One clue to the masculine takeover of Scott is the following knuckle curve of literary history: while *The Heart of Midlothian* is accepted as one of the best of the Waverley novels, it has been marked as an anomaly, "a thing apart in his *oeuvre*."[6] I want to argue that this sense of the book is mistaken, based, I believe, on the unexamined and often buried assumption that the book is different because its lead is a woman, a bias reflecting our general neglect of the subject of heroines.[7] We need to question directly Scott's use of a heroine, and such a heroine, if we are to see why is not an anomaly in Scott's work.

Why should the hero of this novel, one of Scott's greatest novels and clearly in so many ways at the center of his continuing topics and concerns, be a woman? Why would Scott choose a heroine as his lead character or, put more accurately, how is the fact of her gender expressed in what we think this novel is about? What happens to our understanding of the role of the hero when it is filled by Jeanie Deans? Given the connections between *The Heart of Midlothian* and many of the other Scottish Waverley novels in subject and values, what kinds of relations do we see between this novel and the others? What happens to our understanding of the pattern of the whole? My claim is not that it makes no difference that the lead character is a woman but that the differences it does make point to a fuller interpretation of *The Heart of Midlothian* than we have had and also to its proper connection to Scott's other Scottish novels, thereby illuminating them as well. To explain why this is so I must turn first to those other works, to discuss the male roles in Scott's fiction.

Whatever else the Waverley novels might be, they are at the simplest level stories about heroes. Scott has given us Redgauntlet and Saladin, Ivanhoe and Rob Roy. He has dramatized what being a hero can mean. We need only recall the trial scene of Fergus McIvor, the highland rebel in *Waverley*. McIvor's lieutenant, also on trial and certain to be hanged, politely asks the court to be freed, assuring them that he will return with six others of the clan, all willing to be hanged in their chief's place. As the court laughs, Evan responds, "If the Saxon gentlemen are laughing . . . because a poor man, such as me, thinks my life, or the life of six of my degree, is worth that of Vich Ian Vhor, it's like enough they may be very right; but if they laugh because they think I would not keep my word, and come back to redeem him, I can tell them they ken neither the heart of a Hielandman nor the honour of a gentleman."[8] But Scott kens well enough, and his eloquence makes us know it in our hearts just as Evan teaches it to that Saxon court. At the very least, a hero has others who would die for him, while for his cause he would die himself. The attractions of such a heroic code are infused into that stirring prose.

But Fergus McIvor, though perhaps Scott's most alluring heroic figure, is not the hero of *Waverley*, insofar as the term is a novelistic one. The book is about Edward Waverley. As readers have long seen, many of the Waverley novels have a pattern of double characters, part of a larger tension in Scott's work between such dualisms as past and present, Scotland and England, law and justice, romance and reality. Referring to the main characters, Ernest Baker remarked that "Scott's heroes are merely persons to whom a lot of things happen."[9] Much has been written about the passivity of Scott's leads, notably by Alexander Welsh but also by Marian Cusac.[10] It is a constant presumption in discussions of the novels. The lead characters have been deemed passive because of their relation to heroes, such as Fergus McIvor, the grand style, truly heroic heroes, the handsome defenders of lost causes who would seduce young men into reckless adventures in which they themselves will probably die. Against their commitment and intensity, anything less can seem passive.

But readers have also noted that heroic gestures can result in one's head on a stake at the Scotch gate of Carlisle, whereas being less committed can bring adventure without such deforming consequences, can even provide a reward. This is part of the difference between what

George Levine has called real, or practical, and aesthetic romanticism.[11] Fergus dies, and Edward Waverley commissions a grand portrait of them both for the dining-parlour at Tully Veolan. As Levine has said, the final judgment on Evan and Fergus must be doom.[12] Both the chief and the man who would die for his chief also would slit the judge's throat. That degree of commitment is past grace. But after all, grace is not what Evan, or Fergus, or Scott in providing them with such eloquent means for presenting their cause, would ask of us. Grace, mercy, forgiveness—these are the concerns of the other kind of hero, concerns that in *Old Mortality* damn young Harry Morton in the eyes of his fellow rebels.

Yet we do less than justice to Scott's enterprise if we rely on easy psychology, dismissing his eloquence as an unwitting and unresolved reflection of his own doubleness, as if he somehow could not resist the allure of an older and braver Scotland, even as his gentler or more rational self chose the ordered present.[13] Rather let us grant, with Fleishman, that Scott's refusal to "choose between them reflects not a vacillating temperament but a comprehensive vision."[14] We need to return to the trial of Evan and Fergus to learn more of what that vision contains.

Evan's stern and powerful response teaches the ignorant Saxon gentlemen what heroic action can mean. His definition, as simple as it is beautiful, requires nothing less than an absolute loyalty to his chief. Such loyalty either kills or dies, admittedly a limited perspective. And we might say that Fergus, too, can be defined rather simply. As both leader of his clan and follower of the Chevalier, his dedication also means the twin commandments of kill or die. With Fergus and with Evan, we are struck by their certainty. On the floor of that cold prison, Evan is "sure" that he "never desired or deserved a better end than just to die with his Chieftain" (430). What the proper course is, what duty is and has been, what ends and means are right—of these there can be no doubt, and for these no regret. As Fergus assures the Saxon judge, "you have condemned loyal and honourable blood to be poured forth like water. Spare not mine. Were that of all my ancestors in my veins, I would have peril'd it in this quarrel" (422).

Such certainty is exactly what is at issue. And I refer not to the Jacobite cause, though that is no less than an inspired choice for dramatizing such certainty, but to any fixed principles of human action. Fergus knows what a hero is; he knows what he should do and be. But neither Waverley nor Scott nor the reader has that kind of certainty. We may not be as crude as the Saxon gentlemen who laughed at Evan, but we are in much the same position. We are the audience before whom these figures rise up and explain, in actions and in words, the nature of the heroic. Sir Everard and Miss Rachel Waverley, Baron Bradwardine, Fergus and Flora—all appear before Edward Waverley to define and portray the heroic life. And when we go beyond this first novel to the other novels about Scotland, we see others of them rising up again and again with their eloquent words, their noble gestures, their haunted lives.

Perhaps the most famous explication of this heroic code is given to Darsie Latimer by Hugh Redgauntlet: "The privilege of free action belongs to no mortal—we are tied down by the fetters of duty—our mortal path is limited by the regulations of honour—our most indifferent actions are but meshes in the web of destiny, . . . [we] stand bound to act no more than is prescribed" (236–37). Redgauntlet sees destiny as woven by the views of heaven, which determines the direction and the meaning of all his acts, no matter how seemingly random or small. We might also think here of Rob Roy waving away Frank Osbaldistone's offer to save Rob's sons from repeating their father's fate by procuring foreign commissions for them, of Fergus seeing the ghost that foretells his death, of Edgar Ravenswood's gloomy conviction of his avenging role.

These characters assert a necessary correlation between their own principles and heaven's plan, a correlation that grants their views and their acts a divine sanction. Their certainty, therefore, need not depend on outcomes, on what happens or how things happen; it need not depend on anything at all. Indeed, this certainty means not just having or holding firmly to one's principles but knowing that these principles need never and can never be qualified. All has already been decided or revealed. All will proceed as planned. Such certainty can be a license for fanaticism, as with John Balfour's murder of the archbishop in *Old Mortality* or Helen Campbell's of Morris in *Rob Roy*. But Scott's continuing presentation of such attitudes ventures more than the obvious condemnation of their extremes.

It is convenient to be fated. The notion provides a "close identification of individual and community," as well as a feeling of connection to the past and to the natural universe.[15] Most important, it provides an a priori correlation between meaning and act, value and event. There are no pointless lives, can be no pointless deaths. This is the world many critics of Scott have written about, the world of romance, of another time and place, of barbarism and courage, of lawlessness and love. But the critical difficulty lies in interpreting the meaning of this world relative to the lead characters and thus in describing the action of the novels. David Daiches, in what might function as a classic statement that encompasses many critical readings, describes Scott's endings as "reluctant victory of prudence over claims of romantic action," while Welsh concludes that "the center of activity in the Waverley novels at most proves to be the *resistance* to romantic energies."[16]

I want here to suggest yet another way to describe these heroic figures, one that places more emphasis on their role in the dramatic structure of many of the novels. The immediate problem with the dualism of passive and active, as critics from Cusac to Hart (and Welsh himself in his own careful qualifications of his terms) have pointed out, is that it sets up an opposition that is more distorting than useful in describing the lead characters. *Passive* is a poor term. I would also like to point out that so, too, is the term, *active*. Indeed, these terms are the very language of the dark heroes, those would-be Pygmalion figures whose catagories we must surely suspect. Thus Hugh Redgauntlet finds his nephew weak and indecisive and in need of shaping up, Balfour believes Harry Morton lacks the vigor of true commitment and would infuse him with the faith, and Fergus struggles to hide his impatience with Waverley's ambivalence toward the cause. We have too easily accepted these heroic figures' descriptions of others and of themselves. We need to challenge such categories and replace them with terms that do more justice to the divergent tensions that animate these novels.

The dark heroes are active in that they initiate, evolve, and realize plans, give orders, ride around rather rapidly from place to place, kill people, and are generally aggressive in forwarding the means that could lead to the success of their causes. In this sense we must call them men of action. But the limitations of such a definition are obvious. These daring and decisive men exist in a very safe, very determined universe. The notion of fate, of destiny, provides them with a framework of meaning that they need never challenge or explore. Indeed, all the decisions have been made, the acts prescribed, before they ever were born. The notion of fate provides a powerful justification for lives free from the most terrible problem of human enterprise, the obligation to discern, to evaluate, to decide.

That obligation is terrible because it carries with it precisely what the dark heroes will not confront, what their concept of destiny is designed to evade. Their definition of action leaves out one of its most basic aspects, the weight of responsibility, made heavy by the knowledge that events could have been different had we so chosen, could yet be different if we so choose. There are moments, such as Balfour's restless night dreams or Rob Roy's first response to the news that his wife has killed Morris, when the weight descends, when doubt appears, and with it conscience and regret. But it is cast off at once as these men of action ride forward to whatever fate has provided for them. And cast off, too, are all suggestions that, instead of directing their energies to shaping others into participating in their preordained fates, they can and should shape their own lives, that they can choose to act so as to create their own destiny. They are, indeed, provided for. And for all their vitality they remain, I would say, passive in their acceptance of their roles, preferring the simplicity, the familiar clarity, of defeat and doom to the unknown consequences of a changing life.

These figures are condemned to the past not because they prefer the past to the present but because they prefer to have no notion of time at all. They are, in fact, warriors against time, fighting, like Cuchulain, the inevitably onrushing tide. Their causes exist as causes because they have at least once already been lost. And each new outbreak relives that defeat. Glory and dedication are in direct proportion to hopelessness. For this to stop being true would mean to allow for change, for redefinition, exactly what these noble warriors are fighting against.

Thus the principles of the Covenanters are so pure that even their victory, being necessarily temporal rather than absolute, cannot satisfy and is defined as loss. And the Jacobite cause beautifully illustrates that to allow for change, for the meaning of things to become other than it has been, would be to deny the very tenet on which rests the claims to rightness of that cause. The pure and changeless principle of the Stewart claim to divine right stands against the historical reality that the Stewarts, as monarchs, are no more. Indeed, the Jacobite cause only came to exist once it had first been lost. The purpose of the heroic figures is to defend these lost causes and to stand inflexibly against the encroachments of time and the meanings of history, rejecting their own and others' potentials for choice, and fighting all those who would moderate their insistence on destiny.

Yet the polarity between fate and free will, like the other dualisms invoked to explain Scott's characters, is itself too reductive to be of much critical use. The problem is one of balance, or rather the false assumption of it. The commitment to fate on the part of the heroic figures need not and does not mean that the two alternatives have anything like equal weight. We must be careful, I think, of giving too much weight to *Waverley* when we look for patterns in the novels, merely because it balances fairly evenly Fergus and Edward Waverley. But the heroic figures can be as benign and flexible as Rob Roy, his rigidity being transferred to his wife, as obsessed as John Balfour, or exist only piecemeal as it were, as an aspect of the lead character, in Guy Mannering or Edgar Ravenwood. The point is that the heroic figures do not function as representatives of a vision we might choose, any more than the lead characters function as the proper or progressive alternative. The either–or approach, which accounts for the heroic figures as one side of a dichotomy, offering an anachronistic view of the meaning of life that Scott and his main characters—and presumably his readers—are attracted to yet ultimately reject for a moderate and modern view, has dominated Scott criticism. If we abandon it we can look anew at the function of these figures in the structure of the novels. To understand that function, and thus its relation to the function of Scott's great heroine, we must move to the other aspect of the novels, the lead characters.

"We are not living in a boy's adventure tale."[17] So says the captain in Conrad's "The Secret Sharer." With his scornful reply that "we aren't indeed! There's nothing of a boy's tale in this," Leggatt asserts both the heroic quality and the reality of his life. He is a boy become a man, the tale has come true. Behind his scorn lies the exhilarating belief that he really is living an adventure tale, that the truth is not that such tales vanish when we grow up but that only when we grow up can such fictions become real. But heroes in life, like heroes in books, need an audience, a witness, someone whose understanding, which is itself an act of belief, transmutes into truth what would otherwise be only leaden fantasy. Heroes these days need someone to believe in them because without that someone, as the players in Tom Stoppard's *Rosencrantz and Guildenstern Are Dead* discover, tragedy is some fools in costume railing in the rain, death a failing to reappear. A scorn similar to Leggatt's is offered by Scott's heroic figures to the young men who come to witness and possibly join their causes, a scorn that insists that the game they play is real.

The analogy with Conrad is initially useful in thinking about Scott's fiction by showing us that we have been sophisticated in our approach to narrative structure in Conrad in a way that we have not in Scott.[18] We see the crudeness of that insidiously continuing premise in readings of Scott's work, that his double characters represent alternative ways of life. Borrowing loosely from the many impressive approaches to Conrad makes it suddenly easy to see other ways of approaching Scott.[19] Like such characters as Leggatt, Kurtz, or Lord Jim, whom we know do not represent a way of being we should consider following, the heroic figures can be thought of as forces that shape our understanding of life. The lead characters would then be the interpreters of those forces, the characters whose act of mediation is the very process of discerning and choosing that defines the truly heroic life. Evan and Fergus know how to die, know how, in Ephraim MacBriar's grand definition in *Old Mortality*, to keep company with "the spirits of the just" (341). But their world of spirits can never be ours. Scott's novels examine the world that can be ours, the possibilities for heroic action when we do not live in an adventure tale, boy's or man's.

The Bride of Lammermoor offers a character who is simultaneously both heroic figure and lead. As Levine has remarked, Edgar Ravenswood fails to read history and is doomed to the past.[20] In this he reminds us of Fergus or Balfour. In a way that looks forward to the plot of Charles Maturin's *Melmoth, The Wanderer*, Ravenswood is torn between his inflexibility—the conviction that he has been fated to be an avenger in a lost cause and thus fated for doom—and the power of his heart to change by loving Lucy. And also like Melmoth, Ravenswood fails, having only the courage that cannot believe there is anything left to win. The ambiguous credibility of the apparition of Alice at the fountain does not mean that we are to accept the supernatural but that Ravenswood will. With choice posing as necessity, he rides off to die on the sands as had been foretold, embracing the false bride of destiny and teaching us that in the Waverley novels evil is the evil of despair.

Ravenswood stands at an extreme along a line of lead characters the other end of which may be Darsie Latimer in *Redgauntlet*, who is never tempted by the notion of destiny. Even Hugh Redgauntlet's invoking the need to provide consecrated ground for Darsie's father's head, now on the gate at Carlisle and "the perch of the obscene owl and carrion crow" (378), is not compelling enough to convince Darsie to accept his fate as a Redgauntlet and relinquish "the privilege of acting for myself" (236). When Darsie protests against Hugh's proposals on the grounds that "I must see some reasonable hope of success" (378), we know he will never join those heroic figures, with their disdain of life and circumstance, their rejection of the victory that would release them from the certainties of a hopeless fate. He is redeemed, as Ravenswood would not be, by the power of hope. Far from being passive, Darsie affirms his right to be active. In a novel characterized by a lack of external action, his struggle with Hugh Redgauntlet is precisely over the issue of whether he is to be passive or active, whether he must accede to the destiny determined by his birth or assert the right to choose.

But since Darsie's commitment to forming "my own resolutions upon the reasonings of my own mind" (236) existed long before he met Redgauntlet, in part because he had been unaware of his lineage, the encounter with his uncle, unlike those between Edward Waverley and Harry Morton and their heroic figures, does not function to teach him the responsibility of choice. We must look for some other reason for the long encounter between the two that constitutes the major action of the book. Why does Darsie meet his uncle? What is gained besides the actual recovery of his name, his family, and his estate?

The answer, I think, points to nothing less than the path to redemption. Unlike Ravenswood, Darsie learns to look on the face of fate, to acknowledge his bond, and still believe in the power of choice, the obligation to make himself rather than be made by another. In *Redgauntlet* the bond is symbolized quite literally by the hoofmark on the foreheads of the family, a mark representing violence and death, a mark that Hugh Redgauntlet has and that Darsie must recognize and see on his own forehead a well. In the superb scene before a corrupt judge, Darsie repudiates any connection with Redgauntlet, then, looking at him, suddenly remembers that face from childhood; he's not sure why or how. For Darsie is, indeed, a Redgauntlet. And to deny that is to deny the truth of history, though to accept it does not also mean to accept a determinism that is finally ahistorical. Darsie must recant his denial and admit of some connection, however unknown its nature, however obscure the obligation it confers. Learning to understand the nature of the connection is the subject of the Scottish Waverley novels.

Not to recognize and acknowledge the horseshoe mark, with its echoes of Cain that look forward to Leggatt's romantic self-definition as a wanderer marked by heaven, is also to be inflexible, though not in the same sense as Redgauntlet and the other heroic figures. Often in the novels the failed fathers represent this kind of inflexibility: Mr. Fairford in *Redgauntlet*, Godfrey Bertram from the time he becomes a judge in *Guy Mannering*, Mr. Osbaldistone in *Rob Roy*, Reverend Staunton and David Deans in *The Heart of Midlothian*. Whether in their particular opinions they stand for the past or the future, the glory of God or the glories of accounting, these figures are fixed and unchanging. Whatever progress means in Scott's fiction, it cannot be linked with law-abiding citizens. And it will not come from eradicating Jacobites, or even from the inevitable passage of time. Only those who are willing to feel the allure of the lost causes, on whichever side, are capable of bringing progress. It requires the flexibility, if not actually to change sides, at least to be able to imagine them, and to extend sympathy to the other, darker life.

This is why the lead characters do have adventures, do find themselves, through their acquaintance with the heroic figures, participating in some of the great recorded moments of public history, moments that, without those figures, they would never have shared. What they learn, what we learn as well, is not that adventure is an anachronism, nor romance an adventure tale to be outgrown. Adventure and romance do exist, but not as the whole story, not as all that life is about. What they learn is precisely that there is no either–or, no highland robber or Glascow merchant, that Rob Roy and Nicol Jarvie, much like Redgauntlet and Darsie, are relatives after all. That is why the other Glascow merchants with whom the Osbaldistone company did business are the ones who turned on their former associates and are not related to Rob Roy.

To deny the relation between the daylight and the dark, whether you are on the side of a doomed fate, like Helen Campbell, or of logic and self-help, like papa Osbaldistone, is equally to mistake reality. And we might notice how much the problems in *Rob Roy*, as well as in the other novels, result from denying family relationships. *Guy Mannering*, a study of the destructive family consequences of such a denial, again reminds us that the rleations that Scottish Waverley novels defend are not simply those of blood. Upon being commissioned a justice, Mr. Bertram upholds the civic honor of the office by evicting his old friends, the gypsies, from his land, breaking the "friendly union" between his family and "[T]he knaves" (61). As the gypsies are driven off, Meg Merrilies turns to remind him of what he has broken, of the loyal hearts he has lost: "ride your ways, Laird of Allengowan, ride your ways Godfrey Bertram! This day have ye quenched seven smoking hearths,—see if the fire in your ain parlour burn the blyther for that" (72).

The heroic figures appear in order to testify to their own reality, though not, as they would have it, to convince the main characters to join them, nor, as some readers would have it, to teach us to repudiate them. Meg Merrilies, Redgauntlet, Rob, Fergus—all rise up to require that we admit our ties to them, though what that means is different from what they think. On that admission depends Scott's definition of heroic action and his lead characters' opportunities to shape their own lives. In *Guy Mannering* young Harry Bertram must actually follow Meg when she calls, must fulfil his promise to be, in Julia Mannering's horrified words, "engaged to a madwoman" (391), if he is to outgrow his false identity as Mr. Brown. Moreover, these engagements cannot be broken in a moment or a day, cannot be put behind us in the past, which is why we hear of Waverley's continuing aid to the Sons of McIvor, as befits one who has "worn their tartan" and been "an adopted son of their race" (429).

In ways that look forward to the captain's relation to Leggatt, Scott's leads bear witness to a darker world and mediate between that world and a presumably more civilized society. If their mediation succeeds, they provide a new definition of heroic action, not the fatalistic decisiveness of the dark heroes but the fuller, braver, and more dangerous ability to force their own fate, to save their ship, in Conrad's terms, through their sense of responsibility, for themselves but especially for others. Their acts are directed not by providence but by their own understanding and by hearts that will not repudiate their debts to the lawless, the mad, the wrong.

The new kind of heroic action is well dramatized in *Old Mortality* in Harry Morton's relations to John Balfour, that fanatic old warrior who wrestles with the evil one each day before dawn. Balfour enters Harry's life one evening to begin the train of events that form the story. Harry immediately acknowledges their bond, agreeing to hide Balfour on learning who he is. Harry's obligation is based on an old and unpaid debt his now-dead father, Colonel Morton, owed Balfour for saving his life. But if that debt, so quickly acknowledged, were enough, there would be no novel. It appears at the very beginning of the story precisely because it can be no more than a beginning, the first word and not the last. Indeed, we can say that *Old Mortality* is the story of Harry's learning his true relations to Balfour, relations that cannot be circumscribed for either of them by that initially recognized bond.

The bond Harry first acknowledges is a debt of honor, part of the chivalric code of a gentleman and a warrior. That heroic gesture affirms a world that believes in heroes and thereby believes in the efficacy of masculine-defined values to direct our actions and so make our history. Appropriately, the debt was contracted in battle, and the connection between such a debt and a war is reinforced by the similar exchange of heroic gestures between Harry and Lord Evandale, as each saves the other's life. They could equally have killed each other, on the public field of battle or in that private heroic landscape, a duel. The code, the gestures, belong to the world of the heroic figures, to Fergus and Redgauntlet, even to Balfour, though he is a corrupt version of the type. Harry's true legacy from his father, only symbolized by the gold chain of victory whose 3000 links his miserly uncle counts, is this code and its debt of honor through which he first affirms his own links to a lawless world.

The first problem with heroic codes in general and debts of honor in particular is that they are formal descriptions of our ties to each other. Harry feels he has nothing in common with Balfour, that this strange man really is a stranger, one to whom he can confidently say, "I have endeavoured to repay a debt due to the comrade of my father. . . . [B]ut you will excuse me from engaging myself either in your cause, or in controversy" (64). Against this polite and notably cold description of their relations Balfour offers an alternative view, one that we must notice turns out to be the true one: "[T]he son of my ancient comrade is to me as mine own, and I cannot behold him without the deep and firm belief, that I shall one day see him gird his sword in the dear and precious cause" (65). Harry learns that he will, like Harry Bertram with Meg Merrilies, *engage* himself, that his ties to Balfour, far from being limited to a night's shelter or some other concrete payment of a debt of honor, far from being limited to the debt of honor itself, are deeper, more irrational, and more lasting than any notion of honor can entail.

For codes of honor summarize and crown the masculine-labeled ideologies of our culture. And that is all they do, all they can mean. They assert their claims in adventure tales, or in the daylight rationalizations of heroes whose conscience troubles sleep, or in the dreams of young men who know not yet what they will do. Such codes decorate and thus disguise a way of seeing that is both merciless and cruel, in which the hero is always a warrior, the warrior a murdering brute. To be willing to die on principle curiously justifies being willing to kill. Harry learns that he is tied to Balfour not by a masculine code of honor but by what that code would mask, every person's potential for hate and violence and doom. And he learns that his obligation to shelter Balfour lies not in a code of honor but in everyone's obligation to acknowledge deeper ties, the ties that code denies, the human ties that lead to mercy and connect the madmen to the sane.

All this becomes clear in Harry's last encounter with Balfour, a scene that justifies Graham McMaster's insight that the novels move "away from realism toward fantasy, allegory and symbolism," and reminds us of how much we need a study of Scott's symbols.[21] Harry's reasons for seeking out Balfour years after they rode in the same cause provide a narrative excuse for this final rencontre, one that invokes and transforms their first meeting. This time the meeting occurs in Balfour's home rather than in Harry's, in a waste and wild landscape, in an "extraordinary and secluded" (404) cave. Harry is guided on his mission to ask mercy for Edith and Lord Evandale by a little girl. This messenger of gentleness and feminine courage assures him that in this landscape she is not afraid, that "grannie says we need never fear onything else when we are doing a good turn" (402). Harry now is also armed with goodness, a depth of generosity as yet undeveloped that evening so long ago when he could be induced to save a stranger's life only by the invocation of his father's debt. Unlike the little girl's, however, Harry's fuller goodness is not innocent, not naive. Cold and reserved so long ago, imagining he had nothing more to engage him with Balfour than to repay a debt, Harry now attempts to renew the acquaintance that has so deeply affected his life, and to draw upon the very power of influence with Balfour he had formerly been assured could not exist.

This time the meaning of Harry's relations to Balfour is clear. On first seeing Harry, Balfour assumes he is the ghost of conscience Balfour has just routed. Indeed, Harry is that ghost, and Balfour must fight his terrible battle yet a second time that morning in the cave. But Harry, as that ghost, no longer represents a crude commitment to a heroic code, because that is not what conscience means. He faces Balfour, his evil one, acknowledging their links yet engaged in a struggle of hope against despair, of the possibility to "[T]hink better of mankind" (407) against the martial fatalism that would trap him in Balfour's imperatives of "fight—yield, or die!" (410). Harry rejects the familiar code that leaves no choice but to kill or die and insists, even in circumstances that appear to leave no choice, on the right to choose.

All this is dramatized in the physical struggle between the two. Determining that Harry will accede to his view, that Harry is necessarily trapped and must fight. Balfour throws away the bridge that leads to his hiding place. But in as superbly literal symbolic act, Harry actually leaps "the fearful chasm" (410) that divides the cave of fatalism, of despair and doom, from the path of freedom. That leap, Harry's rejection of Balfour, frees him from Balfour. Yet his freedom comes not from denial but from sympathy. He feels for Balfour what he has come to ask Balfour to feel for Evandale and Edith, the mercy that Balfour denies to them and to him, as Balfour had also denied it to those "grey hairs" (405) of the archbishop he slew so long ago that haunt him still.

Harry's commitment to mercy and Balfour's rejection of it, whatever its general religious basis in new versus old testament thought, is related particularly to the novel's analysis of the difference between masculine heroic and feminine heroic values. Like Fergus, Balfour is a heroic figure whose understanding of reality is based on the principles of a point of view that, by its very fixity, is inadequate to interpret that reality. This same mistaken sternness is exhibited in Guy Mannering's suspicions of and duel with Mr. Brown. *Old Mortality* presents more fully and starkly than such examples as *Waverley* or *Guy Mannering* the bitter consequences of this position. It also presents more fully the alternative. Harry Morton engages himself deeper than most of Scott's leads in the wrong cause, and one result is the clarity with which he and the reader see what the right cause might be. Balfour may deny Harry at the end, but Harry will not deny him. The debt is properly paid at last, not as a debt of honor but as a debt of humanity, with the imaginative sympathy that a sense of humanity brings.

Scott's lead characters share an ambivalence that the heroic figures call feminine weakness, but that proves the basis for their salvation. The character who could be dissuaded from leaving Milnwood by his uncle's breakfast-table reluctance to part with a gold chain and by his housekeeper's mutterings about awaiting an inheritance that will allow him to marry, seems, like Edward Waverley and Darsie Latimer, vague, uncommitted, easily swayed. And by such fragile chains of circumstance as the too-hot spoonful of porridge that scalds Harry's uncle's throat, thereby inflaming his ill humor toward his nephew, does Scott point up the connections between the persuasive influence of externals and an open vision. These young leads are characters for whom circumstances matter, and thus characters for whom being indecisive also means being flexible. The adventurers and adventures they encounter will deeply affect their views. These are characters who, by their very openness, are capable of responding to what happens to them and thus capable of believing in change and choice. This openness contrasted to an apparent strength that is actually blindness is also the explicit subject of Austen's final novel, *Persuasion*.

Scott's lead characters are witnesses in a sense the heroic figures never intended. They do not make zealous converts, never fully become what others envision for them, a point that only enrages Harry Morton's comrades in arms. Yet they are not zealots for the very reason that they could be converted at all: their willingness to accept other versions of reality than the ones they have known. This does not mean that they are without firmness. But they are without fixity. What they accept, by their gestures and their deeds, is not the rightness of those lost causes but their rightness as a presence in our lives. To the extent that this acceptance is continuing, it represents one of the most constant values in the Waverley novels, the willingness to understand and to forgive. Through that willingness emerges a proper sense of time, an historical perspective.

Scott's dark heroes are wild fatalists who know their connection to the darker side of history and human possibilities. But that is all they know. They are without hope for the future. The townspeople in the Scottish novels, the judges, the fathers, the businessmen, all the upright representatives of the patriarchy, deny their connection to that darker side and base their hope for progress and salvation on the belief that they have nothing to do with it. Both the dark heroes and the upright townsmen are wrong. What Scott's lead characters are about is both recognizing their connection to the darker side—Conrad's heart of darkness, if you will—and learning to hope as well. Failing to do both must limit even such a "brave and humane" (421) man as Colonel Talbot in *Waverley*. The difference between a Colonel Talbot and so many of the leads is the power of sympathy, and thus of mercy.

The Scottish Waverley novels insist, to borrow Percy Shelley's paradox, that this is a "power girt round with weakness," the weakness of a point of view wavering enough to respond to the allure of other points of view, even those that bring evil. Our masculine-dominated culture, strong in certainties, has disparagingly called such weakness feminine. Shelley, and Scott, have simply understood the same point, but without the disparagement, and also without the sense that the feminine properly belongs only to the female. Scott "has been unfixing the boundaries of male identity ever since Edward Waverley rode out from home to be kidnapped, 'educated,' seduced, and otherwise feminized."[22] We can all be feminized, we can all escape determinism without simply denying the past, we can all hope to make better history, if we become the right kind of hero. And that is a heroine.

This essential dualism, hope for life despite, yet because of, the knowledge of death and loss, is a central human dilemma and becomes a major fictional problem for nineteenth-century British novelists. The gothic, by which I refer to the historical literary movement from

Horace Walpole's *The Castle of Otranto* in 1764 to Maturin's *Melmoth, The Wanderer* in 1820, is continuously concerned to dramatize the confrontation with despair. Melmoth himself seems the brother of Edgar Ravenswood. My larger hypothesis is that the emergence of this dilemma as a major topic helps to account for the prevalence of heroines in nineteenth-century British fiction. Myra Jehlen, in her discussion of feminist criticism, offers a related point. She sees the emerging subject of the novel as the tension between the interior self and the demands of society and proposes that "this interior life, *whether lived by man or woman, is female.*" [23] Her qualification is important, that female characters are not seen to represent real women but rather the inner self of either sex. Similarly, I would say that the heroines I am interested in represent not women's values but human values, those values our culture so often belittles by calling female and that I am here calling the heroic feminine.

These heroines and this concern for the inner life do not appear newborn within the novels of Scott or of Austen, nor is their ancestry limited to gothic fiction. Richardson's influence on Scott, and on all of nineteenth-century fiction, is profound. Readers have long recognized the ambivalent play in *Clarissa* between conventions of femininity, the powers to understand and care about others, and the developing sense of self.[24] That ambivalence about traditional feminine values coupled with the complex meaning of mercy and its religious dimension in the novel are part of what makes Clarissa such an elusive as well as influential heroine. Without doing more here than acknowledging Scott's debt to Richardson, we can see Scott's own great heroine, Jeanie Deans, as herself an example not only for us but for the many novelists who came after him and were influenced by his work. Once we see the pattern in such novels as *Waverley, Redgauntlet, Old Mortality, Guy Mannering,* and *Rob Roy*, in which the lead character represents not the passive or weak alternative to the heroic figure but rather the mediating vision that alone can incorporate that figure and thus break out of adventure tale into history, out of myth into time, then we can turn to the problem novel, *The Heart of Midlothian.*

In spite of being considered uncharacteristic of Scott, *The Heart of Midlothian* and its peasant heroine have long been admired. Georg Lukacs calls Jeanie Deans Scott's "greatest female character." [25] David Daiches says the novel shows that "there is the possibility of heroic action in modern life . . . in the unpretentious faith and courage of a humble Scots lass" or, as Fleishman put it, "genuine nobility is here found and developed in a woman of the peasantry."[26] Yet there has always been something missing from these discussions. For example, though Fleishman has taken up the question of why nobility should appear in a peasant, he says nothing of why that peasant should be a woman. Readers have traditionally not examined the question of why heroic action is dramatized through a heroine.[27] Instead, there has been the continuing problem of trying to place Jeanie in relation to the patterns of other Scott novels. The general assumption is that she does not fit. Thus Welsh, discussing how *The Heart of Midlothian* does express the pattern he has described of passive and active heroes, makes what has always seemed to me the startling claim that the pairing is between Reuben Butler, who is Jeanie's fiancé, and George Staunton.[28] Such a misreading stems in part from the problem with Welsh's categories and from a kind of mechanical application of the term *passive* that puts a minor figure in the lead character's role. Even critics who go beyond the labeling of Reuben as hero that mixes up the meaning of hero between lead character and male good guy, who recognize Jeanie as the lead character and in that sense the hero of the book, still make the unexamined assumption that she cannot be a hero in the way the other leads have been. Francis Hart sees Jeanie's leading role but agrees with Welsh that Reuben is the moderate hero and then terms Jeanie a "heroic fanatic," a category that hardly fits the double pattern of the novels.[29]

These repeated difficulties about Jeanie's role emerge in part from the implicit, and perhaps unconscious, critical assumption that because she is female she cannot occupy the same position in the structure of the novel as Scott's other lead characters. Certainly, the difficulties shrink away once we make the simple yet enormously important concession that Jeanie does, indeed, occupy the same position as Edward Waverley or Darsie Latimer or Harry Morton. We can then begin to look at the central issue of her relations to a dark heroic figure and to ask what seems to me the most useful question to bring to *The Heart of Midlothian*, how those relations are illuminated and transformed by making the hero a heroine.

Granting Jeanie's lead role, we see that the character to whom she stands in most dramatic relation is George Staunton.[30] Within Scott's canon, it is both predictable and unusual that the center of the novel should be Jeanie's confrontation with George at the parsonage at Willingham. Like Harry Bertram, Jeanie finds herself engaged with a madwoman, the peasant girl whom George Staunton seduced and deserted. Madge Wildfire's madness functions as a lurid talisman of how women are victimized by men, not randomly or personally, but as a given of the relative cultural definitions of women and men. But unlike either Harry Bertram or Harry Morton, and in a symbol that superbly captures the novel's acknowledgment that what we call the givens of nature are truly the inventions of culture, Jeanie Deans is led not to a cave but to the bedroom of a young English gentleman. What she confronts there is the same evil, the evil of masculine codes that privilege culture as nature, choice as inevitability.

For much of the story Jeanie thinks she can have nothing to do with George. But Jeanie must go into that bedroom, must confront the sexuality that defines George's power and that is at the center of the masculine heroic mode of controlling women. She must also confront both sides of the Orc cycle, the father and the son, if the reader is to understand her cultural relations with them.[31] George will become, quite literally, her relative, her brother-in-law. And his money, sent to her by her sister over the years, will buy for Jeanie's family the farm neighboring their parsonage at Roseneath, thus solidifying their future place in the new world.

George Staunton is an important variation on the dark heroes of Scott's novels. We meet him at his best, as a public figure. He is Geordie Robertson, generous and loyal friend to Wilson, condemned thief, repentant sinner, intelligent organizer, and daring leader of the Porteus mob. If, as Welsh has observed, most of Scott's heroic figures turn out to be a bit villainous, Robertson moves to that category rather soon in the novel, having more in common with Balfour than with Fergus.[32] Robertson's most damning feature is that, apart from the sense of justice, however skewed, he shows as leader of the mob that hangs Porteus, he has been moved to become an outlaw not by any political or religious principles but simply by that most demeaning of motives, egoism and its resultant lack of self-control. Handsome, charming, and courageous, he is yet a heroic figure without a cause, even a lost cause, to direct his actions.

Though without the principles that can be so alluring in Scott's heroic figures, George does share their fixity. He is an intense, excessive, obsessive man, and his obsession takes the form of a conviction that he is damned. We first meet Geordie "skulking . . . among the scattered rocks" of a "sequestered dell" (114), where he gives a dramatic presentation of himself to Reuben Butler "in the name of the devil" (115) and sternly dismisses him with the assurance that "the eye that seeks to trace my motions shall have reason to curse it was ever shrouded by eyelid or eyelash. Begone, and look not behind you"

(117–18). Geordie's guilt is self-inflating, and we hear the difference between this heady language and Balfour's unselfconscious ravings as he faces his devil. Geordie has been an actor. He performs again that coming night, threatening to take the role of the infamous Muschat and murder Jeanie at Muschat's Cairn. There he assures her, in language so desperate that it sounds "rather like that of a fiend than of a human being," that "you see before you a wretch, predestined to evil here and hereafter" (159).

We see Geordie's point. Like Redgauntlet or Ravenswood, Geordie insists upon the inevitability, the divinely directed necessity of his fate. Unlike others of Scott's dark heroes, he also insists that his destiny is to do and be evil. Nonetheless, he shares with them the security, the release from responsibility, that the notion of predestiny can give. For Geordie, too, has been provided for. By presenting the dark hero without a cause and with the conviction that the particular quality of his fate is evil, *The Heart of Midlothian* makes explicit the criticism of the masculine heroic vision that has been implicit in his work all along: its refusal to bear the weight of any real choice. In that first conversation with Jeanie, Geordie moves from introducing himself to claiming that he has destroyed not only Effie and her baby but his mother and Wilson as well. This is an affirmation of responsibility that, by its very excess, is really a denial. Geordie's point is that everything seems to go badly for those around him but he cannot control that; fate has decreed it, he really has no choice at all. So he takes the only honorable option, acceptance of all the crimes. And we might note that Jeanie, who does understand responsibility, immediately extracts the one conclusion he wishes to obscure: "Then you are the wicked cause of my sister's ruin?" (160).

In that meeting at the Cairn when Geordie explains to Jeanie that she can save Effie's life by lying to the court, by saying that Effie had told her sister she was pregnant, Jeanie replies that "I wad ware the best blood in my body to deep her skaithless, . . . but I canna change right into wrang, or make that true which is false" (163). But Geordie can. These are the kind of reversals in which he excels. Geordie's belief that he is predestined for evil makes his evil actions the necessary fulfillment of God's plan, and in that sense good. And surely one point of the references to acting is that Geordie sees himself cast in the role of villain in a script he has not written and cannot change. Whatever he does, however thoughtless and destructive, is divinely directed, has a larger purpose, a meaning for good. Geordie may not change right into wrong, but he changes wrong into right.

Geordie is a chameleon in his genius for combining free will with predetermination, for reversing the moral significance of things. And with startling appropriateness, Scott literally gives him double names and a double identity. Geordie Robertson, the wrong, turns out to be George Staunton, the right, son and heir of the Rector of Willingham. The portrait of Geordie/George combines in one character those supposed antipodes in Scott's fiction: the lawless yet adventurous Scottish past and the law-abiding and upright English future. The point of the combination is not the antipathy of these contrasting modes but their identity. The nature of this identity is revealed in the fine second section of the novel, when Jeanie travels to London to ask a queen's pardon for Effie.

Jeanie's walk to London involves only one significant step, the meeting at Willingham with Reverend Staunton and Geordie Robertson metamorphosed into George Staunton. Here the often suggested link in Scott's work between the proponents of society and its outcasts becomes a major theme in *The Heart of Midlothian*, embodied both in George's double identity and in the relations between father and son. The minister and judge beget the outlaw, a figure of seductive evil reclining in the heart of that sweet parsonage, as George describes himself, "like a crushed snake" (340). Father and son share a masculine code of honor that we can no more applaud in its upright form than its adventurous one. The wrongness of that code as a basis for understanding or action is brought out by using a heroine in ways less easily seen when the lead character is a man confronting another man. If the masculine heroic masks an inhuman notion of war, it also masks an inhuman notion of love. Turning to that notion permits Scott not merely to offer another aspect of the inhumanity of the heroic vision but specifically to enforce the connections between the masks of society and those of wildness.

We see why the familiar confrontation between lead and heroic figure occurs in the darkened bedroom of an English parsonage rather than in Balfour's cave. When Reverend Staunton, discovering the two in that bedroom, is struck with horror that George may have some passion for Jeanie, that he may make a "low and disgraceful marriage" (354), we suddenly realize how the evil of the lawful father's world is tied to the evil of the lawless son's. For if George could seduce Madge and then Effie, his father, despite knowing of his son's immorality and Madge's pregnancy, could prevent George from righting that original wrong, the wrong that began so much of the present evil. We may plausibly suspect, then, that he would also prevent George from being so "disgraceful" as to right his wrong to Effie. That Jeanie has the same suspicion we see by her seemingly odd insistence that George not tell his father their true connections. She knows she cannot rely on the minister and judge to choose the path of truth and justice in which the honorable forms of society reflect our relations to each other. She knows that Reverend Staunton would have his son deny his ties to Effie in the name of family honor and would thereby, like Geordie, change wrong into right.

As do so many of the novels, *The Heart of Midlothian* attempts to define human values in opposition to what the culture calls heroic values but which are no more than martial values. The novel's attempt is complicated by the fact that our human values must somehow also be heroic while traditional heroic values often look as if they were the most human. Geordie, like Redgauntlet, like most advocates of masculinity, is adept at depicting cultural constructs as if they were truths of nature. He bases his appeal to Jeanie to lie for Effie on the idea that she should abandon cold principle and follow "natural affection" (164). But Jeanie's principles support human values in a way that George's and his father's do not. In this sense we may call them properly heroic.

Jeanie's role helps us to see the significant point of the apparently weak lead characters, that, either from the beginning or through a process of education, they stand for an idea of heroic action that both encompasses and supersedes traditional masculine codes of honor and courage, Evan's "the heart of a hielandman" and "the honour of a gentleman." The lead characters' relation to that code, and thus Scott's definition of heroic progress, rather than being a pattern of attraction followed by rejection, as it has traditionally been described, is more properly the reverse: an initial rejection followed by a process of involvement through which comes an affirmation of permanent connections. The point has special clarity when dramatized in a woman. Jeanie never could fight. But her walk, a form of action that does not make for grand gestures, guides her to the home of the dark hero. And that walk also asserts choice, responsibility, hope, commitment to forgiveness—qualities that in the Scottish novels repeatedly connect the leads to the dark heroes and define true heroic action.

Again and again, the difference between the masculine heroic and the feminine heroic in Scott's fiction, like the difference between the old sexual heroines and the new heroines of Austen's fiction, is between what is asserted to be absolute or inevitable, a truth of nature, and what allows for and acknowledges change. The question *The*

Heart of Midlothian asks and Jeanie Deans faces, expressed as an issue of conscience, is what the grounds are on which we can win over doom, what powers we have that will give us, at least for a time, the victory that is life. Jeanie's refusal to lie and her decision instead to walk to London embody the answer that there is only one power that can combat death and the despair that comes from the knowledge of death. That power lies not in our stars but in ourselves, not in a belief in predestiny that can make even death purposeful, but in an admission of our shared fate.

This is the community principle on which Jeanie bases her successful plea to Queen Caroline. She reminds the Queen of the Queen's own death, and that when that hour comes, the thoughts of what we have done for others can most sweeten our despair. That scene, a plea for a sister, pleads for a kind of sisterhood as well. It is one that can include queens as well as peasants, men as well as women, the good girls and the bad. Indeed, at the center of the plot is Jeanie's sense of her bond with, and her obligation to, her sister. And I point out the symbolic value of Scott's making Jeanie and Effie half sisters rather than full-blooded sisters. What unites them is the father, what they share is their lives under his dominance. And such dominance is felt even by a queen. The claims of sisterhood replace the masculine idea of brotherhood. As depicted in the novel, that is the vision that has posed so long as natural and universal, but which in historical practice has always been an artificial and exclusive principle, a matter of elitist codes and factions, of being the right sex and the right color and the right class.

We mistake the meaning of Jeanie's walk to London if we read it as heroic in the sense of being a physically brave or impressively grueling activity. For it represents a kind of courage that Scott's heroic figures cannot sustain. When Effie, at her trial, with sentence pronounced for doom, tells the court that "God is mair mercifu' to us that we are to each other" (252), she expresses the traditional masculine heroic perspective. Her relations with George have taught her well. But what is newly heroic about Jeanie's walk is that she takes it on the chance that we might be more merciful to each other. That kind of hope is heavier to carry than Effie's sight of the doomster or Geordie's desperate courage in offering to sacrifice his own life if Effie could be freed.

Like Harry Morton, Jeanie leaps the chasm of despair. Her leap is not as graceful as Harry's and rather slower, requiring as it does all the various comic conveyances that help her along in her walk. But the issues are the same. Balfour's imperatives of "fight—yield or die" offer the same trap, the same denial of choice, as Jeanie's alternatives of a sister's death or a kind of spiritual death for herself in telling a lie. We are back to the heroic code, to Evan's and Fergus's kill or die, and to the essentialist and reactionary presumption that underlies that code, that the givens of the world we find ourselves in do not allow the changes that come of choice. Jeanie does not succumb to those supposedly immutable givens and leaps to freedom. Never believing she is fated to do evil, to herself or to Effie, she chooses to follow conscience, not because she fears God but because she does not fear men. Like Harry Morton, who made his excursion to Balfour's cave on the same chance, Jeanie's admission of our ties to each other frees her to plead for mercy because it frees her to hope.

And that, finally, is the point. If we think that the great human virtues are manly and martial, the resolution to fight, yield, or die, and that the kingdom of man is finally composed of knights who have earned their places forevermore, then the values that insist on our connections rather than our differences and that prefer mercy to justice and revenge will be seen as merely feminine. Redgauntlet offers a fine instance of this perspective when he dresses Darsie, whom he considers to have been brought up "delicate and effeminate" (240), in women's clothes. From such a perspective the lead characters, when they are male, can be considered weak and passive. But this is not the perspective the novels allow. Scott turns out to be "less a dealer in heroes than" many novel writers.[33] The very virtues so often asserted by hostile males to be female are victorious in the novels, virtues that stand not as female values but as feminine, human, and heroic values and as the only forms in which the future can continue and contain the past. In our sense of connections, both spatial and temporal, both with other places and with other times, rests our hopes for the future. These hopes, though they may vary as to specifics, can be defined. They are the belief that we have the power to direct our lives, that our choices can affect events, that we can change the future by our decisions and our acts.

We must, at last, recognize in Scott's work the link between what are traditionally thought to be feminine values, those softer virtues of flexibility and forgiveness, and what that work offers as a sense of history and of progress. Scott's novels are not historical merely because they dramatize the great events of Scottish history or connect large events with individual lives or give "living human embodiment to historical-social types." [34] They are historical because they require that both their lead characters and their readers acknowledge their deep relations, their sisterhood, with people and beliefs and events that it may be easier to condemn or to reject or, worst of all, to forget. In Meredith's *The Egoist*, Willoughby Patterne salves his outrage at a servant who had dared to quit by pronouncing that "Flitch is extinct!" Scott's novels insist that Flitch, and all he reminds us of, cannot be declared extinct, that the past is never simply past, that our sense of time and of the present, as well as our hopes for a better future, cannot depend on such conclusive and atomizing powers.

Scott did not create Jeanie Deans because he thought she would make a better lead character than all those noble young men. Rather, I imagine, and his 1830 introduction says as much, he heard Helen Walker's true story and reshaped it into a fiction structured like many of his others. But because Jeanie is a woman, she transforms and thus extends the meaning of the pattern of feminine heroism for men while still standing within it. Moreover, if Jeanie, being a woman, is free from conventions applying to heroes, she is also, being a peasant, a short, stocky, freckled peasant, free from the conventions of traditional sexual heroines as well. We might call Scott's creation of her unconsciously feminist, except that the point might be that our reading of Scott has been unconsciously masculinist. As I have tried to suggest, the lead characters continually embody the rejection of limited masculine notions of the heroic life and the affirmation, because of their empathy with the dark heroes, of more sisterly values. Jeanie's heroism, unmarred by readers' gender-based expections of what being a hero means, is easy to see. And if it has been less easy to see the heroism of such noncommittal young men as Edward Waverley or Darsie Latimer, Jeanie's heroism can release us from preconceptions about them as well.

Through Jeanie Deans and *The Heart of Midlothian*, both long considered anomalies in the pattern of the Scottish Waverley novels, we can see more clearly what the pattern is about. When the heroine becomes the hero, the novel offers a new definition of what heroism can mean. In Scott's fiction that definition has been offered all along. It is directly linked to his idea of history, his sense of time as, to borrow from Blake, the mercy of eternity. But with the use of a female lead in *The Heart of Midlothian*, that definition fulfills its promise as a vision of progress, which includes recognizing gender as a cultural artifact and revising, and reevaluating, the qualities labeled male and female.

The Heart of Midlothian and the first great peasant heroine also stand as part of the influential beginning of a century in which novelist after novelist will use a woman lead to express the central issue of his or her fiction. *The Heart of Midlothian* can direct us to look again at some of the other great heroines in nineteenth-century British fiction. As the story of Jeanie and Effie suggests, the progressive human community, as imaged in many nineteenth-century novels, may well be a sisterhood.

4

Gaskell's Daughters in Time

> It's queer how out of touch with truth women are. They live in a world of their own, and there has never been anything like it, and never can be.
>
> JOSEPH CONRAD

> There's a stake in your fat black heart
> And the villagers never liked you.
> They are dancing and stamping on you.
> They always *knew* it was you.
> Daddy, daddy, you bastard, I'm through.
>
> SYLVIA PLATH

It's queer how out of touch with truth even the most insightful writers can be, how even someone who could look deeply enough into the human heart to write "The Heart of Darkness" and "The Secret Sharer" could distribute truth according to sex. We must suspect Conrad's use of the Cain story, that his belief that we are brothers and are our brothers' keepers really does refer to brothers rather than to brothers and sisters, that mankind means men. Certainly, Marlow's words on women show us one of the limits of Conrad's own power, great as it is, to touch the truth. It may be that Percy Shelley's Demogorgon is right, that, finally, the deep truth is imageless. Yet the history of literature is a parade of its images, of attempts to touch the truth.

Conrad follows a long tradition of British novelists who took the risk of trying to offer truth, of believing, in George Levine's words, "in the possibility of fictions that bring us a little closer to what is not ourselves and not merely language."[1] Nineteenth-century novelists continually defined that "what," that something "really out there after all," in anti-heroic terms.[2] The link in fiction between realism and the anti-heroic has long been understood. I want to extend that insight, to argue here for the link between realism, the anti-heroic, and the frequency of women as the lead characters in nineteenth-century novels. To touch the truth, to leave the world of our own, demands understanding, forgiveness, love. These sympathetic powers, often developed by female characters, lead to a sense of connections, the very sense that Marlow feels and understands as brotherhood, however dark the knowledge that binds us may be. Thus Marlow's literary ancestors and Conrad's literary inspirations, characters who took their own dark journeys prior to which they too were merely savages, and whose routes marked the way for Marlow's, include such famous creatures as Emma Woodhouse, Gwendolen Harleth, and Isabel Archer. They also include the less famous characters of Elizabeth Gaskell.

Critically, Gaskell's work has not fared well. Much has been made of her ability to describe the curtains in Mary Barton's house or the landscape around Monkshaven and the relations between landowners and whalers there.[3] But these kinds of appreciations are too easily linked to a traditional blindness about gender as well as a masculine belief that women novelists—Burney, Austen, Gaskell, Charlotte Brontë (not Emily, who is bizarre, nor Eliot, who has that masculine mind)—describe or mimic their worlds rather than invent them. Evaluating works by a woman writer in terms of their reflection of the writer's life or the society outside the novels too often connects to thinking that women lack the creative fire to be like Yeats's golden smithies, forging art out of the unpurged images of life. In the specific case of Gaskell, tributes to her descriptive ability grant her work the kind of mimetic realism no one respects, that which merely reproduced fact. This has worked to deny her fiction any substantive realistic power, to see it as an eclectic mix of reportage and sentiment.[4]

Even recent readers of Gaskell's work who do not simply repeat the old strictures have tended to place Gaskell as a mother figure whose literary vision and voice articulate the dependent feminine role within the patriarchy. Carolyn Heilbrun, from a perspective that agrees with Coleridge and many other readers that "great minds do tend to be androgynous," asks of Gaskell's novels: "[I]s there a passage which does not betray the gender of its author?"[5] And the question is not a compliment. Heilbrun, who has written a brilliant analysis of the woman as hero in late nineteenth-century fiction, faults Gaskell for writing within conventions, sometimes playing with them but never radically challenging the structures a patriarchal society has made up and called true.[6]

I suggest that Gaskell's work is radical in ways her critics have not yet done justice to. Gaskell's novels, like those of Dickens or of Scott (who is an enormous influence on her), are engaged in something other than recording sympathetically her observations of urban life and memories of country life or speaking up for the powers of the female role within a paternally ordered culture. Coral Lansbury, in her fine full-length study of Gaskell's work, argues persuasively that the resolutions of the novels, far from being naively optimistic, should be read as the fictions they are, patterns that do not verge from reality because they are reflections distorted by sentiment but because they are not reflections at all.[7] This insight recalls to us the prophetic and reforming quality of Gaskell's novels. It may well have been improbable in Manchester for relations between worker and employer to find solutions through individual friendships, or for a worker to die in an owner's arms, or for a woman to rescue bodily a factory owner from an angry mob. But realism in fiction has never been so simple a matter as to be measured by what has happened or probably would happen in life.

Like so many other Victorian novels, Gaskell's works offer a complex definition of the real, one that insists on the profound interdependence of the private and public realms, one that also envisions for everyone a feminine future better than the masculine present and past. To get to that definition we need new kinds of questions, not those that trigger our own fictions about the factual situation in another time and place but those that may guide us to the different truth Gaskell's novels tell. A literary lie is, after all, another name for a novel. And Conrad, a great mind who unarguably had his own troubles getting past a paternally ordered world, who may not have been androgynous, must have known somewhere that not only women but both men and women, insofar as they write novels, "live in a world of their own, and there has never been anything like it, and never can be." And living in a world of one's own has been, at least in the history of literature, one of the best ways to be in touch with truth.

A moment in *Cranford*, the idyllic novella that has often been used to denigrate Gaskell's fiction as escapist, directly addresses the subject of truth as opposed to a world of one's own. Miss Matty, the spinster heroine, about to open a tea shop, first asks the shopkeeper presently selling tea in Cranford if her enterprise would lesson their business. Mr. Smith, the narrator's father, who does not live in Cranford, scorns these scruples, announcing that "such simplicity might do very well in Cranford, but would never do in the world."[8] Mr. Smith lives in the town of Drumble, and Drumble, in this novella, comes to stand for the world, the real world, the world presumably in touch with truth, with Cranford presumably that never-never land where women live. In Drumble human nature reveals its true self as competitive, dangerous and endangered, even wicked.

But the brilliance of this story is that we never see Drumble, we never visit it. Drumble remains outside the boundaries of the novella, an invention, a "cartographer's conspiracy," given no more reality in the story than that other outside place, the India that Miss Matty's brother, Peter, ran away to when still a boy and that he so impulsively returns from in his old age. The cheating rogues that Mr. Smith so constantly watches for in Drumble are as fantastic as the flying cherubim Peter tells of shooting down in the Indian Himalayas. One is the practical, clear-sighted realm of business and the other the dreamy and heroic realm of high adventure. Yet in this novella both are alike in two fundamental ways: they are masculine and they are unreal.

Like so many nineteenth-century novels, *Cranford* in its small way offers a debate on the nature of reality. *Cranford* does not insist that there are no rogues or cherubim, no devils or angels, no competitive businessmen or heroes. Rather, it insists that the values those businessmen and heroes have believed to be trivial and naive, the values of women who live in a world of their own, far from being out of touch with truth, are a powerful force in creating what we call reality. As Nina Auerbach put it, "the cooperative female community defeats the warrior world that proclaims itself the real one."[9] Since the true or the real is what we are continually in the process of making, the feminine values of Cranford, though gentle remnants of a fading past, also turn out to be the best hope for the future and must be carried into our understanding of what we are and do. They are the values we must use in creating ourselves.

And surely that is part of the point of how the narrator functions in *Cranford.* Daughter of Mr. Smith, native of Drumble, Mary Smith nonetheless writes not of where she lives but of where she visits, the life of which so clearly brings life to her mind and heart. Mary comes from and literally belongs to that outside world. Yet we never see or know of her in it, because what is significant in Mary's life takes place in her relation to Cranford. She is not to be understood as a sympathetic but somewhat removed observer. To believe that would be to accept Mr. Smith's external definitions of action and event. Mary is a convert, discovering in Cranford a truth her father cannot tell and seeing through the eyes of Cranford to the fictions he takes for truth.

We see how much the pattern of this novella owes to Scott. The doppelgänger forms of upright citizen and heroic figure that appear so often in Scott, in Nicol Jarvie and Rob Roy, Mr. Fairford and Hugh Redgauntlet, Reverend Staunton and Geordie Robertson, appear again in almost mythic form in *Cranford*, in Mr. Smith and in Matty's brother, Peter, while in India as the Aga Jenkyns. Peter's unforgivable crime in the eyes of his father, that patriarchal tyrant who ruled Cranford until his own death, and still ruled through his elder daughter until her death, was to dress up as a girl and croon over a mock baby. Peter abdicated masculinity and declared his propensity for the feminine. His father, the Christian minister so reminiscent of Geordie Robertson/George Staunton's father, responded by physically beating him and driving him from home out to that other masculine realm of danger and adventure. Only after the masculine authorities in the family, both father and elder daughter, are dead can Peter abandon the masculine life of adventure and stop being the Aga Khan. He can at last return to the feminine world that he early preferred and to which he belongs.

Gaskell's point is much the same as Scott's. Both the businessman and the adventurer, seemingly so different, are identical in presenting versions of human nature that are aggressive, that offer a fixed understanding of human nature, one that does not value the pliable, the passive, the weak. Instead of these two figures, which for Gaskell as for Scott merge into one, Gaskell offers an alternative that must be familiar to Scott's readers. Miss Matty Jenkyns is a lead character who is not particularly aggressive or assertive, yet who stands, however waveringly, against these battling figures to represent the idea of human nature the story supports. The distance from Edward Waverley to Miss Matty is but a short one after all. For both are persuadable characters, alike in their sensitivity to those who surround them, though Miss Matty shrinks from disagreements at the tea table, and Waverley fights in a war.

The connection to Scott is developed past its original in one important way. Edward Waverley, Harry Morton, Darsie Latimer—these young men stand for what we can simply call human values, the values of kindness, mercy, and love, the same values so beautifully dramatized in Jeanie Deans. In *Cranford* these are Miss Matty's values and also those of the obligingly feminized Peter and Captain Brown. Yet *Cranford*, as the story of the village of Amazons, explicitly and fully defines the world in which those values can flourish as a feminine place. The feminine has been given its own town and its own world. And the town and that world fill the whole novella. The examples of Captain Brown and of Peter when he returns from India make clear that these values can appear in men. Nonetheless, they are the values of a world of women, not, as in Scott, values culturally defined as feminine yet dramatized as necessary for both male and female lead characters in what is still dramatized as a masculine-dominated context. Scott's focus remained more on what men needed to learn whereas Gaskell's moved more to what women could teach.

Yet for both novelists, and this may be the center of what Gaskell took from Scott, these feminine-labeled values are directly linked to a sense of time, of history. The special quality of *Cranford* is that in it values the culture has characterized as feminine are tied to an idea of time and are also explicitly celebrated as feminine. Gaskell's full-length novels offer what *Cranford* only suggests, a developed examination of the nature of history and an exploration of how our ideas of history are intertwined with how we define truth, reality, and ourselves.

The immediate difficulty with *Ruth*, that declaredly unconventional novel about a young woman raising her bastard son, is that Gaskell offers such an apparently cowardly ending, killing off her heroine by having Ruth nurse her seducer through the cholera and take the fever herself. This is a level of self-sacrifice many readers don't much admire. If we see the novel as liberal propaganda, aimed to portray the conditions of life for fallen women in order, in Meredith's words, to "[h]elp poor girls," or in Trollope's, to feel their "misery is worthy of alleviation," the ending does seem cruel.[10] Is there mercy or is there justice? Is Ruth, having earned the right to live, yet required to die? Did Gaskell fail in the courage of her radical convictions and at the last conventionally destroy her lovingly created sinner, or were the convictions limited to no more than a partial redemption?

An answer may lie in avoiding the presumption that the intention is the realization, that the novel may be judged according to the degree to which it fulfills Gaskell's declared social purpose.[11] After all, *Ruth* has no obligation to be social history or propaganda. And its achievement should not be measured by the extent to which it may realize our projections of the plight of seduced women in mid-nineteenth-century England. Wihtout denying the reforming purpose of this novel or its real public impact, I want to look at the fictional conventions it inherits and transforms.

When we consider British novels whose subject is fallen women we must inevitably find our way back through Dickens and gothic and sentimental fiction to the novel and the heroine who defines the type, the sublime Clarissa Harlowe.[12] Ruth is a latter-day Clarissa. Richardson's other, less successful heroine suggest the literary price of an earthly reward. Pamela happily marries Mr. B. He has not, of course, actually seduced her, and if he had, such an ending would presumably not have been possible. But it should not have been possible anyway, given the terms of their struggle, which is why the plot of *Pamela* seems to me flawed. Happily, *Ruth* descends not from *Pamela* but from *Clarissa*. And the struggle Ruth wages does lead to victory, great victory, although it also leads to death. There are many ways in which the patterns in *Ruth* recall those in *Clarissa*. I want to suggest just a few here, those particularly that might help to distinguish what is special and important about *Ruth*.

Ruth is a gentle and innocent ingenue whereas her seducer is the familiar evil Pygmalion from so many eighteenth-century novels. Mr. Bellingham is handsome, charming, clever, and wicked. A gentleman, he seems to have all the strength, the power, and certainly the money on his side. Indeed, their respective positions are so unequal during Ruth's first encounter with Mr. Bellingham that the character in Richardson's novel she may most resemble is not Clarissa but Rosebud, the little servant at the inn whom Lovelace decides to spare. But Ruth does not remain so unequal. As with Lovelace and Clarissa, Bellingham's victory over her body becomes her victory over his soul. The novel is structured so that from their first encounter to their second, more than ten years later, their positions have been reversed. The little, trembling rosebud has become a daunting figure. When Bellingham, never understanding her, imagining that the old imbalance still applies, begs her to marry him, Ruth, who does understand him, is repelled. And Clarissa's fabulous cry that "my soul is above thee, man" echoes in Ruth's insistence to her old seducer that she no longer loves him and will never love him again. She will never marry him, never live with him, so that their son will never be like him.

But this brings us to the great distance between these two novels, both of which dramatize so intensely and so starkly the power relations between the two sexes. In *Ruth* there is a son. And, more importantly, there is sexual passion, the passion that generations of Richardson's critics have only been able to locate through their interpretations of Clarissa's dreams and Richardson's subconscious. Ruth openly admits her past love for Bellingham during that conversation on the Abermouth sands. She was not raped, she was seduced. And even though, like Tess so many years later, she knew not what she did, she deeply loved her seducer. While Tess walked indifferently, listlessly, away from Alec D'Urberville, Ruth had to be thrown off, blocked by Bellingham's outraged mother at his bedroom door. And even then, in that Welsh mountain village, she literally ran after the carriage that carried her beloved away.

Unlike Clarissa's attitude to Lovelace, who had drugged her to virtual unconsciousness during the crucial, and single, event, Ruth's superiority to Bellingham is not tied to a denial of sexuality. Gaskell offers us passion and then purity, consummation and then innocence of heart. Ruth has loved him, she has lived with him, she has, at least momentarily, preferred death to life without him. Yet, as one of the relatives of those dying of fever whom Ruth nurses can testify, "She will be in the light of God's countenance when you and I will be standing afar off" (425). What accounts for the difference between the two heroines is Gaskell's commitment to the power of time.

Ruth is a novel about redemption, about the transforming power of time. The subject of a fallen woman is an evocative vehicle for examining the active relations between character and event that constitute a personal history, because the whole notion of a fallen woman assumes that one's status is fixed, that there can be no more personal history, just an endless repetition of that one defining event. One can lose one's virginity only once, one can fall only once. As Byron, a master of these categories, put it, "the woman once fallen forever must fall."[13] This is the simple message of poor Aunt Esther, in Gaskell's first novel, *Mary Barton*. But in *Ruth*, Gaskell does not give an event the Hegelian status of being, as if it were outside time.

The subject may be clearer if we briefly compare *Ruth* to a novel more or less contemporary with it that also uses the fallen woman, Dickens's *Bleak House*. Though written six years later and by a novelist who was socially committed to helping fallen women and who consistently supported Gaskell's work and strongly praised *Ruth*, *Bleak House* uses the conventional literary view of the fallen woman. She is irredeemable or, more precisely, redeemed only in death. Is Lady Dedlock's crime the ambition that denied her love for Nemo, or the passion that fulfilled it without marriage and thus produced Esther Summerson? Certainly, her ambition alone would not have resulted in that hunted death. And even if we feel both ambition and passion make Lady Dedlock a fallen woman, can we conceive of an Esther Summerson who has known illicit sexual love?

Though born a bastard, Esther is beyond the reach of circumstance, placed there by her own lack of desire, her inherent purity of heart. Those two qualities are, indeed, the same. Lady Dedlock is damned because she has wanted and has gotten what she wants. Much of the plot of *Bleak House* depends upon an antisexuality, a suspicion of sexual passion, that can only see it as a sign of an uncontrolled person or a corrupt heart. Dickens would not have understood Blake. He was too fond of producing his own Thels and approving of them. Lady Dedlock's fate, though tragic, is inescapable. Indeed, the movement of her whole story is the attempt to escape the inescapable, to get away from the fact that will haunt her and her lover to their graves.

The achievement of *Ruth*, as social history, as intelligent fiction, is that it insists upon the power of circumstance, the very power that Clarissa vanquished and that Lady Dedlock was not allowed to invoke. Choosing neither prostitution nor death as the fate of its heroine, the novel simply imagines a new set of circumstances, that a person, having once passed into the world of experience, simply lives on, lives more or less as other people do. In fact, Ruth's affair with Bellingham is the beginning of her life. The ignorant, fifteen-year-old farmer's daughter turned dressmaker's apprentice vanishes in the light of the long process of understanding what she has done and become. That is her trip to the Congo.

Ruth is a novel of education, a form that nineteenth-century novelists continually used for exploring subjects quite different from the issue of an individual process of maturation. In *Ruth* the heroine to be educated is a kind of character defined as past educating, a heroine, who has already been made what she must ever remain, when she was successfully seduced by a wicked Pygmalion. She is, in Gaskell's words about Esther, Mary Barton's aunt, past hope. The subject not only offers ideas about change, as we would expect from a novel of education, but also casts an argument about the issue of reform the implications of which extend beyond any personal history.

Reform in its political aspect is an explicit topic in *Ruth*, and the election process appears in the novel in a way that looks forward to Eliot's use of it in *Middlemarch*. Mr. Bellingham reappears late in the novel metamorphosed into Mr. Donne, the Liberal candidate brought in by Mr. Bradshaw, a leading businessman in Eccleston. Everything about the candidacy is shady. A London parliamentary agent, approached by the Eccleston dissenter, Mr. Bradshaw, finds the rich and bored Mr. Donne to run for the seat. This arrangement substitutes for appropriateness and commitment. Bribing the voters gains the election. And thus the old Tory interests are challenged in the name of progress. We think of Eliot's reformer, Mr. Brooke, running on a platform of land reform while his own tenants' houses crumble.

But while Mr. Brooke is the heroine's ineffectual uncle, Mr. Donne is the heroine's quite effectual seducer. In what must constitute in Eliot's novel an implicit but conventional acceptance of the ultimate justice of the electoral process, Mr. Brooke is booed by the voters and abandons his election, and Mr. Bulstrode, Eliot's corrupt civic leader, is forced to resign from his official positions and abandon his role as a spiritual and political force in the town. Moreover, Eliot's Will Ladislaw and Dorothea carry us into the future by their own involvement in politics. But in the darker and more radical vision of *Ruth*, the corrupt politicians, both Mr. Donne and Mr. Bradshaw, sustain their public success. Ruth and her son, Leonard, find their future in medicine. The point in *Ruth* is not that there are corrupt politicians, politicians who are having trouble getting or keeping power, but that, unlike in Eliot's novel, politics itself is rejected as a mode of reform.

And at least one reason why the novel rejects politics is that it is a world deliberately without women, a world of men who hold office and of men who put them into office. Women literally do not vote. Indeed, they can have nothing directly to do with the process at all. And because their relation to the political process is radically different from men's, because they stand outside, they are in a privileged critical position twoard a world that understands itself as a central, if not the central, mode of defining human behavior. They may decide that what is important is political reform, joining the process through women's suffrage and through women holding office. That, of course, has been the main historical choice women have taken. But they may also, as in Gaskell's novels, use their external perspective to offer a critique of politics itself, one that presumes that there is a necessary link between the nature of the process and its exclusion of women, one that is capable of imagining, precisely because of its excluded position, that social action outside politics might be our better hope.

Politics, though long characterized as corrupt, has at least as long been characterized as a major form of describing civilization. How familiar we are with the idea that a people can be understood by its government, its laws, its political process. We need go no further than Hobbes and Locke and Swift to find the primacy of this belief in English thought. And how familiar as well is the assumption that not only a nation but human nature itself can be understood by its political forms and, just as important, that the measure of human progress can be taken by looking at the development of those forms. Politics is history, the outward form of the inward truth. For those who believe in change, in the improvement or decline of civilization, there is a dynamic relation between political forms and character. History, in this mode, is public, measuring not only the past of a people but pointing the way to the future. Such public history not only describes but creates. And making history can be understood as participating in whatever political process defines a government in action.

Mr. Donne and Mr. Bradshaw are making that public history in *Ruth*. Yet we need not be taken in by their own sense of their importance and power. It is time for us to recognize once again that familiar pair, the businessman and the hero, a serious version of that comic couple in *Cranford*, the man from Drumble and the man from India. In *Ruth*, one is a hard-headed and practical manufacturer, the other a handsome and charming man of leisure. But they are both frauds, both false versions of the kind of public presence and action that can shape a culture's future.

Even further than *Cranford*, the source for these two goes back to Scott, to *The Heart of Midlothian*. That book, with an insight that will reverberate in nineteenth-century fiction, literally makes identical the criminal and the hero, and just as literally represents the near relation of that criminal adventurer with the successful community leader. The metamorphosis of Geordie Robertson, the outlaw who has seduced Effie Deans, into the young English gentleman, George Staunton, echoes strongly in Mr. Bellingham's reappearance as Mr. Donne. And just as George is actually the son of the upright English minister, magistrate of the town, Reverend Staunton, so is Mr. Donne related, in spirit and interests, to Mr. Bradshaw. In *Ruth*, as in *The Heart of Midlothian*, the forces of seduction, of dissolution, of self-indulgence, are in cahoots with the forces of law and spiritual order. These seemingly different kinds of vision are united in an aggressiveness that defines the political process and is at odds with the values the novel would support.

For Gaskell, as for Scott, what is at stake is a way of understanding history and therefore a way of understanding, and thus defining for the future, both character and event. How are we to judge what we are and do? The answer offered by Mr. Donne and Mr. Bradshaw depends on fixed definitions, on human nature as essentially static, on easy interpretations that do not require the complicating awareness of a sense of time and a fallible self. Mr. Bradshaw, destructively inflexible, simply disowns his son when Richard is discovered to be a thief. But he is not humanly allowed that simplicity. The decision does such violence to his feelings that he suffers a stroke. Mr. Donne, too, is used to having people do and be what he wants. If his manners are more tranquil, his temper is not. Both are standard figures of public authority, encompassing between them two major areas of social, political, and economic power in England, the new manufacturing class and the older class of inherited wealth.

But Mr. Donne is also Ruth's seducer and Mr. Bradshaw the righteous citizen who fires her and exposes her sin. Part of the brilliance of the novel lies in connecting these two and also showing us what that connection has to do with the role of the feminine in creating and interpreting history. The forces that use women are tied to the forces that condemn them. The masculine powers enforcing the political, legal, and social rules of the culture are the powers that literally violate women and oppress the feminine spirit in whomever it appears. Blake knew that long before, when he heard the harlot's curse in "London." Gaskell understood it at least as well.

And she also understood that the alternative to this satan masquerading as the forces of right is not a turning away from the corruptions of the public realm to a private, albeit feminine, world. Gaskell's novels affirm Paul Smith's comment about the later work of Julia Kristeva, that a "stress on individuality cannot . . . be understood as an end in itself, nor can it be taken to be logically and historically *opposed* to political discourse, nor romanticized as suffering or martyred dissidence."[14] Gaskell's answer was that the gentle virtues of the private realm must be transposed to the public. Juxtaposed against the activities and characters of Mr. Donne and Mr. Bradshaw, the novel offers a true reform movement, in Ruth. Her private story of personal growth, her slow climb upward from that terrible fall, transforms her from a typical Galatea to a Pygmalion who can remake herself. That story becomes more than a plea for understanding the plight of fallen women, or a stirring account of victory over sin, or an example of the redemptive power of Christian faith.

When we come to evaluate Eccleston, when we write its history, what story, since history is a story, do we select? Most histories of nineteenth-century Britain, even now, assume that change is marked by the victory of the Liberals over the old Tory interest, by the new success of the manufacturers, and that these are the stories to tell. *Ruth* offers an extended critique of that assumption, a claim that the life of a community does not lie in these large public events and cannot be measured by economic and political forms. If we ask why not, the answer the novel gives is clear. These traditional modes of describing the historical process not only leave out great numbers of people but also violate another mode of measuring progress, a mode whose values are traditionally characterized as feminine, a mode that measures by the principles of mercy and love. Ruth Denbigh, through the account of her true reform, represents that mode.

The last third of the novel, in which Ruth is exposed and redeems herself as a volunteer nurse during the cholera epidemic, is crucial for exploring the question of what we should call history. Unless the community is changed by Ruth's story, it remains a personal history. What is impressive about the novel is that it does not merely pit fake public progress against substantial private progress but examines how private progress can and ought to become public. Our public realms must take up the values we have relegated to the home. One simple way to describe the plot of *Ruth* is that the fallen woman becomes the angel in the house who then, and this is the essential step, becomes the angel in the town. And the whole town, even Mr. Bradshaw, learns the lesson of forgiveness and the power of change.

The message of the novel is clear. As long as history, as the record of human progress, is measured in traditional public terms, in the terms of political or economic moves, there will be no progress, because the values behind that kind of measuring deny and even attack the best of the human spirit. Moreover, the ascendance of these false measures can be marked by a society's unjust treatment of its women and is characterized by a rejection of what are classed as feminine values, a belief that to be loving, merciful, and generous is to be weak. But there is something deeply astray about a society that cannot be merciful. Those supposedly feminine, and thus less effective and desirable, values are the real measure of progress, the true story of a community's growth or lack of it, and only when they are publicly accepted as such can a community, a society, improve.

The traditional masculine values of assertiveness and domination, however much those who hold them may picture themselves as the leaders of the future, are linked philosophically to a rejection of change, a belief in inherent authority and fixed truth. They represent a denial of history. Change is made by those like Thurstan Benson and Ruth Denbigh who actively practice the values of forgiveness and affection and whose vision is strong enough to effect change in the towns in which they live. In these lie our hope, if the future is to free itself from repeating the past. In this sense Carolyn Heilbrun was right, Gaskell has a feminine story to tell.

Is *Ruth* an historical novel? Is Gaskell an historical novelist? Avrom Fleishman has said that "[w]hat makes a historical novel historical is the active presence of a concept of history as a shaping force—acting not only upon the characters in the novel but on the author and readers outside it."[15] I have been arguing that *Ruth* does present a concept of history as a shaping force, both inside and outside the novel, the force of traditional gender values. To extend the point, the novel argues the existence of more than one concept of history, both inside and outside its pages, and the need for principles to select the right one, the one that allows for progress rather than repetition. Perhaps it is better to say that the novel mistrusts standard definitions of public history, the record of national, political, and social movements, of big events, because the principles that determine the importance of these events cannot evaluate what the novel offers as the primary processes of personal and community development. Thus we cannot trust the official public version of Ruth Denbigh's history, which marks her as permanently fallen, and must turn instead to a new definition of public history, one that offers principles according to which we cannot merely measure but actually encourage and, therefore, in some sense, can create Ruth's growth.

The linking of two male characters to represent the practical and the adventurous, the yin and yang of traditional masculine definitions of reality, along with the contrast between their public history and a private history with public consequences, is found not only in *Cranford* and, in more realized form, in *Ruth*; it is a constant pattern in Gaskell's novels. One of the traditional critical difficulties in approaching Gaskell's work has been the frequent claim that it is a divided canon, that the Manchester or social reform novels (*Mary Barton*, *North and South*, and *Ruth*) have little to do with the nostalgic rural novels (*Cranford*, *Cousin Phillis*, and *Wives and Daughters*), while *Sylvia's Lovers* may have little to do with either.[16] The sense of divisiveness too often has led readers to approve of one sort of work at the expense of the other.[17] But if we reach beyond the country/city dichotomy in Gaskell's settings, we can see that the locales change but the subjects, the questions, and the underlying structures do not.

What John Lucas termed "the nature and problems of social change," and what I have defined more specifically as the hostilities between traditional public movements of history and personal changes with extensive public effect, provides the basic structure of Gaskell's novels.[18] All her works ask what progress means. And all her answers juxtapose masculine-defined notions of aggression and economic power with virtues the culture has labeled inferior and relegated to the feminine and the home. Gaskell's work argues the practical as well as the moral need to bring those virtues out of the home. The novels offer an analysis of social problems that locates the fault in, and therefore points the solution to, the wrong-headed devaluation and displacement from the public sphere of the values of compassion and harmony. England may now be a masculine world. But only by retrieving the feminine, and by defining the public and the private spheres as places where both men and women belong, can it make a history truly called progress.

We see the basic choices clearly in *North and South*, in the contrast between the workers' strikes and riots and Margaret Hale's friendship with Bessy and Nicholas Higgins. That friendship, linking Higgins to Mr. Thornton, may have been the beginning of more factory reforms in Manchester than all the strikes and riots and political votes. This is surely the point of the dinner scene late in the novel. Mr. Thornton testifies to Mr. Colthurst, "a rising member of parliament" (512), who seems to be in the novel precisely to receive this testimony and thus make a private lesson public, that "I have arrived at the conviction that no mere institutions . . . can attach class to class as they should be attached, unless the working out of such institutions bring the individuals of the different classes into actual personal contact. Such intercourse is the very breath of life" (515). And by life he means social and public life, the life of a culture as a whole.

Mr. Thornton describes the tension as between class and class, but that is his specific experience of a larger tension the novel creates between two ways of understanding human relations and thus two ways of making and interpreting history. Gaskell's first novel, *Mary Barton*, foreshadows *North and South* in contrasting the story of a father involved in nationally known events (here, such workers' efforts as trade unions and the People's Charter offered to Parliament rather than the crisis of confidence in the Church of England that leads Reverend Hale to give up his living) with the heroine's more significant, ultimately more publicly significant, story. Even the particulars of its ending are very close to those of *North and South. Mary Barton*'s own use of the class issue includes an explicit description both of what the values are that must be used to make the future and of what their sources can be.

Mary Barton offers an early version of the link between Mr. Thornton and Nicholas Higgins, in the terrible bond that ties Mr. Carson to John Barton. Though it be to learn of his son's murderer, Mr. Carson descends from his house to the lodgings of his worker for that required scene of "actual personal contact." The scene does bring "the very breath of life" to Mr. Carson, for it brings the mercy of a forgiveness that alone can relieve his grief. This initial scene leads to yet another contact between the classes, when Mr. Carson questions Jem and Job about John Barton's political views and motives, and it finally results in Mr. Carson changing his attitudes and his practice to his Manchester employees. Many improvements, both existing and yet to be carried into execution, "take their birth from that stern, thoughtful mind, which submitted to be taught by suffering" (451).

Mr. Carson's direct teacher is, of course, the Bible. But the message of the Bible is a feminine force in these times.[19] As Ellen Moers put it, this was an age in which the "feminist impulsion" found its expression in a "Christian humanitarianism."[20] The biblical message of love is carried throughout *Mary Barton* by the women, by Aunt Esther, by Margaret even as she goes blind, by Alice, by Mrs. Barton, and by Mary herself. But it is taught to Mr. Carson even more immediately in a small but symbolic incident he witnesses after leaving Barton's rooms. Mr. Carson sees a little girl on the street suddenly knocked down by a rough boy. She is bloody and crying. Yet "the little sweet face" begs her nurse to release the boy, saying "He did not mean to do it. *He did not know what he was doing*, did you, little boy?" And she puts up her mouth, "to be kissed by her injurer" (428). Mr. Carson goes home, reminded by that vision of feminine apparent weakness conquering masculine aggression to read again where he has seen those words before. So would Gaskell's stories remind us all. Mr. Carson does read, learns the great lessons of love and forgiveness and, through that personal education, changes the public history of Manchester labor relations.

All of Gaskell's major works juxtapose these two senses of public history, one aggressive and one emerging from loving private relations, to have us arrive at similar conclusions. I have already discussed the community vindication of the gentler virtues in Miss Matty's success in Cranford as a noncompetitive shopkeeper and in Ruth's acceptance by and influence over the people of Eccleston. Through the creative resolutions of fiction, if not of fact, the novels invent possible answers to the problem of how we live in time and, therefore, of how we can draw the future in our own image, and what we would have that image be. And those answers, that image, are feminine. I want to turn now to this same problem and the particular answers and images offered in Gaskell's later fiction, focusing on *Wives and Daughters* and on the great but still neglected novel Gaskell described as "the saddest story I ever wrote" (6:xii), *Sylvia's Lovers.*

The tension between public events and personal history with public effect in Gaskell's fiction is the expression of an even more fundamental dualism that forms the structural basis of her work: the tension between father and daughter. Gaskell's version of the Pygmalion myth takes on a primordial form as the struggle of the old and publicly validated male authority to control and contain the young female energy. The Pygmalion myth, for all its narrative aura as a story of romantic love, is played out in Gaskell's fiction in a more essential way as fathers raising their daughters. And the argument of Gaskell's work is that strength and health, for women, for men, for England, must lie with the daughters who can throw off that shaping, killing, paternal influence. Wearing neither of the familiar and lying disguises of artist or of lover, Pygmalion looms as the daddy figure he always secretly was. Galatea must repudiate him, turn from the conservative public interests he represents, and create herself.

Yet many traditional readers, themselves perhaps conservative fathers, have admired Gaskell's fictional fathers. Critics have often suggested that the central character in *Mary Barton* is John Barton, and that Gaskell erred on the side of feminine sentimentality, the need to tell a domestic love story, by making Mary Barton the lead instead. John Gross finds the novel weakened by the shift of emphasis from father to daughter, and J. G. Sharps, noting that Gaskell had early considered calling the work "John Barton," draws the conclusion that what "primarily interested Mrs. Gaskell" was the tragedy of John Barton's life and "Mary's romances [were] of secondary importance."[21] But to suggest this is to judge in masculine terms, to reduce the heroine's story to that of finding a husband, and precisely to miss the point. However sentimental we may judge Gaskell's treatment of

Mary Barton to be, her developing decision to place Mary as the lead of this first novel, in spite of her quite conventional feeling that "John Barton was my hero," would turn out to be essential to Gaskell's enterprise (*Letters*, 42). That original move begins a literary vision that continually challenges and discredits established masculine definitions of value and meaning, including masculine conventions of narrative. Gaskell's novels question and reject the very attitude of mind that would judge John Barton's story to be the more significant.

What Gaskell's novels finally are up to is replacing the stories of our fathers with the stories of our daughters. Through that replacement, righting the old wrong of displacement of the feminine from history, the novels can offer a new understanding of history and a new history to tell. They can also indicate what kind of new history needs to be made outside literary history. That new history has not yet, as we say, come true, because the values of the masculine world still dominate, in our time as in Gaskell's, what we select to call history and so much of the history we make. But that new history, if not yet true, is being told as fiction, in nineteenth-century British fiction, in the novels of Gaskell, again and again.

Unlike Gaskell's first work, the last and not quite completed novel, *Wives and Daughters*, does not offer us a particular public story of events in contrast to the heroine's life. As in *Cranford*, public history lurks somewhere off the rim of the story, in the political fortunes of the Cumnor family, in Roger Hamley's scientific discoveries in Africa and scientific meetings in London. But these are distant and shadowy events. The masculine world of public events, of labor relations, of liberal elections, of wars and impressments, so prominent in the previous novels, is now no more than a ghost. This is not to say that the issues themselves have changed, but rather that Gaskell's veils for containing and expressing those issues have become more translucent.

The father–daughter tension, Gaskell's original and continuing choice for embodying in character the masculine–feminine disparity of values, strolls forth at last as her explicit subject in this final work. Why the choice should be father and daughter is clearer when we recall the spinster, Miss Pole's, sublime remark in *Cranford*, "[M]y father was a man, and I know the sex pretty well" (115). We might also think back to *Frankenstein*, to the father–daughter parallels U. C. Knoepflmacher has so beautifully pointed out between William Godwin and Mary Shelley and Victor Frankenstein and the monster.[22] Presenting the disparity of values through a father and a daughter allows Gaskell to play on both the authoritative aspect of masculine definitions of life and their diminishing power, along with the inevitability of the ascendance of feminine values. Time is on their side, for daughters are making the future, fathers conserving the past.

In spite of a title, probably not of Gaskell's own invention, in which male roles are conspicuous for their absence, *Wives and Daughters* places the tensions between father and daughter as its central event.[23] It is tempting, not only from the suggestiveness of the title but also from many of the plot details, to argue that the novel's central subject is actually mothers and daughters.[24] Certainly, the relations between Hyacinth Kirkpatrick and her daughter, Cynthia, are of major importance and it would also be plausible to describe the book as a story of two sisters, Cynthia Kirkpatrick and Molly Gibson. If Cynthia has a bad mother, Molly has no mother. And yet, of course, that is not true, for Molly has many mothers, though not the one who gave her life. She is surrounded by mother figures, concerned and kind women like the Miss Brownings, Betty and Miss Eyre, Mrs. Hamley and Lady Harriet, all reaching out in loving support to this appealing girl.[25] Yet in spite of the abundance of mothers in the novel, none has the importance to Molly, or the centrality in the plot, of the father with whom she goes "riding together down the lanes" (510).

To diminish the doctor's importance is to diminish Molly's achievement as well. It is also to ignore Gaskell's whole representation of the replacement of masculine values by feminine values and thus to miss the political point of the book. Appealing as it may be to see in *Wives and Daughters* a women's tradition of mothers and daughters, we cannot make Gaskell's fiction feminist that way.[26] The tradition the novel does treat seems to me even more important in its public significance. Because her concern is more than personal but also public and social, Gaskell explores the masculine inheritance that, if we are to move beyond domestic relations, we must all face and, we would hope, transform.[27]

Wives and Daughters tells the story of how Molly, shy, agreeable, obedient, dutiful, grows out from under her doctor father's powerful sphere. And Mr. Gibson's sphere is powerful not simply because he is a dictator, though, of course, he is, but because Molly loves him, deeply, truly and, the novel insists, appropriately. *Wives and Daughters* is a brilliant work, in part because it delineates people's forms of dominion over others without any melodrama and hardly any drama, reminding us that so many struggles take place without rebellion or defiance, take place quietly among good people, among families, among people who really do share warmth and affection and love. The process of change in such a sphere will be barely marked and slow. *Wives and Daughters* traces that change with a lightness, a gentleness that is itself a source of hope. Progress will come, if it can come in such quiet ways.

When we meet Mr. Gibson in the early pages of the novel it would be easy to conclude that progress has come. Mr. Gibson seems a development from the briefly introduced Mr. Davis, the clear-sighted doctor in *Ruth*. Mr. Gibson is a father "very willing to gratify his little girl," even in ways that involve "a little trouble on his part" (7), and we first watch him using care and intelligence and "a little natural diplomacy" to arrange for Molly to go to Lady Cumnor's annual party at the Towers. And when, at the end of that gala day, Mr. Gibson comes home to find that Molly has somehow been left behind at the Towers and gallops off dinnerless on the long ride to bring her home, we can only feel that Molly has a very fine papa, indeed. And their mutual delight on the ride home, Molly's relief to be away from the constraints of the Tower, and her assertion that "it is such a comfort to know that I may be as rude as I like" (28), suggest a relationship with neither coldness nor oppression.

Gaskell's fathers are almost all particularly fond of their daughters. John Barton and Nicholas Higgins are both rough men who can be softened by their daughters' smiles, and Reverend Holman's heart is broken in *Cousin Phillis* by his daughter's sighs. Reverend Hale in *North and South* turns to his daughter as his main support in the crisis of his life, to mediate between him and his wife, while Daniel Robson sees in Sylvia the light that animates his home.

In this company Mr. Gibson is exceptional not in his love for Molly but in the sane and thoughtful way in which he tries to raise her. He is a doctor as well as a father, an honorable category for Gaskell no less than for Dickens. We are reminded of Allan Woodcourt, Esther Summerson's loving doctor in *Bleak House*, whom everyone must surely admire. In Dickens's world, there can be no better fate for a girl than to marry a doctor. Mr. Gibson too is a modern doctor, the new doctor, brought in sixteen years before the story opens to aid and then replace old Mr. Hall. Moreover, this modern doctor is at ease with the gentry in a way unheard of by his old-fashioned predecessor, is as dedicated as he is competent, and publishes papers in medical journals as well. Clearly, in so many ways Mr. Gibson seems more to represent the future than the past.

The novel does offer us one of those standard backward fathers, one of those traditionally primitive male authority figures, in Squire Hamley, who loves the past as deeply as he loves the trees on his estate, planted when he was a child and grown old along with him. The squire continues "the primitive manners and customs of his forefathers" (44) of the eighteenth century, and we suspect there is some connection between this preference and the fact that he is "obstinate, violent-tempered, and dictatorial in his immediate circle" (44). Yet surely the claim of the novel is that the squire's form of backwardness, obvious as it is to his community as well as to his readers, is not the most dangerous form. As Meredith would elaborate so comically in *The Egoist*, we are in greater danger not when we recognize the primitive but when we fail to recognize its civilized disguise. The supposed proponents of progress, as Blake and Percy Shelley and Meredith and Matthew Arnold also remind us, can enslave the elements without freeing themselves.

Of all Gaskell's fathers, none is so committed to the future as Mr. Gibson, freed as he is from the irrationality and old prejudices of such local country gentlemen as the squire. That makes the doctor a peculiarly fit character through which to explore the question of what the past should bring to the future, of what being progressive might mean. For the doctor does repesent the past, because he stands for a vision of the future that, though decorated with all the latest social and intellectual advances, though carried on "in the best modern way," yet is doomed in fundamentals merely to relive old ways. Part of the greatness of *Wives and Daughters* is that its primary representative of living in the past should be such a forward-looking practitioner as Mr. Gibson.

The squire and the doctor, seemingly so different, one so old-fashioned, ignorant, and rough, the other so scientific, rational, and up-to-date, share fundamental qualities. Both place control above feeling, and both are authoritative, even tyrannical, with their families. If this seems strong to say about the witty doctor, we recall how Mr. Gibson first sent Molly to the Hamley's, saying that there was a secret reason but requiring her to submit unquestioningly, "to be an honourable girl and try and not even conjecture what the reason may be" (64). This is an apt example of Mr. Gibson's notion of what honor means in a girl and of what he thinks his little Galatea's relations to him should be. Molly's single unsuppressed response to his announcing his coming marriage results in his immediately turning away from her, mounting his horse, and riding away. Mr. Gibson's power to get his daughter's compliance depends a great deal on what he sees as his firmness and the novel presents as his withholding his love. The squire would control his children through tightening his heart and his pocketbook, the more modern doctor simply through tightening his heart.

The buried heart, the will to control, the cynical realism, are familiar elements in Gaskell's fathers, just as familiar as the fact that they are all in some way stern men who intimidate their daughters. Mr. Bradshaw's self-control is so rigid as to cause his breakdown. John Jenkyns, the dead father in *Cranford*, broke his youngest daughter's heart and drove away his son with his domineering ways, and thus killed his wife. The consequences of speaking "in his old way—laying down the law" (69) were so dreadful, actually destroying his family, that he became humble. The embittered Mr. Robson leads a riot and is hanged, while John Barton commits murder. We recall what happens when Mary Barton's mother dies: "[O]ne of the good influences over John Barton's life had departed that night. One of the ties that bound him down to the gentle humanities of earth was loosened, and henceforth the neighbors all remarked he was a changed man. His gloom and his sternness became habitual instead of occasional" (22). We see a similar though less dramatic shift in Squire Hamley when his wife dies. Having lost "her pleasant influence over him," the squire has no one to smooth his rough temper and realizes that he is "becoming a domestic tyrant" (285). Without an external force of kindness and affection, the squire's heart hardens into an aggressive willfulness.

The doctor's heart has long since hardened as well. If Mr. Davis from *Ruth* is an early version of Mr. Gibson, his ties to the squire suggest that his closer relatives are the familiar duo of Mr. Donne and Mr. Bradshaw. In *Ruth* Mr. Davis and Mr. Donne/Mr. Bradshaw form a simple contrast. Their descendants in *Wives and Daughters* are Mr. Gibson and Squire Hamley. But these two have more complex connections than simple difference, and understanding their relations leads us to see what Mr. Gibson has in common with Mr. Donne/Mr. Bradshaw. For if Mr. Gibson really is a more rational, more intelligent man than Mr. Bradshaw, he nonetheless shares that domestic tyrant's conviction that he can and should put away feeling at will, and that to do so is to be superior to, in advance of, other people.

Mr. Donne, of course, found putting away his feelings for Ruth impressively easy. Neither Mr. Gibson nor Mr. Bradshaw would boast that degree of ease. Yet the doctor, telling himself that as a professional he knows the physical ill effects of experiencing violent emotion, "had rather a contempt for demonstrative people," and "did not give way to much expression of his feelings." Thus, as the poets warned, does science replace the sympathetic imagination and lead us astray. Preferring to be "his own cool, sarcastic self" (122), admiring his own control, the doctor "deceived himself into believing that still his reason was lord of all" (33). We see that his sense of being modern and advanced, of belonging to the future rather than the past, is entwined with his sense of being superior as a man of reason and strong will.

The tension here is not between reason and emotion, between self-control and the lack of it, as Mr. Gibson and Mr. Bradshaw choose to believe, but between an open and a buried heart. As Craik has pointed out, Mr. Gibson "deliberately suppresses feeling, and so, . . . does violence to feeling unwittingly."[28] For all his love of his daughter, Mr. Gibson continually suppresses expressions of affection toward her and, using the rationalization that his decisions are for her own good, makes choices that protect him from strong emotion. Buried in Mr. Gibson's heart is his memory of "poor Jeanie" (54), the woman we must surmise is his first and his only true love. Yet we are given no clue about what happened to that love. Mr. Gibson's first marriage, to his boss's niece, who "was good and sensible, and nothing more" (32), is more appropriate and convenient than passionate. His second marriage, to Hyacinth Kirkpatrick, is downright cold. He needs someone to control his cook, he needs someone to chaperon his daughter.

We can hardly account for these significant decisions in Mr. Gibson's life as examples of a strong heart governed by reason. Mrs. Goodenough may be forgiven on the occasion of Mr. Gibson's first wife's death for "gasping out her doubts whether Mr. Gibson was a man of deep feeling," though she judged "by the narrowness of his crepe hat-band" (33). Mrs. Goodenough's doubts were right. Mr. Gibson's "general plan to repress emotion by not showing the sympathy he felt" (152) too often results in not feeling the sympathy, in preferring "willfully [to] shut his eyes" (372). The process works not only for sympathy but for pain and anger, and thus provides the doctor with some degree of domestic harmony. We see that Mr. Gibson is a descendant not only of Gaskell's previous characters but of Austen's Mr. Bennet, that other famous father who also likes to be "his own cool, sarcastic self." And when Mr. Gibson's willful blindness toward his wife no longer worked, he "was not a man to go into passions, or ebullitions of feeling; they would have relieved him, even while degrading him in his own eyes; but he became hard and occasionally bitter in his speeches and ways" (476). Thus feeling when repressed burrows into self-deception, deliberate ignorance, and ultimately a false and cold view of life.

For Mr. Gibson, putting away his feelings does not simply mean that he hides them from others or tempers them with reason but that he really puts them away from him, that he lives and acts without, and often against, the guidance of his heart. It is not simply that he is not ruled by feelings. What we come to realize is that the doctor does not respect feelings at all. He does not like to express them because he does not like to have them. For him, to consult one's heart is to fail in objectivity. And Mr. Gibson holds objectivity dearer than the people he cares for, dearer even than the capacity to care. We may recall Percy Shelley's warning that "the great secret of morals is love."

Is this an advance over old ways? To ask the question is to begin to free ourselves from those alluring masculine definitions of modernity that focus on scientific and rational principles of control over our environments and ourselves while turning away from the visions of feeling, definitions that cherish a buried understanding that control is a form of authority and an aggression against the past. To free ourselves from such definitions is to have learned the lesson that frees Blake's Milton from his satan: "I know my power thee to annihilate/ And be a greater in thy place & be thy Tabernacle." The lesson of history is the lesson of repetition, of the eternal return. Gaskell, no less than Blake or Nietzsche or Percy Shelley or so many other nineteenth-century writers, warns us to step out of that repetitive cycle, to relinquish the self-assertive victory that is its own defeat, and to make a new kind of history with new definitions of what progress means.

A defining attribute of Gaskell's particular representation of how we can move successfully from the past to the future is that the story that repeats itself is masculine and the one that offers real change is feminine. As Blake and Scott had already suggested, the key to the future must be forgiveness, which by its very nature allows that the future can be different from the past. The step Gaskell takes is to make explicit the tie between that fundamental Christian virtue and traditional feminine virtues. The novels argue that the virtues of mercy, forgiveness, and love have been devalued by society, classified as feminine, and supplanted by the preferred and presumed masculine virtues of assertion, justice, and rationality. And the cultural result is as unworkable as it is wrong. As Blake tells us, "He smiles with condescension, he talks of Benevolence & Virtue,/ And those who act with Benevolence & Virtue they murder time on time." (*Milton*,

Book 2) How do we envision, how do we portray in our art, a new generation who could break out of this cycle of generation? Gaskell's lovely and original answer is that redemption can imaginatively be depicted through a domestic history in which fathers are replaced by daughters rather than by sons.

That replacement process directs the plots of most of Gaskell's fiction. Once we begin to see that in the novels the spiritual and emotional hopes are embodied as daughters, we can explain why such odd things happen to the sons. Many readers have pointed to Gaskell's differing presentation of daughters and sons. Sharps observed that "Mrs. Gaskell seems to have had an inclination for introducing into her stories selfish sons and unselfish daughters," while Aina Rubenius noted wryly that Mrs Gaskell "did not accept the conviction of many parents that a brother had an undoubted right to consider himself superior to his sisters."[29] But these insights need to be extended if they are to imply more than Gaskell's dislike of the social practice of preferring sons.

One of the peculiarities of Gaskell's novels is that, unlike most generational patterns in British fiction, the main family line is traced through a daughter, and the usual female role of extraneous sibling, if represented at all, is filled by a son. Moreover, that son often exists only to be absent. This is true of Peter, the Aga Jenkyns from India, in *Cranford*, John Barton's dead boy in *Mary Barton*, Reverend Hale's sailor son, Fred, wanted for treason and hiding in Spain in *North and South*, Mr. Bradshaw's weakling forger banished to Glascow in *Ruth*, Mr. Robson's surrogate son, Charley Kinraid, the sailor carried off to a man o'war, to glory and a French prison, by a press gang in *Sylvia's Lovers*, and Squire Hamley's great hope, poor Oswald in *Wives and Daughters*. Certainly, Gaskell's own brother disappeared at sea. But to let that bit of biography stand as an explanation of such an important plot pattern seems a bit disingenuous. Like so many readers' assumptions that Gaskell wrote novels as a sort of grief therapy, to compensate for the death of her little boy, it is to use psychology in politically suspect ways as an alternative to rather than a part of interpretation.[30]

The pattern of absent or simply irrelevant sons is so prevalent in the fiction that we may read in it a rejection of the standard assumption that the future of the family and the British nation will be carried through its sons. On the contrary, in Gaskell's novels those sons leave home, they leave family, they leave the country, they leave the world. Again and again the novels point out that the sons just aren't around, that we cannot count on them at all. Characterized by absence, they are also distinctly ineffectual, even burdensome, in their moments of presence, often bringing disturbance and conflict to the sisters struggling with responsibility at home. We need only think of Margaret Hale's brother, Frederick, visiting England incognito with a charge of treason to evade. His longed-for return as the hope of the family brings joy but also danger, the terrors of near discovery at the railroad station, and the shame of Margaret's protective lie. So much for the dreams of being rescued from the difficulties of their situation by the beloved son and heir.

The pattern of the absent son also includes the dream that the son can make life better and the too frequent reality that he will add to the difficulties of the struggle. In some sense, Gaskell's sons are all foreigners, remembered and familiar and beloved, yet living some other life in some other world. They cannot really make history, because they are not part of the community. If they are alive, they are adventurers, but in the old-fashioned and undesirable sense of Scott's dark heroes. They are impulsive, passionate, and childlike. They have, as we are told in a startling description of Fred Hale, "the instantaneous ferocity of expression that comes over the countenances of all natives of wild or southern countries" (293). They may tell fantastic jokes, like the Aga Peter, or turn Catholic, like Fred Hale, or emigrate to Canada, like Jem Wilson in *Mary Barton* and Edward Holdsworth in *Cousin Phillis*, or go to Africa, like Roger Hamley, or simply to war, like Charley Kinraid in *Sylvia's Lovers.* But they all go, and because they are the sons, because they fit the old conventions of the heirs, the young, brave men of action, those that are at home watch and hope, and believe that when those young men return a better world will begin.

But, of course, and this is Gaskell's point, it doesn't. Some never return, and many return briefly, long enough for those at home to learn that there will be no heroic rescues in these reunions. Fred Hale, though rich in Spain, comes back without the English money to pay a doctor's fee for his dying mother. Charley Kinraid simply comes back too late, and precipitates Sylvia Robson's tragedy. Charley's "bold and fervent" plea to "come with me" for "your marriage is no marriage" and "shall be set aside" (404), is no match for the solid reality of Sylvia's baby's cry. What happens while those brave sons are gone, the very stories Gaskell tells, cannot be "set aside." Sylvia is a wife and mother. And even Miss Matty Jenkins, about whom we might wish to say that nothing has happened to her while the Aga Peter was away, has, nonetheless, grown into an old, poor, spinster. For, at the very least, time has happened to her. Peter brings her a pearl necklace, for "that little delicate throat which . . . had been one of her youthful charms." And Miss Matty is obliged to remind Peter that "I'm too old." But it is "just what I should have liked years ago—when I was young" (182).

The lesson of Gaskell's novels, like those of Scott, is that the heroic figures cannot rescue us from life, cannot put us outside time. Scott's dark heroes are usually attached to the past, to a cause that can no longer be won. Gaskell's heroic figures, on the other hand, tend to be attached to our dreams of the future, as sons and heirs, as adventurers in new worlds. But Gaskell's claim, quite as strongly as Scott's, is that these adventurers do not really lead us into the future, that they offer no proper sense of time or of place, because their only inheritance is to be doomed to repeat the violence of the past. That is why Margaret Hale's last sight of Fred is his wrestling with a brute at the railroad station, why Roger Hamley's letters hint of unmentionable dangers in Africa, why Charley Kinraid sails on warships, and the Aga Peter's stories are of mutinies and gunpowder and touches with death. And even those not actually having adventures, like Jem Wilson or Edward Holdsworth, are men of action who strike out on their own.

This is not to say that the novels utterly reject the world of these sons. We turn back to *Cranford*, both to Mary Smith's statement, "For my part, I had vibrated all my life between Drumble and Cranford" (185) and to a plot resolution that returns the Aga Peter to Cranford for good, to live out his old age in harmony and affection with Miss Matty. The sisters who stay at home continue to love those whose imagination takes them to the big world of business or adventure. The novels do not repudiate the imaginative charm of such choices, though they do condemn the values and qualities that are activated through making those choices. And the novels also condemn their masculine claims to being better choices, to being more realistic, more courageous, more socially productive and historically significant, than the choices of the daughters and sisters who stay at home.

These sons and brothers, even the Aga Peter, even builders of a new railroad in Canada, even fighters in some of the famous battles of their times, do not play a role in choosing and making the future of their families, their neighborhoods, their towns. They are the people who left. That is the extent of what Gaskell's fiction would allow their sphere of influence to be. They leave in their place their sisters, the daughters who will carry the weight of creating here and now a new and better world. And perhaps the sadness of these novels is related to our present perspective, with its knowledge that the "new and better world" did not come, that the worlds of the sons, with their emphases on the values of individualism and competition and aggression, won, that what actually lay ahead for these communities was the Boer Wars, the Great War, and the continuous aggressions we live in now.

Wives and Daughters dramatizes Mr. Gibson's masculine notions of control as fictions through the truer insights of his daughter, Molly, one of those women of "steady every-day goodness" (254) whom it is so much harder to be than a standard heroine. We recognize Molly, as we have been recognizing others like her since Austen in *Northanger Abbey* first described Catherine Morland's thin awkward figure, ignorance of the principles of drawing, and affectionate heart. Whether we think of her as an anti-heroine or simply a character outside the conventions that accompany heroines, Molly is familiar to us. She is a character of limited power in her world, both because she is a female of limited means and because, as Gaskell arranges it (as had Austen and Charlotte Brontë before her), her story begins when she is a child. And it is a story that plays out its feminine/masculine version of one of the most familiar and most loved of narratives, one that has been with us since David and Goliath or Jack, the Giant Killer or the Tortoise and the Hare, the narrative of the ostensibly weak but true hero who triumphs against the odds.

Realism, as I have already suggested, is anti-heroic. But another way to say that, one that invokes so many of our tales that would define the heroic, is that the notion of realism often includes the repudiation of aggressive notions of the heroic in order to light up for us what real heroism would be. If there is one shared quality of fiction and reality it is that both are played out in time. The trouble with the heroic, and thus the reason why it is so insistently both the subject and the enemy of the novel, specifically the realistic novel, is that it is not. That is the point of Scott's distinction between his dark heroes and his lead characters and of Gaskell's distinction between fathers/sons and daughters. What the distinction means in her work, that the heroic is the masculine and the anti-heroic the feminine, also implicitly means that the hero of a fiction of reality will be a heroine. And that heroine will win her victories along the amblings of time.

We see that victory in a minor way, in Aimee Hamley. Though French and a servant, everything Squire Hamley despises, and very young, gentle, obedient, and shy, she wins the old squire's affection and, finally, the full control of her boy. This foreign interloper replaces the dead son as the daughter who will direct the Hamley future, being, as we are explicitly assured, the person most capable of raising the family heir, her child. Molly too is young, gentle, and obedient, though not shy. We might describe Molly as a cross between Austen's Fanny Price and Catherine Morland. Certainly, Molly has Catherine's eager and frank ways. And, like Fanny at Mansfield Park, this apparently powerless little girl becomes the central figure in renovating her world. Yet the limits of the comparison can help us to see what is special about Gaskell's creation. Molly's influence reaches out beyond a family to a community. And part of the reason why is a quality that must remind us of another of Austen's heroines. Like Emma Woodhouse, handsome, clever, and rich, Molly Gibson is gifted with self-love.

Never actually at war with her father, nor outwardly acquiescent but filled with dark, bitter thoughts, like Jemima Bradshaw, Molly has a strong sense of self that continually presses on the bonds that would control her. Thus, whereas her father decrees that she must have only a minimal education, it was "by fighting and struggling hard, that bit by bit Molly persuaded her father," who was "always afraid of her becoming too much educated" (35), to let her have French and drawing lessons. Yet in the long process of outgrowing her father the French lessons don't matter much. What does matter are Molly's modes of human relations in comparison to those Mr. Gibson prefers. He seldom has a word to say to those old friends, the Miss Brownings, but Molly's visits to them bring energy and expressed affection. And it is Molly alone who teaches us, as she so fearlessly teaches Lady Harriet, that the Miss Brownings, in spite of their difficulties in wearing the right wig, are characters rather than caricatures, real people after all.

Molly's major form of transmuting her father's values into her own is dramatized through their differing approaches to the two great tragedies of the novel, the deaths of Mrs. Hamley and Oswald Hamley. Mr. Gibson is a fine doctor, always ready to go to a patient, and able to do good when he arrives. The novel offers ample testimonial to his skill, but that testimony appears only in details at the edge of the action. Both the patients we see him attending in the foreground of the story slowly and inexorably die. If *Bleak House* seemed to offer, both to Esther Summerson and to the reader, advice reminiscent of what many a mother is said to advise her daughter, that the way to salvation lies in hitching your wagon to a doctor, the events of *Wives and Daughters* give less reassurance in that direction. The professional life of social action cannot do much against the continuing pains and losses of life and is, in fact, in central moments ineffectual. As Meredith was to put it so wittily fifteen years later in the "Prelude" to *The Egoist*, "We drove in a body to Science the other day for an antidote" to our modern malady. "Before daybreak our disease was hanging on to us again, with the extension of a tail. . . . That is all we got from Science."

The real doctor is, of course, Molly. She is no more able than her father to stop those Shelleyan necessary evils of "chance and death and mutability." But she can address the unnecessary evils, in a way that he cannot. As Mrs. Hamley tells her, "You give one such pleasant sympathy, both in ones' gladness and in one's sorrow" (95). The pleasant sympathy that Mrs. Hamley is so grateful for on Molly's first visit deepens throughout the story, makes Mrs. Hamley's dying more tolerable and pierces the darkness of her husband's grief. By the time Oswald dies, with his remaining son away in Africa, only Molly, the borrowed daughter, can reach the Squire's heart. And she revives the Squire not only through her kindness but because, with Roger crucially absent, only Molly holds the secret of Oswald's marriage and his child, the new life, the Hamley heir. As she had rescued Cynthia from Mr. Preston's blackmail through effort and sense as well as love, showing the strength but also the power usually granted a brother or a father, so Molly, along with Aimee, rescues the Hamleys. In both cases what she restores is the future they by themselves would have lost.

The strongest part of Molly's character is a warm, loving heart. But she combines that obvious quality with a natural sense of her own value and an eagerness for experience. This is what protects her from the lesson of self-denial as the key to goodness and thus enables her to become the strongest force for good in her community. Commenting on Roger's advice to think of others because "you will be so much happier for it," Molly responds, "No, I shan't." She goes on, with a depth of insight that Roger himself feels, to make one of the most luminous remarks in the novel: "It will be very dull when I shall have killed myself, as it were, and live only in trying to do, and to be, as other people like. I don't see any end to it. I might as well never have lived" (154). And her story might as well never have been written.

Doctoring, so respected in *Bleak House* and even in *Ruth* as a hope for the future, is no longer automatically good. Nor is the presumably feminine spirit of self-sacrifice, seen both in Ruth Denbigh and in Esther Summerson. Bringing health to a society must have as its primary tool a heart that is both expressive and self-assured. For Gaskell as for Shelley, the discoveries of science cannot take us into the future if we reject the passion to imagine what we know. Yet, in opposition to the patriarchal narrative tradition of benevolence and of womanly service as the pure essence of the gentle sex, Gaskell's fiction has moved on to argue directly for what was certainly implied by Ruth Denbigh's initial sexual affair, that a warm heart includes our own hungers, our own desires. The lesson for us of the doctor and the daughter is not only that we must have feelings but also that we must value their expression and their fulfillment as an essential part of our connections to other people. Affection must be visible and its receiving as well as giving be accepted as a public value, if we are to create and strengthen the ties that can bind us, as for a while they bound John Barton, to "the gentle humanities of earth."

Molly Gibson's life is a success story, though Gaskell did not live to write its final lines. Roger, we believe, came home and married the strong and gentle woman whom he had at last learned to love. This happy ending, envisioned if not realized, culminates a line of such conclusions and the lessons they imply.[31] Jane Austen told a similar story in *Mansfield Park*, in Edmund Bertram's switch of affection from the flirtatious and weak-principled Mary Crawford to sisterly Fanny Price. Adam Bede turns from that kittenish and immoral victim, Hetty Sorrell, to Dinah Morris. And although Gaskell's own novels before *Wives and Daughters* do not also borrow from this familiar pattern of a threesome, they usually conclude with the victory of the heroine, her success at last. Miss Matty ends as the toast of Cranford society, with her beloved brother at her side. Ruth, of course, dies, which is always a limited form of success. Yet she dies only after her own reintegration into the community and their public tribute to her. And Richardson with his two heroines had already shown us that death may sometimes outshine life as a way to reward the victor and end the tale.

An initial variation on the typical pattern of Gaskell's endings is in *Mary Barton*, where Mary rescues Jem Wilson from death at a public trial, but then goes off to a new world to make a new life with him. I have been arguing that the disappearance to other worlds is masculine, as opposed to the feminine choice of heroines who would make the future at home (with home meaning both the public and the private place). Although Mary is a force for community good in her strong action to effect the outcome of Jem's trial, her subsequent move to Canada with him does not fit the pattern. I believe that in this first novel Gaskell, her aims not fully worked out, thought escape from the slums to be the best hope for the Manchester worker. Whatever the reason for this ending, after *Mary Barton* Gaskell's heroines would never again be allowed the solution of simply moving away. They stay, and their staying is part of what makes the difference.

Gaskell's fullest version of her heroine's success may be in *North and South* in the fate of Margaret Hale. "That woman," as the last two words of the novel term her, not only sees her values of personal kindness and contact between classes prove more effective than more aggressive ways, she also gets the money and the man. Margaret is rich, she is the investor who can float Marlborough Mills once again, and she is declaredly loved. We have often been delighted with the fate of heroines who receive only the last of those three, or, perhaps, the first and last. But if to be rich and loved is a familiar happy ending for women, the middle condition, to be a principal investor in a factory, is a new kind of reward. It is the reward of the economic power to effect a community. Mary Barton and Ruth Denbigh save their lovers' lives through a heroic and public effort. Margaret makes a similar effort when she stands in front of Mr. Thornton facing the rioters who would break down his door and is bloodied by a stone aimed at him. But Margaret is also given another kind of heroism, slower and less grand but with more extensive effect. She saves her lover's business. This is possible not simply because Margaret is rich, although implicit in any reward of riches, if there are enough riches, is the possibility of investment.

The significant point, of course, is that Margaret actually does invest. And she invests because her values explicitly include a commitment to a future that is not only hers but is also the future of her community. One of the great insights of *North and South* is that it imagines a situation in which personal and community success are not only connected but literally identical. That is the lesson that Mr. Thornton, committed originally only to public success, must learn. That is also the lesson Margaret, and many a heroine committed initially only to personal success, must learn as well. Margaret's investment, unlike her physical heroism, will both reopen the factory and rescue the man she loves. Reading the novel through an understanding of women and money James gave us in his portrait of Isabel Archer, we may suspect that generous gesture. For Margaret's investment is also a divestment, as she quickly turns her newly acquired money and power over to a man. Yet we still need to value the radical quality of giving a heroine not only the power but the wish to rescue a factory and a man, first with physical courage and then with business sense. And the claim of the novel's ending is that Margaret, through her financial decision, will help the future of Manchester workers, as she has already influenced the quality of their working conditions.

These happy endings, and the successful futures they foretell, are not offered to the victorious heroines alone. One of the problems with the Cranford community of aged Amazons, a problem that must shrink our hope for its successful future, at least until Martha marries, is that it is a world without a man in the house. And if we think back for a moment to *Ruth*, we notice that the woman who teaches Eccleston the redemptive power of time has herself a teacher at home, Thurstan Benson, the primary force in her education. Many readers have noticed the femininity of Mr. Benson, how much his gentle qualities, small stature, and delicate health are details used to characterize him as feminine. Particularly striking is the comparison of him with his larger, sturdier, more active sister with her "masculine tricks" (111). In the Welsh mountain village where they meet Ruth, it is Mr. Benson who must teach his sister the proper interpretation of Ruth's story, the compassion that must preface any active aid.

This reversal of traditional gender traits recurs in the novels, and many readers have suggested that it is characteristic of Gaskell's work. Coral Lansbury's insight that Gaskell's characters are often androgynous can form the basis for our understanding of how the novels deliberately play with our assumptions about gender.[32] Deirdre David has pointed out that in *North and South* Mr. Higgins and Mr. Thornton become less conventionally masculine as they fall under the influence of the gentler virtues represented by Reverend Hale and his daughter, Margaret.[33] Margaret's movements are full of "a soft feminine defiance" (70). And yet, when she first meets Mr. Thornton, though he is used to "habits of authority," she "seemed to assume some kind of rule over him at once" (70). The text is full of comments that tell us that soft, quiet Margaret, both in relation to the world and in relation to her own family, is "a powerful and decided nature" (54) and assumes the control that directs events. Her tall dignity and assured presence are explicitly contrasted with her father's weak timidity and desire to be led. We cannot conclude that Margaret is masculine and Reverend Hale feminine, because the point is more complex.

For all her strength and decisiveness, Margaret embodies and preaches those virtues of gentleness, sympathy, tolerance, and deep and expressed affection, those "gentle humanities of earth" that, along with those other qualities of weakness, fear, and dependency have been relegated to the feminine role. In her softness and her power, Margaret teaches us that those humanities, so long unrespected by the masculine realm of competitiveness and aggression, realms that see themselves as the true reality, must be taken up by us all. The man who can look on the workers' suffering "with contempt for their poorness of character" (98) shows us that the choice of competitiveness is the choice of ego, the choice that reads in the misery of others proof of the value of self. Are we so blinded to fact, to time and place and circumstance, as to call such a self-flattering vision realistic?

Against that unseeing vision the novel places a commitment to a more encompassing view, one made visible by the power of sympathy to help us be disinterested enough to reach the truth. That commitment can be held by both men and women, as can either of the negative poles of masculine aggressiveness or shrinking feminine dependency. The point is precisely that the gentle humanities are neither literally female nor culturally feminine qualities, though we have designated them as such. Instead, they unite qualities that culture has traditionally considered separate: the power to reach out with feeling for others and the power to be strong and firm within ourselves. Gaskell's point, of course, is that to be able to sympathize is also to be intelligent, adventurous, and brave.

We mistake the novels then, if we read in their endings, their pattern of fathers supplanted by daughters, a defense of female ascendancy. Daughters, in Gaskell's novels, give us and their communities and their lovers the future. And that gift has a dramatic validity in the novels that we cannot theorize away. We are not offered portraits of men rescuing the future for their women and their towns. But neither are we offered a straightforward conclusion that what lies ahead is a woman's world. What we should say is that those who lead us into the future don't biologically have to be women, although, historically, for the time and place of Gaskell's novels, they are. That this will vary in a better time and place is often built in to the end of the story. Thus in *Ruth* the heroine ends as a sort of Moses figure. The future is explicitly left to the men, to Thurstan Benson, who already understands love and mercy, having been the source of it all along, and to Mr. Bradshaw, who has learned to understand. With values properly human, they can guide the future in Ruth's stead by educating her son. We see the same point years later in *North and South*, in Aimee Hamley making the Hamley future through educating her son. In these two moments in which Gaskell provides a glimpse of who will follow the ascendant daughters, both are sons. The new world, we are to conclude, may be male or female, but fundamentally it will be based on more generous values than the present, if it is to be new at all.

Gaskell's novels are not realistic in showing us what is but in showing us what might be. These portraits of little towns and country neighbors, of faded ladies and flowering girls, of strikes and riots and class conflict resolved into harmony, of lovers united and unforgivable sins forgiven and redeemed, all may be dreams in narrative. But they are dreams that could come true. This is not to say they will, that there is any sense of the inevitable about that pretty future the novels invoke. The novels offer visions of how we can shape history that are possible but, precisely because we actually can shape history, are not inevitable. We really are to understand these books as dreams, while remembering, to borrow Delmore Schwartz's phrase, that in dreams begin responsibilities. These works do not ask us to believe in progress. Instead, they depict for us what progress, if we were to choose to make it, would have to mean. And central to that meaning is a turning away from the very values of assertiveness that the present still affirms as the measure of a future that outshines the past.

Lives and novels don't always work out as we would wish. Many readers, among them Elizabeth Barrett Browning and Charlotte Brontë, protested the heroine's death that ended *Ruth*.[34] Nonetheless, that novel's ending does promise hope. There are others of Gaskell's works that do not. Because progress is not inevitable, there are dreams that don't come true, where the struggle for the future different from the past is made, but the struggle is lost. We see it in the languid eyes and lost dreams of cousin Phillis, the daughter who has outgrown the innocent world her father made, only to find her new world composed of pain and loss. We see the pattern most brilliantly in the last novel before *Wives and Daughters*, *Sylvia's Lovers*.

Sylvia's Lovers is a dreadful tale, depicting, as seldom has been so depicted in English fiction, the hopeless disasters that our choices of passion can bring. As Kester, the Robson hired hand and lifelong friend to Sylvia Robson, tells her near the end of the story, "It just spoilt yo'r life, my poor lass," and "Phillip's life were pretty well on for bein' spoilt" (502). Sylvia herself concludes about the feelings and events that shaped her fate that "I think I shall go about among them as gnash their teeth for iver" (524). Her meaning is religious, that she will be damned. But without the religious dimension her faith provides, her description of what remains to her is fitting enough. In a Christian universe Philip's correction is probably right, that "God pities us" (524). Sylvia will not be damned to hell for eternity for the curse that refused Philip forgiveness when Charley Kinraid, the sailor Sylvia loved and believed drowned, came back to tell her that Philip had known Charley's fate and kept it hidden in order to marry Sylvia himself.

But in this world Kester is right. Sylvia's story is of a life spoiled, irretrievably spoiled. If the moral of the story were enough, if we were to read *Sylvia's Lovers* as a Christian parable and not a novel, we might perhaps conclude that Sylvia's life was not spoiled, or that it was, but that the loss was bearable because it happened in a just cause, because through her sufferings she learned the lesson of forgiveness.[35] Sylvia did learn that lesson, but it cost her not so much her life as her self. Crushed by events, all that is left of Sylvia is "a pale sad woman, allays dressed in black" who dies "before her daughter was well grown up" (530). The hopes of the young farmer's daughter who walks to Monkshaven in 1796 to sell her butter and eggs and buy cloth for a pretty new cloak are never to be fulfilled. And the energy of the girl so "full of frolic and gambolling life" (13) is turned to hate and bitterness and sorrow. Why that hope is not fulfilled, that energy turned inward for destruction, is the subject of the book.

Even a brief description of Sylvia's sad fate calls up for us the similar fate of another, presently more famous, country girl created twenty-eight years later, Hardy's Tess of the D'Urbervilles. The maiden we meet at the "club walking," keeping warm in her thin white dress because she "had a private little sun for her soul to bask in," continues her walk, into the chilling landscape of Flintcomb-Ash Farm and finally to the rocks, growing cold in the night, of Stonehenge.[36] We meet Tess with a red ribbon in her hair as we meet Sylvia about to choose red material for her cloak, and for both the color foretells their doom. These details may also remind us of Eliot's Hetty Sorrel and the seduction narrative all three echo, the tale of little red riding hood. But *Sylvia's Lovers* and *Tess of the D'Urbervilles* (and indeed *Adam Bede*) are connected more fundamentally through their plot structure.

Both plots unfold by means of the relations between the ignorant and lovely young heroine and the two men who want her, whom she chooses between. And the options, in both novels, share essential qualities. Alec D'Urberville and Charley Kinraid, though one is a newly landed gentleman and the other an impressed sailor, both can be categorized as adventurers. They are men of action, physical, sensuous men, romantics of the flesh, who prefer doing to thinking or saying and who live intensely in the present. They are drawn to the smiles, the blushes, the drooping eyes of the rural maid, and to the mouth each so quickly finds a way to kiss. Charley takes his victory at the game of "kiss the candlestick" at the Corney's New Year's party, whereas Alec claims "the kiss of mastery" (45) as the price of not racing his gig down the steep hills of the road to Trantridge.

We do need to qualify this similarity. Alec D'Urberville may be an adventurer, but he is a decadent and corrupt version of the type, in this more resembling Mr. Donne, Ruth's seducer, than the hearty Charley Kinraid. But though Charley is honorable to Sylvia and Alec dishonorable to Tess, we cannot see this as a difference in basics. For Charley's character too is darkened by tales of other girls he has betrayed in the past. And although Alec is himself unambitious, he is the immediate product of an energy that has raised his family to a class now theirs by effort rather than by birth. We see a similar energy and upward mobility in Charley himself, who uses the active courage of his type to rise to lieutenant in the navy and marry a lady with a good dowry. In this sense both would-be Pygmalion figures represent new ways.

Philip Hepburn and Angel Clare also embody versions of a common character. They too represent new ways, but as the thinkers, the talkers, the teachers, the educated men who believe that they see in the world around them fresh meanings that are framed from values beyond the merely material. Angel and Philip tend to think themselves in advance of other people, in class and education for Angel and in common sense and reason for Philip. When Philip tells Daniel Robson that "laws is made for the good of the nation, not for your good or mine," he sees as regressive Daniel's angry response of "Nation here! nation theere! I'm a man and yo're another; but nation's nowhere" (43). Philip wants to improve Sylvia, to modernize her. With her mother's blessing, he wants her to learn the lessons of reading and ciphering and geography, as Angel wants to teach Tess modern questions and ideas. Each believes that he is more interested in rescuing that country girl than in ravaging her, and neither really can admit the extent to which his passion is stimulated by what Hardy memorably calls "the aesthetic, sensuous, pagan pleasure in natural life and lush womanhood" (133).

Though Philip is a shop clerk and Angel a gentleman, they are both intellectuals, turning away from the life of the body for the life of the mind. This is not to say that they are unaware of external reality, for both also share a primary commitment to practical life and what they see as forward-looking ways. Thus Philip is a successful clerk at

Foster's shop, a good businessman who is promoted to partner, whereas Angel is preparing himself to be in business as well, as a farmer, and apprentices at Crick's dairy to learn the trade. Yet both suffer from a classic problem of those who see themselves as more intelligent and rational than their fellows. They deceive themselves, about their motives, their feelings, their desires.

The point in exploring these connections goes beyond my strong hope to suggest the as-yet-unrecognized depth of what Hardy, as well as so many other Victorian novelists, learned from Gaskell.[37] Both use these three virtually identical elements, the ignorant, luscious, and life-giving woman, the active, physical man, and the contemplative, sensible man, along with a plot that develops by means of their changing relations, to dramatize the novelist's sense of the ties between the larger dynamics of history and the passions of individual lives. The distinction between the novels does not lie so much in the particular variations each gives his or her version of character or even in the fact that Hardy's heroine loves the intellectual man of business and Gaskell's heroine chooses the physical adventurer. This last distinction melts when we translate it into the language of Cranford. What we would say there is that one picks Drumble and the other India. The trouble with both of these presumably progressive choices is that neither can transport us into a better world.

And yet there are fundamental differences between the two novels that can help us to discriminate the special quality of Gaskell's sense of our lives as occurring within history. One way to get at that quality lies in the issue of choice. We could say about Sylvia Robson that she rightly chose passion but wrongly chose the man, the man who seemed the more passionate but really was not. Charley was a true lover, but Philip loved her more deeply, and Sylvia could not see that until she heard of Charley's marriage, and knew "that Philip would not have acted so" (461). The reunion, the forgiveness, finally come in part from her being able to value the strength of his heart at last. But Tess—for Tess there never was a right choice at all.

We are told of Alec's meeting with Tess that "she might have asked why she was doomed to be seen and coveted that day by the wrong man and not by some other man" (35), a remark echoed in Tess's own wish that Angel had chosen her to dance with that early day at the club walking when she was a virginal sixteen. Implicit in such words and in the action of the novel is the sense that Tess has been fated, marked out somehow, if only by the red ribbon in her hair, to a march of circumstances in which love and salvation always appear too late. We know that Angel would not have been the right man when he met Tess. Indeed, he is only made a better man by the trial occasioned by learning of Tess's fall. We must and do hold Tess responsible for her tragedy; her own desires were part of its making. And yet, encompassing the fact of personal free will, and encompassing also the historical pressures of being a peasant girl in nineteenth-century England, is the larger directive of simply being human and a woman, of being a child of nature, the sport of fate. As many readers have seen, Hardy's brilliance lies in part in having made it impossible for us to select any one of these factors as determinate.

Yet I would claim that finally Tess is a victim, of men, of masculine history, of nature, of her own self. We cannot imagine that her beautiful vitality could have become other that what it did become, a crushed life on a blighted star. In Hardy's work the relations between our private lives and the historical forces that shape our cultural history are fundamentally at conflict. Perhaps, more precisely, the conflict lies between our hopes for happiness and both the private and the public forces that mark our fate. We are not only touched but touched immeasurably and uncontrollably by the circumstances that surround and create our lives. The fading of the sea of faith, the new intellectuals and new leisured gentry, the changing ownership of land and new values of crops, all the issues that make up the situation of rural England and the attitudes to peasant women in the nineteenth-century, will force our paths. So will our own dreams and passion. Even time itself, the simple movements of day and night, will kill us at the last.

Tess's story has an inevitability that Sylvia's does not. This, of course, is always a tricky argument to make, since I am somehow claiming that Gaskell's novel could have been other than it is. It is a claim perhaps only visible through the light of Gaskell's other novels. They do tell a different story in the sense that they tell the same story with a different outcome. Margaret Hale's life, Molly Gibson's life, fulfill the promise that in Sylvia's fate is merely broken. As Andrew Sanders has put it, the characters in *Sylvia's Lovers* "are not prisoners of fate."[38] We know with Gaskell in a way we do not with Hardy that people can find their road to the future and that when they do not the reasons are not the givens of human life.

I do not mean to put Hardy's work of the side of inexorable fate and Gaskell's on that of free will. They are both historical novelists, both committed to exploring the consequences of definitions of gender that have been historically defined. However determined by the givens of time and place they may establish their characters to be, inherent in any notion of living in history is the possibility of change, of life, and our definitions of it and of ourselves, becoming different than it is. Fate in historical fiction always combines the inevitable and the chosen, and for the critic to aim to measure the relative weight of each is a foolish task. Yet in Hardy's novel the extent to which fate, or its modern equivalent, the processes, both random and significant, of history, plays jokes on the heroine is explicitly offered as a subject of speculation. *Tess of the D'Urbervilles* is about what happens to us in these modern days. And what happens is dreadful beyond what we deserve or can control.

In *Sylvia's Lovers* what happens is also dreadful beyond what we deserve. But Sylvia Robson does have a choice, though not finally the choice of a right lover for, as with Tess, both lovers are the wrong choice. She has a choice about how she feels, not so much in terms of how she loves, but of how she decides to respond to the uncontrollable circumstances, the jokes fate plays. At the mercy of events larger than she, Sylvia must still understand them, interpret them, measure them in human terms. And the large claim of the novel, a claim that Hardy's book, more pessimistic if not more tragic, would not make, is that the meaning Sylvia gives to events can itself transform what happens to her.

Sylvia chooses what she believes is the right attitude to take, the brave and honorable stance in facing the trials of her life, the attitude of heroic firmness. What this means, in actuality, is that she is harsh in her judgments, relentless in her views. Sylvia translates her intensity of feeling into rigidity, believing that to feel strongly is to stand out against change. That kind of confusion has been familiar to us since *Sense and Sensibility*, when that sensitive seventeen-year-old, Marianne Dashwood, assured us that "at my time of life opinions are tolerably fixed" (93). And in Sylvia's life as in Marianne's, there are voices to challenge that view, to remind her, as Kester says, that "Niver's a long word" (337). Kester, Jeremiah Foster, Hester Rose—in them Sylvia has the guides not possible in Tess's universe, where no one's vision is wider than circumstances. But she also has less positive influences, influences through which her bright joy in life is permanently, irretrievably faded into a dull grey, that serviceable color she rejected for her new cloak so long before.

To identify intensity with fixity is to deny time. It is also to imagine, along with Scott's dark heroes and their lost causes, that change, that a history in which the future is different from the past, is a form of weakness, a way of giving up. It is to look on life as conflict, where duty lies in being permanently loyal to your own side. That is one reason why, as a married woman, poor Sylvia haunts the fields and ocean walks that return her happily to "the free open air" (361) of the older days from which she was torn away. But history, the larger forces that effect Sylvia's life, the time and place and circumstances that shape her present and influence her future, for all their power, are not immune to her desires, if she but understand her own power to free those desires from the chains of a fixed heart.

Sylvia's Lovers is situated "at the end of the last century" (1), in the past and precisely in that past near enough to be accountable for the present. Most of Gaskell's longer fiction, even that set in an earlier time, offers dreams of what could be, visions that show us what we must carry with us from other days. But *Sylvia's Lovers* is not so much a dream as the reconstructed background to the reality in which we now live. Gaskell's novels are dreams because we, as a community, as an entire culture, need to become other than we are. But she also offers, in this sad story, a visionary account of why we haven't become so, of what has gone wrong, of how we got to be who and where we are. When her story is told, Sylvia is long dead. But the consequences of her choices are the way we live now.

The story uses once again the primary structure of Gaskell's fiction, the pattern of father and daughter, and a simple way to describe the source of Sylvia's failure is to say that she never outgrows her father's values or, more precisely, she outgrows them too late. Pygmalion has successfully shaped Galatea. Daniel Robson passes on two essential, dangerous qualities to his daughter, his love of a world of adventure and his power to sustain his resentments. Daniel Robson is an old-fashioned man, but there is nothing old-fashioned about the values he represents. They are the same values of Charley Kinraid, that portrait of progress, the specksioneer turned navy lieutenant, and of the gang who impressed him against his rights and his will. They are also the values of the citizens of Monkshaven who burn the inn where the press-gang stays and of the judges who hang Daniel Robson at York for his part in that burning. Even more extensively, they are the values of France and of England, of the governments that sent their people to fight at St. Jean d'Acre even as they had during the Crusades. These are the heroic values, the martial values, the values of aggression, of firmness, of war. And one reason why this Monkshaven story suddenly reaches out to depict a famous foreign battle in a faraway land is to remind us that the values that break and shape that little isolated community are the same values that direct the rest of England and also England's relations with Europe and the rest of the world.

The problem with those martial values is clear on the morning of the battle at St. Jean d'Acre. Charley Kinraid's "heart was like a warhorse" as he moved to the "walls where the Crusaders made their last stand in the Holy Land. Not that Kinraid knew, or cared one jot about those gallant knights of old" (451). And thus history, without memory, repeats itself in an endless cycle of aggression, of victory and defeat. And the real tragedy of *Sylvia's Lovers* is that fame even now, even as I write this essay, even as you read it, rests with the fighters at St. Jean d'Acre and the press-gangs at Monkshaven and not with the story of Sylvia and her lovers.

Sylvia sees the world of adventure her father and Charley talk of at the quiet farm as the change from a winter's night to "life, and light, and warmth" (103). Like cousin Phillis, she directs her own deep joy and energy into dreams of a fuller life in another world. The insight of the novel is that this fuller life, this world of adventure, is inseparable from the inflexibility, the hard heart, that is Daniel Robson's other legacy to the daughter "vehement in all her feelings" (137). It is a legacy similar to that available to Molly from Mr. Gibson, although the larger world the doctor represents is more that of Drumble than of India. But Sylvia, unlike Molly, does not throw off this masculine inheritance until too late.

Such a story, such a failure, might seem to fit a familiar pattern of the novel of education, or rather of failed education. But that would leave *Sylvia's Lovers* in the realm of novels about individual lives, however much those lives may speak to us all. The special difference about the novel is that Sylvia's loss is primarily the loss not of her happiness but of her profound responsiveness to life. As Sanders has commented about Sylvia, "something vital in her has vanished with Charley Kinraid and died with Daniel Robson."[39] Her responsiveness is lost to Sylvia herself but, more important, it is lost to those around her, to the world that knew her radiant heart. The young girl swept away into hysterical tears by the press-gang's raid on the sailors returning to Monkshaven from Greenland possesses a depth of sympathy that can warm that cold northern town. But her absorption of the values of aggression and stern flexibility petrifies that heart and leaves Monkshaven without the blessing of her tears.

Sylvia does not bring us into the future because her education in forgiveness, the final warming of her heart, remains only a private lesson after all. Unlike the lesson of Mr. Carson in *Mary Barton*, Sylvia's lesson is never learned by her town. This point helps to explain the final lines of the story, which suddenly place us in the present, in a Monkshaven "now . . . a rising bathing-place" (529). From this present perspective we look at the story to see what it has brought us, to see what the continuity, the line of history, has been. And the message of the story is that there has been no continuity, that the feelings and meaning, the lessons of this love story, have not redeemed the sad past by brightening the present. They have not made a difference to a town whose progress can be marked by its becoming a resort. Without that difference, that continuity, we remain with only the dislocating possibility of reliving such past losses yet again.

Sylvia's Lovers explicitly ends with two versions of history, the private and the public. The point is that the discrepancy between the private and the public truths, between what really happened and what lives in public memory, goes on to this day. That public version, the one we all live in outside the story, is still characterized by the harsh paternal values of a world that prefers judgment to mercy, that celebrates martial victories and molds Sylvia's story into a "tradition of the man who died of starvation while his wife lived in hard-hearted plenty not two good stone's throw away" (530). The private version is not even remembered directly, but known only by hearsay, by a bathing-woman who knew an old man when she was a girl who "could never abide to hear the wife blamed. He would say nothing again the husband" (530). Those old man's words so barely recalled are all that remains to Monkshaven of the insights of mercy and thus of the power of what has been to transform what will be.

We see in this late novel what we haven't seen since *Mary Barton*. The child of the future, the daughter, Bella, goes off to Canada at the end of the book. That exit, unlike Mary Barton's in Gaskell's first novel, does fit with the pattern of the fiction. Bella makes this trip to Canada precisely because we have failed at home, failed to feminize our values, our reading of events, and how we choose to make history. Bella is gone for the horrible reason that the daughters have not found a future here, in a world that only repeats the cruelties of the past. This does not imply that the future is in Canada. It too may only be another warrior world.

The public failure is why, even when readers say the novel has a happy ending in the deathbed forgiveness and reconciliation in love of

Sylvia and Philip, that happiness is superseded by a larger sense of disaster, loss, and waste. The private feminine answer, or the personal message of Christianity, is not by itself enough. Nor is the fact of the novel itself, that not only the bathing-woman but, more directly, the narrator, recalls the story and had now told it to us. For it has not, at least not in the time in which the novel ends nor in the time in which we read it, made a difference in our shared lives, any more than it made a difference to the citizens of Monkshaven.

Our personal responses are also not enough. We reduce the book if we read it as suggesting we might be content with those final scenes. Gaskell is not simply a Christian novelist, carrying the living message of a forgiving heart. That route, as the novel itself explicitly dramatizes, leads to the noble and self-effacing life of Hester Rose. Ineffectual in bringing happiness or averting catastrophe, unfit to be a heroine, Hester plays out her role in Monkshaven by founding alms-houses for poor disabled sailors on the Horncastle road. This is, indeed, good work. But it is the kind of work that always exists in a world of destruction. "Pity would be no more/if we did not make somebody Poor." We can hardly confuse Hester's almshouses with a better world.

Gaskell is not only a Christian novelist but a feminist historical novelist. She presents the values she would have us affirm and also depicts for us how we must affirm them, publicly as well as individually, as a community moving forward in time. In Paul Smith's words, "any discussion or even enactment of dissident individuality is condemned to social marginality unless it can embrace or be embraced by more widely insistent claims."[40] There have always been people who have learned the lesson of love and mercy. And we have told ourselves that such individuals can influence the general progress of culture unawares. We recall Wordsworth's tribute to the "little, nameless, unremembered, acts/Of kindness and of love" and Eliot's belief that "the growing good of the world is partly dependent on unhistoric acts." Gaskell might well agree. Nonetheless, her fiction makes a greater demand, that we do become aware, that we learn the lesson publicly as well. She shows us what kinds of members of a community now can teach us, whom we must listen to. They are the dissenters, the simple Christians, the women. We see them as the childish, the escapist, the ignorant, the weak. In this man's world, this real world, they are the very people we consider out of touch with truth. They are the people we do not now let define the direction of our culture, undervalued people having much in common with Gaskell herself.

5

Paradise Reconsidered: Eliot's Edens Without Eve

> They do not find what they seek, and we cannot wonder. The ancient consciousness of woman, charged with suffering and sensibility, and for so many ages dumb, seems in them to have brimmed and overflowed and uttered a demand for something—they scarcely know what—for something that is perhaps incompatible with the facts of human existence.
>
> VIRGINIA WOOLF

The case of George Eliot's fiction provides a useful paradigm for describing the changes that have taken place in writing the literary history of nineteenth-century British fiction. It also, and this is my purpose here, provides a paradigm for rewriting that history once again. Critics of Eliot from the very beginning with the publication of *Adam Bede* stressed the masculine quality of Eliot's work, its breadth of characters and largeness of vision. Neither, with some exceptions, did the arguments change with the awareness that the author was actually a woman.[1] Indeed, traditional approaches to Eliot were characterized by the assumption that she is different from other women writers, from Austen with all her drawing room talk about whom young ladies marry, or from Gaskell with her real-life husband and children. Eliot is an intellectual, a philosopher, a writer who translated German and read Feuerbach, who scorned kittenish beauty and in

Middlemarch defended telling the story of Lydgate's passion for "industrious thought" against the preference for tales of love and weddings.[2] Eliot has a masculine mind.

In recent years feminist critics have reclaimed Eliot, and have argued, to steal Blake's lines once again, that she is not of Adam's party but of Eve's.[3] We can see this clearly in new readings of *The Mill on the Floss*, which stress the community's destructively oppressive effect on Maggie Tulliver's intelligence and sensitivity and desires, rather than admiring, as have so many previous critics from Leavis on, Maggie's power to renounce selfish fulfillment for the sake of a good larger than herself.[4] Within the general project of establishing a women's tradition in British fiction, many feminist readers have come to place Eliot as a major voice, containing in that voice the tensions between creativity and social complicity with the male culture that so haunt women writers. The ties between such opposites as Hetty and Dinah, Maggie and Lucy, or Dorothea and Rosamond point to the divided spirit that characterizes the art of women writing in a man's world. That spirit is shared with other women artists and creates its own tradition of influence and relationship.[5]

This approach, as I think we have all recognized, offers a powerful and profound insight into women's fiction. But the trouble with the older readings of Eliot's work and with many newer feminist readings as well is that both sides underplay what is actually a changing narrative attitude toward women in her fiction and claim Eliot as their own. The masculine view, of course, simply pretended that the issue of women wasn't important, that moments in the novels where the issue couldn't be ignored were flaws, that women stand for something else anyway, that what was important was Strauss and Feuerbach and Comte and ideas about history and the religion of humanity and the big picture.

But the frequent feminist approach has had its own fictions, indicated by the critical preference for skimming past *Adam Bede*, with its male lead, and beginning discussion instead with *The Mill on the Floss*. The idea of a separate women's tradition, when it stands as the whole truth about Eliot's work and not as what it is, the new truth, ignores one of the great insights in the old truth, that Leavis in some sense was right. Eliot's fiction is part of a great tradition in nineteenth-century British fiction. Like Austen, Eliot had a more extensive reputation and impact than Gaskell or Charlotte Brontë. Regardless of Eliot's personal living situation, when we consider her professional situation from the time she published her first short stories, when we think of her novels in relation to their hugely successful critical reception, their publication histories, and the pervasive Victorian claims of their impact and significance, we should see that we are not talking about an outsider at all. Eliot's work has enjoyed, and did enjoy during her own lifetime, the kind of literary reputation and readership most writers, including great writers, hardly dream of. Our recent emphasis on the Victorian oppression of a woman's voice has tended to ignore the massive evidence of the extent to which Eliot's voice was heard. And surely the public power of this women's voice must have had a psychological as well as a literary effect on the writers who came after her. No one was more influential, no one more mainstream, more actively a creator of a great tradition, than the novelist for grown-ups with the man's name.

My point here is hardly to defend the critical fiction of a great tradition. Instead, I want to remind us all that the idea of a separate women's tradition is also a critical fiction. Certainly, it has its value and its allure. When we, as women, say that culture is masculine, we assert a truth both about the cultural values, including language, we have all inherited and about our pervasive recognition that we women have been consistently excluded from that culture, or, rather, that we have been a special and isolated part of it. That sense of being apart, recognized or not, conscious or unconscious, probably informs the work of most, and perhaps all, women writers. But that shared sense cannot by itself stand as the touchstone for marking out a literary tradition. It may not even be the necessary first step. We cannot simply strip away the George Eliot and uncover the Marian Evans or the "Mrs. Henry Lewes."

I am not arguing that an author's sex is or can be irrelevant, that it ever doesn't operate to shape and give meaning to a work of art, as well as to provide connections between works of art. And gender, regardless of our degree of self-consciousness about it, is always a crucial and defining factor in interpreting fiction. It is central to the meaning of fiction. But in what ways? Surely in more than just one. And perhaps differently in different works. Our awareness of gender, our study at last of how it operates and our critical use of it in interpretation, needs to be set free from the assumption that the physical sex of the artist or the reader is the determining or even the major key. Yes it matters that George Eliot was a woman. It matters that I am a woman reading her work and now writing about it. It also matters that Marian Evans wrote under the name of a man, and perhaps not only for reasons of oppression and self-protection. And finally it matters that the books by this double-named writer are again and again about gender and that they were among the most admired and most influential works of the Victorian age.

In offering connections among works of nineteenth-century British fiction, we need to distinguish between separatism as an historical premise, actually operating in Victorian England, separatism as a premise of female biology and psychology, a premise that is probably essentialist and ahistorical, and separatism as a twentieth-century critical and political tool. In terms of a literary tradition, the historical premise of separatism dissolves the moment I ask, separate from what? Was there a man's tradition that was mainstream and to which Eliot's novels did not or do not belong? Were Eliot's novels more influenced by Austen's work than by Scott's? Was there a women's tradition outside a mainstream to which Eliot's novels most especially belong? Someone might argue that Gaskell's or the Brontës' fiction was outside a mainstream (although I have come to doubt that about Gaskell, at least for nineteenth-century readers), but what does that mean?[6] As women writers were aware, reviewers were biased against women novelists. No doubt readers and male novelists, and perhaps even female novelists who wrote critical essays on lady novelists, were biased against them as well. That is why the case of Eliot's achievement and influence is so enlightening in feminist efforts to rewrite literary history.

Would we be able to construct a line of development of nineteenth-century British fiction that, while acknowledging it is a construct, tries to take account of influence and uses some of the well-known male authors and leaves Eliot out? I doubt it. Are Dickens's or Thackeray's or Hardy's novels in some way more important than, or just different from, Eliot's novels, to other writers or to the reading public, in their time or in ours? Are there more substantial links between them than between any one of them and Eliot? Are there more important links between Eliot's work and the works of other women than between it and novels by men? Feminist critics who want to separate Eliot's work from that of her male counterparts have thrown out one of the basic insights of traditional readers of Eliot's fiction, the very insight that drove readers to insist on her masculine mind: in terms of subject matter, of scope, of narrative method, of what they borrowed from previous fiction and what they invented for the future, Eliot's novels define nineteenth-century fiction.

I am arguing that there was no separate women's tradition in nineteenth-century British fiction. I would not make the same claim for nineteenth-century American fiction or for twentieth-century fiction. It may well be that our present sense of the sharp line between male and female writing, Norman Mailer and Marilyn French, Robert Stone and Margaret Laurence, as well as our indignation about how masculinist critics, both male and female, have skewed literary history in favor of male writers, have directed readings back to the nineteenth-century. And I am also convinced of the reality and importance of the patterns of influence among nineteenth-century women writers that the work of feminist critics is at last revealing. For many reasons, intellectual and political, a separate women's tradition has been and still is a necessary critical fiction. But we can surely now afford to acknowledge the real limitations of that fiction. Quite simply, it leaves too much out.

I suggest that feminist criticism take a new step in its project of revising literary history, one that, through the recognition of Eliot's absolute centrality, takes back from the masculine critical tradition not only Eliot and other women novelists but much of the work written by men as well. I propose a new literary history of nineteenth-century fiction that uses our awareness of the centrality of Eliot's work to say that the voice of the mainstream was, at this important juncture, what James remembered from his literary pilgrimage as the "voice soft and rich as that of a counseling angel."[7] One way to get at the centrality and the power of Eliot's work is to examine a particular motif that Eliot borrowed from previous novelists and represented in a new form: the idea of an earthly paradise. The consequences of that new representation would transform British fiction.

Northrop Frye has said about Blake's poetry that "the end of art is the recovery of Paradise."[8] Many nineteenth-century British writers, particularly in the first half of the century, were concerned with that recovery and, like Blake, revised traditional definitions about paradise in the process of depicting it.[9] Eden, at least the eden of present desire, would not be a matter of simple return, for recovery also meant redefinition. Central to that redefinition was a new sense of history, specifically as a recognition that paradise is lived in time and as a responsibility to understand the past if the future is to fulfill our dreams. Another element in that redefinition, at least as it was developed in nineteenth-century British fiction, was the sense that paradise is not only a matter of history but also a matter of gender, and that the two are intertwined.

Why would notions of history and of gender come to be connected in the attempt to redefine and recover eden? Recalling the biblical story provides at least a theoretical explanation. Having been successfully tempted herself by the hunger for knowledge, Eve became a temptress and seduced Adam into sin. Returning to paradise may well mean returning without her, reaching a higher level of innocence that protects that achieved eden from becoming the beginning of a new fall in a ceaseless cycle by replacing Eve with a less adventurous, less dangerous, partner. Presumably, then, continuity would replace repetition, the temporal future would replace the eternal return. But to say all this is, of course, to presume the perspective of Adam. And it is also to locate where George Eliot's novels begin.

Eliot's first novel, like most of the short stories that precede it, centers in a man. *Adam Bede*, that beautiful book "full of the breath of cows and the scent of hay," is about Adam Bede in a way that *Daniel Deronda*, her last novel, is not about Daniel Deronda.[10] The "broad-shouldered man with the bare muscular arms, and the thick firm black hair tossed about like trodden meadow-grass," strides along the high-road of this novel, turning our heads as he turned the head of the elderly horseman passing through Hayslope who stopped to have a long look at this "stalwart workman in paper cap, leather breeches, and dark-blue worsted stockings."[11] We too will have a long look at Adam, the handsome carpenter who looms tall in the forefront of the novel. And we are happy to watch Adam, because he is intelligent and sensitive and good and because what he must learn, a "fellow-feeling with the weakness that errs in spite of foreseen consequences" (214), is a noble and, at least as important, an achievable lesson for him.

Adam's story is deeply fulfilling, both for him and for the reader. A flawed but noble hero, with a "conscience as the noonday clear" (2) but a narrow heart, Adam learns to accept sorrow as a permanent force that only changes its form, "passing from pain into sympathy" (498). Here is the kind of sorrow that expands the loving soul twined round those who have done great wrong. First with his drunken father, then with Hetty Sorrel, and finally with Arthur Donnithorne, Adam accepts that "I've no right to be hard towards them as have done wrong and repent" (480). He accepts that goodness means more than simply to be good himself. The strength that keeps him so easily from doing evil must go out to others less strong. Adam learns the lesson of suffering and is redeemed in this world.

That redemption also teaches one of the most familiar and most suspected principles in nineteenth-century fiction: the correspondence between a "sense of enlarged being" and a "fuller life" (541), between what we dream of and whether our dreams come true. The sad story has a happy ending. Becoming a better person is its own reward, but it is not the only reward. We last see Adam in the midst of good work and quiet joy, surrounded by passionate love, brotherly bonds, heirs, and a warm community, all grouped harmoniously in a recovered eden, a paradise this side of the grave.

Eliot's first novel is a vital nineteenth-century refutation of Samuel Richardson's essential premise that the "[w]riter who follows nature and pretends to keep the Christian System in his Eye, cannot make a Heaven in this World for his Favorites."[12] For Eliot, who salvaged the loving principles if not the system of Christianity, though there is "a sort of wrong that can never be made up for" (551), good can and does come from evil, there is salvation through suffering. *Adam Bede* locates that salvation as a heaven in this world, in a thatched house in a timber-yard in an obscure English village.

The difference here between Richardson and Eliot directs us to that frequent topic in nineteenth-century British literature, particularly in the first half of the century, its fascination with, its complex and skeptical exploration of, the idea of an earthly paradise. The homely timber-yard is not so very distant from Percy Shelley's "Isle under Ionian skies,/ Beautiful as a wreck of Paradise," or Byron's celebration of fiery dust. And it is similar to the earthly paradise that ends *Emma* and *Persuasion* and *Waverley* and *Villette*, that forms the last long movements of *Pride and Prejudice* and *The Heart of Midlothian* and *Wuthering Heights.*

Richardson had, of course, tried out the notion of virtue finding its present rewards in the disastrous happy ending of *Pamela.* But the shared attributes of the earthly paradise that forms the happy ending of these otherwise divergent nineteenth-century works define the relations between character and event and thus the meaning of the reward, differently than did *Pamela.* Usually rural and domestic, tied to a moral vision, these endings depict a world of labor and familial relations that have been earned on this earth through a suffering that leads to mercy and to love. It is a paradise characterized by time, created by change and by death, the mother of beauty. As Keats put it—thus providing us with a happy explanation both of why a primary mode of nineteenth-century fiction is the novel of education and of how that mode embodies an interest in the earthly paradise—"Do you not see how necessary a World of Pains and troubles is to school an Intelligence and makes it a soul?"[13]

Scott, Austen, the Brontës, all offer stories that create the vale of soul-making, stories that dramatize the process of developing a human sympathy. These are novels of education, committed to the power of experience to transform our souls for the better in a way that eighteenth-century works like *Pamela* or *Clarissa* or *Tom Jones* or *Moll Flanders* or, in a different sense, other nineteenth-century works are not. Novels such as *Evelina* or *Frankenstein* or *Melmoth, The Wanderer* or *Pickwick Papers*, whatever their main characters may learn during the stories, are not particularly illuminated by approaching them as novels of education.

Characteristic of the books I consider here is that experience is, or can be, redemptive and that the reward is inseparable from that redemptive power. To become a better person is to live a better life because it is to make life better, even if the effect is, in Eliot's famous closing words about Dorothea Ladislaw, "incalculably diffusive."[14] The premise of these novels, and often the very lesson the characters must learn, is that books are written about and lives are lived in an inevitable, dynamic relation between character and experience.

The representation of the reward may be as briefly joyous as Austen's line at the end of *Emma* about the "perfect happiness of the union" or as suddenly ominous as the lines that close *Villette*, to "leave sunny imaginations hope." Reading both these lines as happy endings highlights the point that the reward is actually the changed quality of experience, the new relation between self and event, not simply the new self (which may be all that later fictions will offer) or the union of self and other (which is only one form the new relations between inner and outer may take). Blurring this point may be why so many readers of *Emma*, seeing that Emma's soul has hardly been made perfect during her story, have chosen to read that final line as ironic, as simplistic contradiction, or as a downright lie. But "perfect happiness," as Emma learns and as Austen's novels continually insist, is to be found precisely in the imperfections of life, in robbers in the turkey coop, in Shelley's "wreck of paradise," in Stevens's perishable bliss. And even, I suggest, in a world where one's beloved has been drowned at sea.

Lucy Snowe may end her story alone, without Paul, but she also ends it with her own new school and with a heart warmed to life again. Without the school, losing Paul would have been a bitter twist of fate, a cruel response of life to the self who has so painfully found the courage to love. But we cannot read *Villette* as a love story, viewing the lover as the significant reward. Lucy's process of soul-making, her efforts and slow courage, have, literally, changed her life. She has a school because she has learned to love. Having both a husband and a business may be the most complete happy ending, but in *Villette*, as in *Emma*, perfect happiness turns out to be a partial, all-too-human affair.

The intimate connection in nineteenth-century British novels between the shaping power of experience and the reward is occasionally more fully developed, as in the long final sections of *The Heart of Midlothian* and *Wuthering Heights*. These two novels, particularly Scott's, have been criticized for their final sections, as if the writers lost their imaginative nerve, abandoned satan's party, and turned in the end to detailed pictures of a mundane moral life.[15] But such criticism misjudges the structure of these novels because it ignores the realistic convention they develop. *The Heart of Midlothian* would be a tidier but not a better or more unified book without the long period of settling down on the Isle of Roseneath. Neither, in spite of the charms of the movie version, does *Wuthering Heights* improve without the second generation, without young Cathy putting posies in Hareton's porridge. To imagine otherwise would be like believing that Wordsworth should have cut out the address to his sister that constitutes the final section of *Tintern Abbey*. Some readers have complained about Austen's fiction that she shows us weddings but not the details of life after those happy endings. Scott and Emily Brontë do show us the details, and the very length of the final sections testifies to the weight these two novels give to the earthly afterlife.

What these prolonged finales and our often impatient responses suggest is that paradise in nineteenth-century British fiction is, in essence, anticlimactic. This point may be accurate in a simple, structural way because true paradise (unlike the innocent, naive, or self-deluded state that may open novels) ends novels. However climactic a particular ending may be, that climax is always eroded, even undermined, by our knowledge that it means that the action of the novel is effectually over.[16]

But our sense of letdown in the endings of the books I am looking at is more than a matter of the general structure of fiction. Particular endings press the notion that the large dreams and illusions of Emma, the brave adventures of Jeanie Deans, the highly wrought fancies of Lucy Snowe, the wild passions of Heathcliff and Catherine, the tragic relations of Adam, Hetty, and Arthur, all are past. The earthly paradise these endings evoke must precisely be understood as less than what might have been if it is to be paradise at all. For the human ideal, the real heaven, which is to say the heaven on earth, can only be lived under Wallace Stevens's "friendlier skies," in a particular time and a particular place, and thus with the familiar limitations that bound all our lives. We must accept those boundaries, marked so brilliantly in Scott's novel by the water that surrounds that "Highland Arcadia," the Isle of Roseneath, in order to realize the ideal in the reality.

The Heart of Midlothian and *Wuthering Heights* dramatize this point in notably loving detail, in their visions of what stories usually leave out, of life after stories end, of that tamer future that justifies the story and renders the wild present past. The very slowness of Jeanie and Reuben's progress into a solid material future full of children and teapots and property asks that it matter to us. We must watch their domestic details with something of the same loving concern we so gladly brought to the thrilling events that made possible that domesticity. The second generation lovers, Cathy Linton and Hareton Earnshaw, to be married on New Year's Day, are united in a quiet happiness inaccessible to Heathcliff and Catherine. In a novel depicting one of the most tempestuous love stories of our culture we are asked finally to care about that quietness, that familiar kind of joy.

Yet these calm lives do not rest as the entire last word. Even in that new world, "under that benign sky," we, if not Mr. Lockwood, are also asked to "imagine unquiet slumbers," as Heathcliff and Catherine still walk the moors and disturb the peace. Roseneath, too, has its disturbances, its living ghosts, as Effie Deans from time to time appears in secret, not only distressing Jeanie but filling that contented domestic ruler with jealousy. The tamer reality that completes these fictions has its own inconsistencies that remind us that completion is itself a fiction and that the real, the true, is incomplete. Arcadia can turn out to be a stocky peasant making cheese, the young Earnshaws leaving Wuthering Heights for Thrushcross Grange, Lucy Snowe running her school alone.

The centrality of the motif of an earthly paradise in early nineteenth-century fiction helps us to explain and, hopefully, to appreciate, both the structure of *The Heart of Midlothian* and at least one aspect of the centrality of Scott. Scott's fiction influenced the work of many nineteenth-century British novelists. We have long granted the point but have not begun to measure that influence because we have hardly begun to interpret Scott. I suspect that one reason critics of this century, in spite of heralding Scott's comeback, have seemed so little interested in effecting it, has been the issue of gender. Talking about Scott's work is tied to talking about the work of women writers, much of it neglected, because the immediate literary tradition Scott can be placed in turns out to be populated largely by women writers. Two powerful inspirations for his own novels are Edgeworth and Austen, and his work is a major, perhaps the major, influence on Gaskell's fiction. In relation to his gothic contemporaries there are also important and neglected connections, as in the striking similarity between Scott's pattern of double heroes and that in Mary Shelley's *Frankenstein.*

The particular motif I am discussing here points up both the relation of Scott's work to that of women writers and its original achievement. The attempt in the final section of *The Heart of Midlothian* to present the familiar and challenging process of real-life fulfillment in all its mundane detail owes much to Austen's fiction in general and to the quieter second half of *Pride and Prejudice* in particular. Yet Scott's novel stands as the first developed portrayal of a situation that fascinated both novelists and poets. Its most direct impact is probably on the work of Emily Brontë. Her novel may well have borrowed its crucial double structure of a wild first movement followed by a long second phase of rebuilding from the extremely similar double structure of *The Heart of Midlothian.* Moreover, the two books characterize the paradise of domestic realism both by the soothingly familiar details of good housekeeping and by disturbing visitations from another reality. These crucial visitations serve to remind us that paradise truly is the "wreck of paradise," that the fictions of earned harmony we create and call realistic have their own illusions of completeness that we must recognize as illusions, if only by recalling another time. As Lucy Snowe will learn so sadly in her own little school, heaven on earth is full of memory and regret, for a more intense life, a more painful, a more beautiful, and most important, a different world.

The vision of paradise as both achievable on earth and as anticlimactic has many manifestations in nineteenth-century British novels. At midcentury Eliot's fiction adds a variation that redefines for her own work and for that of later novelists the nature of the vision. The by her time classic difference between an intense, sensual, but ultimately destructive present, becoming past even as we read about it, like the edenic, "half-neglected abundance" (222) of the Poyser's garden in currant time, contrasted with a hopeful but less scarlet future, is taken up with a new tension in *Adam Bede.* The harmony with which the story concludes is again shown to be limited, to depend on its own illusions of an ordered universe. But in Eliot's novel the tension between the achieved earthly order and previous romantic chaos is additionally defined in terms of the tension between the sexes. This final fulfilling world of domestic realism is presented as a male dominion, while its limitations are highlighted through the discontent of a female. There is a correlation between what Adam learns, what he gains, and the fact that he is a man.

Behind the tall figure of Adam creeps another figure, dwarfed and partially hidden by his striding presence, and shaded as well by its own darkness and dreadful fate. Henry James, though always a suspect critic of Eliot's work as of Austen's, given his own problems with influence, claimed about *Adam Bede* as early as 1866 that "[t]he central figure in the book, by virtue of her great misfortune, is Hetty Sorrel. In the presence of that misfortune no one else, assuredly, has a right to claim dramatic pre-eminence."[17] James is looking through Eliot's book to the ones both he and Eliot went on to write. The dramatic preeminence is Adam's, and his story is great enough to hold that place. Yet James's insight remains. Hetty does lure us away from Adam. Her hopes and misery, her beauty, her emotional and mental and moral stupidity, her fate, all unite in a tale that disturbs a humanistic reading of the novel. When I think what we, as opposed to Adam, have learned. I think uneasily of what to make of that amoral dairymaid.

Hetty's soul-making tells quite another story from the one we have been taught through watching Adam. Transported as a criminal for eight years for leaving her illegitimate baby to die in the woods, Hetty lives through the suffering in order to die on the way home. As Arthur Donnithorne, her remorseful seducer, says, she "will never know comfort any more" (481). One essential attribute of an earthly paradise, its quality of pain and reduced hopes and lost dreams, of something missing, is literally embodied in this first novel as the character of Hetty. Her absence haunts the timber-yard. The scene depicting the happy ending is primarily taken up with Adam's and Dinah's responses to the awful news of her death. A better future exists because, as the narrator puts it, Adam's "better" love for Dinah is an "outgrowth of that fuller life which had come to him from his acquaintance with deep sorrow" (541). Another way to put this might be that the better future with Dinah exists because Hetty cannot be part of it.[18]

Hetty's ghostly presence in the earthly paradise points clearly to her relation to her two fictional ancestors, those other cinderellas whose visionary gleam also vanished in the light of common day.

Catherine Earnshaw metamorphosed into Cathy Linton; and Effie Deans, the pagan peasant with her grecian-shaped head, turned into a proper lady and a Catholic. And Hetty, who could never have found fulfillment to her kind of dreams in that timber-yard, is replaced by the fair, pale Dinah. Because the point, as I have been arguing and as Wordsworth taught us, is that our sense of heaven in this world requires a sense of something missing—these characters are more than simply sacrifices or excluded figures. They measure the difference between what is and what might have been. And to be shut out of heaven, even an earthly heaven, blesses a character with a special appeal. Effie and Catherine and Hetty are the romantic judgment on the real. They are the outsider's judgment on the community. They focus loss and remind the reader that in the end we cannot neatly say that losses have compensations.

But if Hetty and Catherine and Effie share the outsider's position in relation to their respective communities, if in these novels concerned with what the past can bring to the future they are all sacrificed for the future, there remains a crucial difference between Eliot's offering and the previous figures. The future that Effie and Catherine haunt does fulfill their dreams. Effie, who has loved "as woman seldom loves" (216), does marry Geordie. Her continuing unhappiness as an elegant lady married to the great love of her youth establishes a crucial insight about outsiders such as Effie and Catherine and Hetty, an insight not based on moral judgments. There are drawbacks to having one's dreams come true. Scott's portrayal of Effie in the long years of union with her heart's desire had shown both Brontë and Eliot the reasons for developing other endings for their wayward women. The most satisfying, that is to say, fulfilling, alternative is developed in *Wuthering Heights*, though it requires believing in ghosts. Catherine attains happiness with Heathcliff, but only in an unearthly state. Some of us prefer a more fleshly fulfillment. But for Hetty, of course, there are no such pleasant pains, no mixed blessings, no Tithonian ironies, only isolation and suffering and death. Yet the example of Effie does relieve a little the force of that punishment, by reminding us that fulfillment can lead to isolation and death as well. We cannot find it difficult to picture what marriage between Hetty and her handsome lover would be like.

There is another difference between the ending of *Adam Bede* and the endings of its two predecessors. The future of domestic peace Effie is excluded from is quietly directed by her practical sister, Jeanie Deans. *Wuthering Heights*, a novel certainly sensitive to the issue of power and people's struggles to exercise it over each other, intimates a future shared fairly equally by Hareton and Cathy. But the timberyard of happiness that Hetty will never reach, the new Eden at the far end of the vale of soul-making, has developed a peculiarly masculine timbre. It is the domain of Adam Bede.

The original step Eliot's first book takes, identifying a by then familiar and appealing moral vision of life's meaning and its rewards with male dominance, establishes a subject for the rest of Eliot's novels and transforms many of the conventions of nineteenth-century British fiction. That step is not by itself radical or liberating for the depiction of women in fiction. On the contrary, Austen's novels, Scott's novels now and then, Charlotte Brontë's work, Emily Brontë's single masterpiece, all present female characters with an openness to their importance and their potential that is missing in *Adam Bede*. And these previous versions of heaven on earth do not presume or imply male precedence. Emma's energy will always be at least a match for Mr. Knightley's judgment, while Elizabeth Bennet will teach Mr. Darcy to be laughed at. And even that creepmouse, Fanny Price, grows up and becomes the clearest eyed and strongest willed person at Mansfield Park. It would be difficult to argue that there will be an imbalance of power and influence between Fanny and Edmund at their parsonage, any more than between Cathy and Hareton at Thrushcross Grange. Many readers have pointed to how the gender balance is established in *Jane Eyre*, and Lucy Snowe, to her sadness, lives in her earned eden by herself. An earthly paradise need not be masculine dominated, even when envisioned by a man. Scott, certainly, created many a gentle maid who obeyed her father or her brother until her true love arrived to direct her way. But in *The Heart of Midlothian*, where he gives us his large vision of what an earthly paradise would be, he simply makes Jeanie both the spiritual and the practical director of this world, though Reuben is the ordained minister and she stays at home.

The immediate difficulty with offering a reading of *Adam Bede* that is sensitive to gender issues and brings Hetty to prominence is that the novel, and by that I suppose I mean the narrative voice and the plot, is one the side of the men. Adam's story is important in a way that Hetty's or Dinah's is not, both because he is the lead character and because Loamshire is a man's world, a point that is offered not only as realistic but as affirmative. Arthur Donnithorne and his grandfather, Reverend Irwine, Martin Poyser, Bartle Massey, and Adam

Bede, these are the leaders who direct the fate of the community. Adam matters because he is a man. Hetty is not only less valuable than Adam, a minor character, but she is portrayed in strongly negative terms.

What distinguishes Hetty from the selfless Dinah and, more important for the development of the nineteenth-century novel, from those previous flawed and selfish outsiders, Effie and Catherine, is that the moral perspective of the book so thoroughly condemns her. Catherine, though punished as an adulteress, is virtually glorified. Effie, who more resembles Hetty in her illicit sexual experience and pregnancy, is condemned, it is true, but by a narrator who also finds appeal in her character as well as her beauty and gives her full human stature. Effie is granted a lesser crime and a better fate than Hetty. She did not abandon her infant but had it taken from her. That she is brought to trial shows the imperfections of the law. And Scott can depict Effie crossing class lines to marry her gentleman seducer in part because he has endowed this peasant girl with what Hetty has not been allowed, the intelligence and sensitivity to be educated.

We see how the narrative harshness in *Adam Bede* functions by turning to Hetty's harshest judge, Bartle Massey. Bartle states the issue vividly enough: "as for that bit o' pink and white, . . . I don't value her a rotten nut . . . —only for the harm or good that may come out of her to an honest man—a lad I've set such store by" (426–27). The schoolmaster is a misogynist. But from the narrator's perspective his embittered dislike of women primarily signals his own need to learn forgiveness. Mrs. Poyser is able enough to defend her sex against the sneering Bartle, telling him that "I know what the men like—a poor soft, as ud simper at 'em like aa pictur o' the sun" (537). Yet, though Mrs. Poyser routs Bartle in this exchange, though again and again in the novel characters whom we respect repudiate Bartle's views, though such feelings do represent his own educational failure to transform the sorrows of personal experience into a larger sympathy—in spite of all this, Bartle's opinion seems troublingly reinforced, both by what happens to Hetty and by others' responses to her crime. Whereas Mrs. Poyser may talk back to Bartle Massey and to the Squire, in this important matter the voluble domestic paragon must relinquish her sympathy to her husband's harsher view.

The moral judgment of the narrative about the heroine sides with the schoolmaster and the masculine community. In *The Mill on the Floss* we know by the relative characterizations of Mr. Stelling and Maggie Tulliver that when he assures her that girls can only be superficially clever, culture itself is being attacked."[19] But unlike

Mr. Stelling, who as a false teacher represents the falseness of culture, Bartle Massey is a loving though damaged soul who deeply cares about educational progress. And unlike the precocious and heartbreakingly sensitive Maggie, Hetty is intellectually as well as morally stupid and has the heart of a cherry stone. Because Hetty is outside the human community, we share Bartle's and the narrator's evaluation of her as subhuman, as most closely related in her sensual greed to Bartle's female dog, appropriately named Vixen. The enemy of true community progress in *Adam Bede* is not false culture. It is a woman's dreams.

Hetty's crime against the community is not a matter of sex any more than of murder, though it is a matter of gender. Hetty cannot accept an earthly paradise that celebrates the Poyser farm as the good life and validates Mrs. Poyser as embodying the proper feminine role. Hetty is bored in her dairy and cares little for making cheese. She does not want to become precisely what Dinah, taking her place, will become, in that rosy future that ends the book. Hetty wants someone beyond the option for fulfillment actually allowed her, the tall, restrained carpenter with broken fingernails. Why give her loyalty to a world where everyone else knows what is good for her better than she does, where everyone tells her to be grateful for possibilities she doesn't want, where her own wishes cannot even be spoken of?

Hetty imagines herself released from the givens that shape her days, able to shape her days to her own desires. What tempts Hetty, her inexcusable excuse for being seduced, is her own dreams. Given the chance to realize her dreams, to live the romance and escape the reality, she takes it. But my point is not that what Hetty imagines is humanly impossible, literally cannot be realized. For there Arthur is. And he does, in his light hearted fashion, fall in love with her. Rather, the point is that Hetty is allowed no right to him. From the perspective of the community this means not that the English class system is at fault but that Hetty's failure to recognize its constrictions is. A reader cannot simply wish that Arthur would marry her, and feel why not, because the two are by nature so suited to each other. Nature does not define the real in this novel, a particular culture does. Yet the narrative voice does not seem to take account of that, and certainly doesn't criticize it. The problem is that we are to receive the particular culture's constructs as ineluctable givens. And so should Hetty. But Hetty wants, and this is labeled her crime, a different role from the one not only the community but also the novel has defined as possible for her. This is the sense in which, imagining herself to be Arthur's wife, Hetty is profoundly unrealistic. She rejects the masculine and culturally created vision of the earthly paradise.

But, of course, these are my terms based on my perspective, not that of the narrator. Can I talk about Hetty's meaning as if it can be separated from the main story line, as if it tells a different story, indeed a subversive story? The question is appropriate about a novel that would claim that none of us have value independently of the people around us, that all our individual acts and lives reach out to influence and transform the lives of those around us, that we live inevitably in a social, public context. But the complexity within Eliot's apparently simple premise is that the social context is historical rather than absolute, a matter of time and place. Moreover, at least one reason for being aware of the public dimension of our lives is to sustain the insight that other people have hearts and rights independently of our desires. The power of sympathy depends upon the capacity to see and value others apart from their impact on us.

Hetty's story winds through Adam's. But does the narrative see her or value her independently of the harm or good she does to the stalwart lad we, as well as Bartle, set such story by? The answer the moral perspective of the novel, the perspective of community good, gives is no. What we must then answer in a feminist reading of the novel, in any reading of the novel that does not choose to ignore the issue of male/female significance and relative value at the heart of the book, is what to make of that morality.

U. C. Knoepflmacher, in an impressive 1968 essay, suggested that the discrepancy between Eliot's presentation of Adam and of Hetty and her harsh disposal of Hetty reveal that "her moralism and the 'realism' with which she reveals an amoral natural order still are in conflict."[20] Adam is linked to Eliot's belief in the universe ordered by human conscience and love whereas Hetty invokes the inhuman and unconscious natural landscape of Loamshire. I would change the language of this insight to say that Adam and Hetty represent not so much the tensions between moralism and naturalism as a debate on the nature of reality. Their debate helps us to define both the central position of Eliot's fiction in the tradition of nineteenth-century realism and its originality in transforming the conventions of that tradition.

In an essay on aggression and providential death in George Eliot's fiction, Carol Christ points out that in Eliot's plots people die conveniently and at propitious moments, facts that are "strangely inconsistent with Eliot's commitment to realism."[21] Christ's insight is a particularly interesting version of a fundamental sense among Eliot's readers, that there is a basic discrepancy between Eliot's claims about realism, about representing events and people "as they are" (179), and how her novels actually work.

The problem is hardly unique. Such a discrepancy can be pointed to in virtually every major novel in the history of British fiction, and probably American, too. From Aphra Behn to Defoe to the twentieth-century, novelists have been telling us that they are telling it like it is. And the poor reader, though both eager and progressively anxious to receive the word, at last to understand it like it is, has had, however reluctantly, to acknowledge not only that the word seems to have multiplied into many conflicting words, but that even the realism in a single novel is indistinguishable from the visible artistic hand of convenience and propitiousness, as well as from the inevitable arrangements of language itself.

We have long since come to recognize the paradox that art is the opposite of reality and yet may be a primary source of truth. To see truth we continue to turn to the creations of illusion, to the golden bird singing of what is past or passing or to come. In the particular case of nineteenth-century British fiction, the paradox is not so much modified as simply made more piquant. It is traditional in this art form that each new creation announces itself to be a break from tradition, to have moved from fiction to truth, and thus to be free of the artifice and manipulations that make up illusion and instead "to give the loving pains of a life to the faithful representing of commonplace things" (182).

The paradox seems unavoidable when we recall, with Gombrich, with Frye, and Barthes and so many others now, that all representations of reality are presented within a tradition, are recognizably modifications of existing conventions, that "there is no reality not already classified by man."[22] Yet we have not needed to wait for twentieth-century European, Russian, and American critics, for post-structuralist theories of referentiality, to light up the extent of the critical difficulties. We need only recall eighteenth-century British philosophers, the line from Locke to Hume, to invoke the primary epistemological difficulty: the impossibility of ever knowing a reality outside of, and thus freed from, our perceptions of it. Our categories will always shape what we know. And George Eliot's own awareness of empiricism and familiarity with the problem it so fully articulates can be surmised from the qualification she gives in her own famous claim to be calling up a picture of reality. She will offer, she says, "a faithful account of men and things as they have mirrored themselves in my mind" (178). She can tell us not the reality but the "reflection," and, moreover, the "mirror is doubtless defective."

We must acknowledge the fundamental epistemological and linguistic dilemma that places an objective reality, at least certainty about an objective reality, outside a subject's reach, or, to put it the other way, that defines any knowledge as inherently transformed by that subject (though even this phrasing, suggesting something prior to its being known, can mislead). But having accepted the dilemma, we need not then conclude that the topic is closed, that all truth is mediated, all language self-referential, all meaning shaped to some extent by convention, and that's that. In the first place, this insight carries its own presumptions that we may not always (or, perhaps, ever) choose to accept. One basic assumption is that the relation between object and subject is absolute and inherent, that is to say, that this insight is true for everyone and true always. Another assumption is that the everyone, the subject, the person doing the classifying, is normatively a man.

As the history of responses to empiricism and as present responses to poststructuralism show, there are alternate presumptions. Obvious examples are to argue that such epistemological and linguistic insights, perhaps all truths, are not absolutely fixed but are partial and temporal, are inevitably a matter of person and time and place. They are particular rather than universal. They are gendered. And they are political. I also suggest, here in tribute not only to twentieth-century feminist theorists but also to the empiricists and particularly to Hume, that an inaccessible reality and permanent condition of self-reflexiveness is true for our reason, is a logical insight, valid within a certain kind of knowing. But there may be other perceptual modes, such as faith, feeling, imagination, that can outreach the mediating self or, more accurately, radically change knowledge by the sheer act of self-consciousness. I mention such alternatives not simply to assert their power. I want to stress that the insight of a necessarily mediated reality, important as it is, cannot stand alone and certainly does not solve our epistemological or our critical problems with the subject of realism.

Even when we suspend the problems the masculine tradition of philosophic logic reveals, particular aesthetic questions about how to understand realism still remain. Quite apart from the general issue of self-reflexiveness, there are differences between individual works of art, differences that cannot be accounted for under the rubric that all truth is mediated, all representation a matter of convention. We need to make distinctions without which we would have no way of marking some of the differences between the art of Cimabue and that of Goya. Within the conventions that are the language of art there are clearly varying meanings to the ideas of both conventions and representation.

The point is particularly relevant when the art to be considered is nineteenth-century British fiction, with its strong commitment to realism as a central and distinguishing feature of its art. We can, of course, ignore or discount this commitment. We can see it as naive or uninformed, we can see realism simply as a matter of narrative technique. We can believe that art, and theory, are outside history and above politics. But after all, these British novelists did follow Hume and the empiricists, not precede them. And nineteenth-century British realism, at least in the novels, presented clear political and social agendas. As Laurence Lerner has said, "To treat realism as merely another set of conventions is to display such a lack of sympathy with its aims as to be virtually incapacitated from appreciating its products."[23] And frequently hidden within that display is a political conservatism that would suppress realism's often radical calls for cultural change.

The critical and political problem for any reader, male or female, of nineteenth-century British novels is what to make of realism as a specific and informing element in certain works of art. How does *Adam Bede* modify conventions so as to lay claim to realism? One important way to get at an answer to this abiding critical question is through the function of the heroine. In this novel the issue of gender leads us to the issue of realism. The rural carpenter's story called up from a sweeter, better, more harmonious past, entwines notions of realism, of history, and of gender so as to begin a feminist vision that is at the heart of what is radical and historical and amoral in Eliot's fiction.

Through Hetty, *Adam Bede* challenges its own representation of the schooling of an intelligence to make it a soul, and denies its apparently central conviction that "[d]eep, unspeakable suffering may well be called a baptism, a regeneration, the initiation into a new state" (436). Eliot's novel explores the issues of the apparent sense or the randomness of life in terms of the problems with presuming a moral universe when the order, the value, the morality, are male. The community premise of the novel, upheld by the plot as well as by the residents of Loamshire, is that the desire to shape life according to the demands of self is antisocial, unrealistic, and deeply immoral. It is also, and this is the element that will shape Eliot's novels to come and radically invert their perspectives, a feminine desire.

If the moral terms on which the narrative both judges and forgives Hetty are harsh, the greatness of *Adam Bede* is that the novel also, though readers have tended to ignore this, offers other more expansive terms, providing a larger perspective that is itself a criticism of the community ideology. This first novel establishes the masculine–feminine tension that will animate Eliot's fiction. That tension had not really existed in the work before *Adam Bede*. An early short story such as "Janet's Repentance," in spite of the sympathy toward Janet and implicit social criticism absent from Hetty's portrayal, stays within a socially conventional, and masculine-defined, moral frame of justice and mercy, forgiveness and redemption.

I am arguing that the moral vision so long described as the essence of Eliot's fiction, so long the basis for critical admiration of that fiction, is precisely what must be questioned and redefined as no more than a partial truth in our reading of *Adam Bede*. The politics of a literary criticism that makes it the whole truth and sees the holes in it as just inconsistencies in the novels or as necessary individual renunciations is all too comfortable with the traditional role of women as sacrifices to the progress of the culture. The portrait of the feminine in this novel cannot be summed up under the broad liberal rubric of Eliot's religion of humanity. To do so is to accept Adam's lesson as the full human story and thus to ignore, as traditional critics of the novel always have ignored, as many feminist critics still ignore, the other human story the novel tells. For we are given two versions of reality here, one masculine and one feminine. In *Adam Bede* gender is not merely a pervasive narrative tool. It is also entwined with a major, and unresolved, question: who defines the real?

Adam Bede affirms two major aspects of the masculine vision that defines, directs, and evaluates its community life. First, that vision defines reality as the earthly paradise of fulfillment and community progress whose center is work and the home and whose leader is male. There Adam lives, the tallest and most important figure in the domestic paradise. And there Dinah lives, "the sweet pale face" (548) of the full-time wife and mother who has accepted the Methodist male Conference ban on women preaching. As Adam says approvingly, "she thought it right to set th' example o' submitting" (550).

Only Seth, the dreamy idealist, the feminine man whose fulfillment is to be tyrannized by Adam's son, whose self finds no place of its own in this world, would urge, instead of a doctrine that forbids women to preach, a religious "body that 'ud put no bonds on Christian liberty" (550). In the realistic world of daily life in Eliot's fiction, the endearing detail of a sprig of mint to sweeten Adam's porridge, unlike the posies that brightened Hareton's porridge, speaks not of freedom but of gender bonds. Heaven on earth, that Dutch painting, is not a place of Christian liberty for the women who keep it clean and fruitful, which may be why Adam and Martin Poyser and Reverend Irwine can be provided with such contentment there.

The second aspect of that masculine vision, the aspect that has traditionally been so appreciated by critics of Eliot's fiction, is its fine moral sense, the firmness of judgment that knows the weight of our feelings and acts.[24] It is according to that measure, with that firmness, that Hetty Sorrel is condemned. And the same measure applies, whether the individual response to Hetty's acts is pity or horror. I would stress that Hetty's pardon, which Arthur so dramatically achieves, actually extends her suffering and still kills her in the end. Mercy proves as deadly as justice because both see Hetty's crime as reprehensible and Hetty as revealed to be beyond the human pale. The leading members of the community, no matter how sincere their forgiveness, cannot accept Hetty's dissatisfactions as anything but sinful; they do not even realize there is anything to understand. Even Dinah, that most sympathetic soul, can only forgive what she can never really see as anything but a terrible fall. Adam does learn sympathy. And we distinguish between Reverend Irwine's kindly tolerance and Martin Poyser's agonized coldness. But neither Adam nor Reverend Irwine nor Martin Poyser nor Arthur could understand Hetty, or could go on living anywhere near her. That is why Adam's final conversations during that dreadful time, his dramatic confrontations and struggles to understand, are with Arthur, the other man, who simply matters as a member of the community in a way that Hetty never did.

The point may simply be that social concern, realism, and morality are not inherently linked. But I would suggest that the major threat to Eliot's mid-Victorian realism turns out not to be class or nature or imagination but gender. Through Hetty's story *Adam Bede* fatally limits the boundaries of the moral universe and undermines its own definition of the familiar realism of "Dutch paintings" (180) and details of domestic life. The apparent contradiction of a realist art depicting a world of moral order that has troubled readers of Eliot's fiction dissolves when we step beyond Eliot's social liberalism, when we identify it as masculine.

Reality in *Adam Bede* is not the world of earthly compensations and everyday contentment that replaces the romantic, and fantastic, alternative. It is not the world of moral order, even, I would stress, of an order informed by mercy rather than mere justice. Forgiveness is culturally a feminine value, but in Eliot's earthly paradise it, like Dinah, is at the service of a better world for men. The true power of forgiveness, as Blake and Scott and Gaskell knew, is to illuminate. But the people of Loamshire are never illuminated about Hetty's desires. Finally, it is Hetty, or more probably, the feminist reader, who must learn to forgive Adam and the Loamshire community and the narrator for envisioning that any of us can build a better world with the stones of a young girl's heart.

To link the alluring realist convention of an earthly paradise with male dominion is to politicize that convention's use throughout nineteenth-century fiction. Eliot's own later happy endings of domestic realism will be self-consciously marked, and set aside, by questions of power, of gender. The novelist has transformed the realistic convention of those Dutch paintings in order to highlight its artificiality and reveal the ideology that sustains it. Eliot's fiction does not define realism as homey interiors or homely characters, any more than it defines narrative art as the story of an individual's or a town's or a region's moral improvement, in spite of the claims of her narrative voice and generations of masculine readers. Her art modifies that convention so as to lay claim to a new realism, one that ultimately means possession of a feminine consciousness. Of course, Hetty has virtually no consciousness. But her puny rebellion, her vain dreams, her blindness, do begin the great and distinctive feminine vision that will characterize the realism of Eliot's fiction.

The larger perspective in *Adam Bede*, which I am calling Eliot's realism, is neither naturalistic nor moral. It has nothing to do with Dutch paintings or English villages or meadows or the convention of learning to suppress egoism for the greater growing good. Indeed, the traditional appreciation of Eliot's realism and her moral sense has encouraged accepting the images of Hetty as expendable and subhuman, a cherry or a kitten, ignoring the sexism of such image-making. Instead of such a one-sided definition, realism in *Adam Bede* becomes the perspective that can hold together the double fates of both Adam and Hetty and thus the double way we live in a quotidian existence: satisfied and yet dissatisfied; feeling the need for the fictions that give meaning to our lives while admitting the imaginative inadequacy, the relativity, the oppressiveness, of the fictions we now have. The temporal paradise is flawed not only by our wrecked dreams but by all the personal and social biases that make up a part of anything we create, and especially a part of our pictures of the lives we want to live. In spite of Hetty's egotism, her ignorance, her stupidity, in spite of how effectively she is crushed, Hetty speaks to more historical, if less encouraging, realities than the notions of individual moral growth or building better worlds can contain.

If Hetty is hopelessly ineducable in the principles of the religion of humanity, this may point not only to her own limits but to other limits as well. It may be that the earthly paradise and the vale of soul-making and the nineteenth-century novel of education themselves prove to be finite modes for defining reality, for capturing the truths of our lives. *Adam Bede* may well mark a transforming moment in the history of the genre. After the story of Hetty and Adam, a hero's passage through the vale of soul-making could never be told so convincingly or applauded so innocently again. His education frequently turns out to be at someone else's, a woman's, expense. And the cost is almost as frequently her own future, her hopes or her life. The alluring story of growth leading to an earthly redemption that passed for true as well as good, has marked itself as only fantasy and often evil, its realism and its values metamorphosed into the conventions of domination and submission. As for a heroine, her passage must be permanently darkened by our dread not only of watching her obstacles and failings in becoming educated, but also of seeing her attain, and thus all too often merely become, that earthly reward.[25]

Eliot's fiction turns more and more to siding with the insights of the inarticulate and immoral dairy maid. We see the same hunger that cannot be fed in Eliot's second novel, *The Mill on the Floss.* The question of feminine fulfillment, or the lack of it, moves to being the explicit subject of the book, and the heroine becomes the main character. Eliot presents Maggie Tulliver's longings more sympathetically than Hetty's and at the same time points up the inadequacies of the community within which her experiences and her chances for happiness must lie. Maggie is more intelligent, more sensitive, more educated, and of a higher class than Hetty, and morally she is a mixed character rather than simply a blind ego in a pretty frame. With her death we are encouraged to feel some ambivalence about an idea of community progress that requires replacing her with Lucy of the golden curls. And even Lucy when she visits Maggie near the end learns for a moment the great lesson of disobedience. Female sacrifice is losing its appeal.

Along with the sympathetic portrayal of Maggie is a plot that gives her, unlike Hetty, the choice for her fulfillment and has her reject it, presenting her as coming to realize that having your dreams come true by disregarding the world around you doesn't finally satisfy. As Maggie pleads in her famous refusal of Stephen Guest, "Love is natural; but surely pity and faithfulness and memory are natural too."[26] Maggie understands, and before it is too late, the sad truth that Effie Deans only experiences. The trouble with Hetty, and her great appeal, is that she would not, any more than Effie, and certainly with no better results, have given up her romantic chance.

If Maggie is right in turning away from her chance to fulfill desire, in renouncing her earthly paradise, many readers have been dissatisfied with the reasons the novel offers to account for that renunciation. Maggie does not reject Stephen because she has come to understand his limitations, because she shares the judgment of Stephen that Eliot has Philip Wakem explicitly offer her, "I have felt the vibration of chords in your nature that I have continually felt the want of in his" (439). She does not reject him because she has come to see that the charm of being "taken care of in that kind graceful manner by some one taller and stronger than one's self" (334) is hardly the route to self-realization, because the conventions of the love story finally are not enough. Eliot presents Maggie's refusal of love not because Stephen, any more than Philip, cannot finally fulfill her dreams but because she is selfish to want to fulfill them. As Judith Lowder Newton suggests, "the effect is that the poverty of Maggie's options is all but buried in the counterinsistence that she wants too much."[27]

For all its sympathy with a woman's vital and demanding heart, its sensitivity to women's dreams, for all its strong temporal consciousness, *The Mill on the Floss* ultimately turns away from a historical vision and thus from a sensitivity to women's cultural plight. Instead, it turns into a virtually timeless tragedy in which Maggie exemplifies the Johnsonian hunger of imagination that feeds upon life. Fated to meet and fall in love with the handsome Stephen Guest instead of, for example, the equally handsome Will Ladislaw, who is not only a reformer but unattached, Maggie seems to be more at the mercy of her creator than of her historical moment. She has only the power to say no. Maggie is destined by her own nature as much as by her culture to play out her disastrous, and finally noble, fate. She vanishes in a flood of emotion in which renunciation is inextricable from revenge.

But that is not the whole story this novel tells. If Maggie wants too much, she also stands as the human center of the novel, the only important character, her wants being the measure of what interests us about St. Oggs. Maggie's feelings, Maggie's choices, Maggie's acts, are why we read the book. Her death, unlike Hetty's, fills the final pages. And would it really make a difference to reverse "the poverty of Maggie's options?" Would it help to offer Maggie a less guilt-laden choice for her earthly happiness than her cousin's beloved? Would it help if Stephen Guest were a better man? We need only think ahead to Felix Holt or to Will Ladislaw. Would it help if Maggie realized Stephen's limits? We would then see her reject him for being a false version of the hero, the black knight posing as the white.

This novel does not take the one significant step of repudiating for its heroine the very conventions of romance, of seeing that the conventions rather than the heroine are what need to be erased. But it almost does. Implicit in the very problems of Maggie's renunciation is the hint that passionate fulfillment is not the heart of self-fulfillment anyway. For the larger point of the ending is that there is no fulfillment, no heaven on earth, for Maggie. And what of those who conventionally do find romantic fulfillment, what of the Adam transformed through suffering and the new Eve? Instead of the depiction of an earthly paradise earned through sorrow and forgiveness, there remains for them only a single line of text about two unnamed figures visiting the tomb.

The treatment of the heroines of *Romola* and *Felix Holt the Radical* does not reach significantly beyond the insights about women's possibilities and potential established in the first two novels, perhaps even reaches less far. Both are historical novels in the sense that both invoke a specific era in the past that Eliot considers of particular historical interest. But I would say that they are not historical in the sense that they do not successfully represent the meaning of the past in the light of its meaning for the present and for the future. They fail as representation or as prophecy. They do not develop the perception implicit in the stories of Hetty and Maggie—that there is an inherent problem with a humanism that envisions women as martyrs to a better community future; that as long as women function as sacrificial means, one might appropriately doubt the ends for which they are sacrificed.

Both Romola and Esther do find their earthly reward and, at least by the end of their stories, they are both good. They were never very bad. Each struggles to tame the desires that threaten her happiness within the community. Romola is a fascinating version of Eliot's angel of renunciation.[28] Esther Lyon, with traces of Hetty's vanity and Maggie's hunger, develops an intelligent and sympathetic heart. Taught by Felix, she moves easily from being an old Eve to being a new Eve. Esther becomes a good girl and a good daughter and earns her earthly reward as the wife of Felix Holt. For both Esther and Romola the answer of goodness and obedience, one to a saintly life reminiscent of Janet Dempster's fate and the other to a guiding husband, resolves their restlessness and brings peace and fulfillment to an expanded heart. The conventions of closure through spiritual and earthly love shine brightly, perhaps too brightly, perhaps because, at least in Eliot's fiction, their blinding light was soon to fade.

Ten years after *The Mill on the Floss* Eliot presents the issue of women's dreams in an important new way in *Middlemarch.* Dorothea Brooke is good, she is rewarded, and yet we are specifically told what is implicit in the plot anyway, that her story is one of hopes not realized. Dorothea is virtually the opposite of Hetty, but because her sense of dissatisfaction with the possibilities of her life as a woman and her longings have her author's moral blessing as Hetty's did not. Eliot is able to give that blessing, as she could not with Hetty or with Maggie, because Dorothea's strongest desire, the desire that cannot be fulfilled within the givens of life, is the selfless desire to help the world and thus to change the givens of life. Dorothea is endowed with wealth, class, education, intelligence, generosity, and a major role in the plot. We can trace her flaws. But her lack of fulfillment cannot, as it could to a great extent even with Maggie Tulliver, be accounted for as the consequences of those flaws.

Middlemarch parallels the stories of Dorothea Brooke and Tertius Lydgate. But with the differences that has struck many readers, that in this book committed to the moral principle of consequences, of the inescapable results of our acts for ourselves and for others, Dorothea is allowed to escape. Her marriage to Casaubon, like Lydgate's to Rosamond, is an act of blindness to others and deception to self. Lydgate pays for that blindness as long as he lives, giving up his professional dreams, accepting "his narrowed lot with sad resignation," and "carrying that burthen pitifully" (586). But Casaubon dies, not only first but immediately, by a *deus ex machina* that frees Dorothea from the consequences of her mistakes.

Why should Dorothea be released from her stupidity, Lydgate permanently trapped by his? Why is her egotism redeemable, whereas his is not? Should we see that convenient release as indicating her superior character, her less culpable blindness to begin with, her greater capacity to be enlightened by her mistakes? And if we grant Dorothea a moral superiority to Lydgate, does it then follow that we find Dorothea's happy future with Will more admirable than Lydgate's resigned movement to his own death, carrying the "fragile creature" because he "had taken the burthen of her life upon his arms" (552)? No. For Lydgate no less than for Dorothea, for the hero no less than the heroine, "subjectivity is an ongoing construction, not a fixed point of departure or arrival from which one then interacts with the world."[29] Nobility does lie with Lydgate's sad acceptance of responsibility, a learned acceptance that comes not simply from principle but from a sustained effort to keep an open heart. His acquiescence to Rosamond's wishes, his successful London practice, his early death, all speak of his moral weakness and the failure of his dreams. But it is plausible to guess that Lydgate's life, like Dorothea's, contributed "little, nameless, unremembered acts/ Of kindness and of love" that helped the paths of those around him. Though never as good as Dorothea, though losing the struggle to do some public good and losing all the private battles to Rosamond as well, Lydgate suffered, he learned, and he proved himself to have a true heart.

Dorothea's release from that oppressive marriage is a gift. But as with all gifts from the gods, we should suspect it. Freedom does give Dorothea a second chance to make at last the right choice, the choice of open eyes and admitted passion that leads to fulfillment. But the catch is that this gift of a second chance is not so fulfilling after all. Rather than teach us that individual moral failings will damage our lives—the lesson of the two first marriages, the permanent lesson for Lydgate—we learn through this apparently generous ending for Dorothea a harder and more general lesson. Our lives will be limited anyway. Moral failures may trap us, but it hardly follows that moral victories will open the gate. Becoming good doesn't save us. The fault may lie in ourselves. But it certainly, and this is the inescapable point, lies in our times.

Unlike St. Theresa, Dorothea lives in the wrong time and place. We watch the process of her character developing, as we watch Lydgate's. And for both what is at stake is the moral life, the insight to see the vision of connectedness that Eliot's fiction presents as the truth of our human existence. But the difference is that the success of Dorothea's perceptual education, her inner success, regardless of whether accomplished before her actions in ignorance have rendered it too late, is not tied to her outer success. After all, Dorothea's errors are retrieved, both because she has the depth of sympathy to clutch her own pain, to see that "she was a part of that involuntary, palpitating life" (578) and because she has a creator who reaches out to retrieve her from that marriage. But even with this double success, Dorothea's story is one of failure. She never realizes her passion to reform, because she never could. For Dorothea, then, plot will never fit character, what happens to her will be inappropriate to her deserts, and not in the Austen sense of being "happier than I deserve." Reality is inadequate to meet the demands of imagination.

Through the St. Theresa legend, through the social and political contexts that inform Dorothea's life, *Middlemarch* defines itself as historical fiction in a more substantive sense than either *Romola* or *Felix Holt*. It renders explicit the suggested point in *The Mill on the Floss*, that gender is not a matter of essence but of history, that women are at the mercy of their historical moment. And at the present moment, they cannot fulfill their dreams. Maggie and Dorothea, like Hetty and Catherine Earnshaw and Effie Deans before them, haunt the final lines and new worlds, of their novels. At the Red Deeps "the buried joy seemed still to hover—like a revisiting spirit." And Dorothea Brooke's full spirit flows on with an effect "incalculably diffusive." Both remind us of what might have been, of aims not realized.

Middlemarch thus provides a solution to a continuing creative problem, one that lay hidden behind the hero in *Adam Bede*: the need to find a community in which her heroine belongs. Eliot failed to find it in *Romola*, in spite of the extensiveness of the public historical context she provided. Romola merely ends up seeming ethereal. In *Felix Holt* the solution is a sentimental, and masculine, evasion, Esther Lyon's context being at the end simply the place provided for her by her radical husband, "greater and nobler than I am." But in *Middlemarch* the lack of an historical community for the heroine, far from suggesting withdrawal or a truth beyond history, emerges in what will be its essential meaning for Eliot, as an historical truth.

The movement from *Adam Bede* to *The Mill on the Floss* to *Middlemarch* is to increasing moral affirmation of the desire for a better reality, seeing such desire as less and less a matter of egoism, and also to increasing suspicion of the actual world that in this moment in history cannot fulfill desire. In each case, desire is embodied in a female character; the historical and cultural givens are represented as male. And once reality in the time and place of Middlemarch is represented as cultural and as unfulfilling, then the conventional happy endings for Celia and her baby or Mary Garth and Fred Vincy on their farm are revealed not only as old-fashioned solutions but as outmoded fiction, conventions from a fiction that had not yet tied the earthly paradise to a patriarchy. They are pretty pictures, pleasingly realistic rather than idealized. But we understand too much to view them as historical possibilities.

Nor is male fulfillment an alternative. The narrator does assure us early in the novel that Lydgate could have become a scientific success, his love story with medical research could have produced a "glorious marriage" (107). We meet Lydgate at a "starting-point which makes many a man's career a fine subject for betting," and the interest of the bet is that "character too is a process and an unfolding. The man was still in the making" (111). His is the history of an "intellectual passion" (106), one with a sad ending of "frustration and final parting" (107). But in spite of all such narrative declarations, Lydgate's story as we are told it is very much one of human as well as intellectual passion, it being part of Lydgate's masculine blindness, and the narrator's duplicity, to suggest that a character, or a narrator, or a reader, could separate the two. And although Lydgate could possibly have made important discoveries in medicine, an opportunity the times did not afford to women, his prejudices about women are also a sign of the times.

For Lydgate's failure, though it is his responsibility, is ultimately a cultural as well as an individual problem. Lydgate's blindness to Rosamond, his good taste in furniture and women that makes him unable to distinguish subject from object, Rosamond's soul from her long neck and "blue flower" (222) eyes, is a cultivated stupidity after all. It is part of the proper education of a well-bred man, one who has successfully absorbed the gender biases of his culture. That is why Will Ladislaw had to be deprived of a proper upbringing. As a product of the masculine tradition, a representative of his own time and place, Lydgate cannot grant women an independent existence or, more precisely, can only fall in love with their dependency. Dorothea does not move his heart, however much she will come to move his soul.

If Adam's story had traced the male satisfaction in the earned eden of domestic paradise, Lydgate's looks at the snake in the garden, the failure of reciprocal love in an eden based on the illusion of masculine superiority. How can a man, how can anyone, find harmony with another human being when his education had denied her humanity, her very reality as an independent self? What chance has he to make a wise and loving choice? Lydgate does get his heaven in this world and discovers the real horror within that masculine myth. The perfect marriage of the girl all Middlemarch admires with the cultivated stranger so superior to the local suitors becomes a long agony of domestic woe, as even their furniture goes the way of their illusions. Heaven on earth is only possible, can only be realized, in some other place, at some other time, for people other than ourselves. Lydgate's bare house marks the present, for both Rosamond and Lydgate. And Adam's timber-yard, we begin to see, exists in a past eden that may never have been.

In Eliot's final book, Daniel Deronda's new East does not exist in the story at all, but in a future beyond his lifetime. Against these past and future edens that end the novels stand the dreams of women who insist that a reality that enslaves them in the "blessed protectiveness" Daniel provides to Mirah remains an illusion, its falseness measured by the real fulfillment it excludes.[30] Heaven on earth, the domestic paradise, is no place for a woman to fulfill her dreams at all. It is a masculine perception and a male dominion, a realism of ideology inherited through men. Eliot's early heroines, when offered that version of fulfillment as reality, don't take it, Hetty preferring to wander off into seduction, Maggie embracing renunciation, while the later Gwendolen is too damaged and too knowing to receive the offer at all. As for Dorothea, she gets Will, but we are spared having to see it. But Lydgate's story explores the meaning of that ideological inheritance for the man and shows us, for both man and woman, the present nightmare within the dream.

From Eliot's first novel to her last, the center of meaning, where reality lies, shifts from the insider to the outsider, the hero to the heroine. Gwendolen Harleth matters in a way that Daniel Deronda does not, much as Adam matters in a way that Hetty does not. If Hetty is outside her particular community, she is also ouside the human community, hardly a person at all. But Gwendolen, though also an outsider in her social world, represents the only human community the novel offers. Grandcourt is a devil, and Daniel is a saint. Both are incorporal, both extremes beyond the realm of mixed character that Austen long before told us composes realistic fiction and everyday life. In her immorality Gwendolen is a return to Hetty, and the double story of Gwendolen and Daniel has its sources in the original dichotomy of Hetty and Adam. But the meaning of that dichotomy has changed. *Daniel Deronda* offers a different kind of realism from *Adam Bede* because it offers a different definition of reality.

As in *Middlemarch*, the center of the issue in this final book is what constitutes history, how the present can move into the future without recreating the past. We know what the idyll of Mirah and Daniel will be. We have been there before with Adam and Dinah. The historical promise of *Daniel Deronda* is made not through Daniel but through Gwendolen. The even-handed author reaches out for Gwendolen as she had for Dorothea, to kill a husband and release a heroine from the consequences of her mistakes. Unlike Dorothea's, Gwendolen's freedom to have a second chance is not used up through again becoming a wife. Domestic bliss seems both fantastic and inappropriate. Her second chance is not realized within the story at all. We don't know, and perhaps we can't imagine, what Gwendolen will do. All we do know is that her unknown future will not repeat her past. But that is enough.

We cannot view Gwendolen as outside history and Daniel as making it because the only history the novel offers is hers. Daniel's story, like his character, is a masculine fantasy. Thus the dilemma of the lack of historical context for the heroine dissolves when the author does not present a community life that the heroine is absent from. There is no ongoing world of Hayslope or St. Oggs, from which the erring heroine is excluded by her death. There is no Florence or Treby or Middlemarch from which the superior heroine can retire or can move on to a more active world. Part of the brilliance of *Daniel Deronda* is that there is no main line of historical progress to which the heroine may or may not connect. Gwendolen creates the context, her movements are the flow of history.

Buried in Eliot's gender distinction is a question: which reality, Adam's or Hetty's, Gwendolen's or Daniel's, is the historical moment we live in now? And the implicit answer, in the nostalgia with which Adam's past community is presented, in the distance in both time and place of Daniel's future fulfillment, in the movement of the heroines from background to foreground, is that our historical moment, and in that sense our reality, is that of the heroines. They are the way we live now. And the way we live now is within an unclear context we are not part of, one that cannot define its own boundaries, one that cannot realize our hopes.

Eliot's last novel is virtually a rewritten version of her first. Change in Eliot's fiction may be measured by the change in the heroine, from a first novel offering a powerless and amoral peasant who dies for her dreams to a last novel offering a young gentlewoman powerful enough to win over Grandcourt and to end her story insisting that "I shall live. I mean to live" (879). However minimal such a claim may seem, it is a true victory, one literally not allowed to Eliot's first two heroines. That Maggie as well as Hetty dies whereas Gwendolen as well as Dorothea and Romola lives, emphasizes that we cannot match any of their fates with a meaning based on individual moral worth. For Gwendolen is a return to and a vindication of Hetty in one central way: they are both immoral heroines. Maggie, Romola, Esther, Dorothea; all have their blindnesses, their egoisms, their vanities. But none so close to wicked as the first and the last.

Eliot portrayed Hetty as too dumb to be good, and as severely punished. But Gwendolen has her own developed intelligence, her mother, her knowledge of Lydia Glasher, and Daniel's guidance. And yet Gwendolen is one of the great bad heroines in English fiction. Many heroines die for less. Or live, as James's Isabel Archer will, to face her marital trap. But Gwendolen will live free. Her presentation is an advance over Dorothea and a confrontation at last with the problems hidden in the initial creation of Hetty. Gwendolen does not find fulfillment, and she is not good. But the crucial difference between her and Hetty is that the reasons for her lack of fulfillment are not simply made a matter of her own failings, with her hunger assuaged by death. Nor does her moral education mean, as it so often has with Eliot's heroines, noble renunciation. Eliot neither kills her nor makes her happy nor makes her good. Gwendolen remains a restless and dissatisfied soul, one who "shall be better" (879), one who may find fulfillment, but one who lives on to struggle with both her desires and her world. Eliot provides no moral conclusiveness either of character or of fate.

Beyond the moral issues, beyond all questions of sex and renunciation, of individual right and wrong, the works of this most moral novelist tell of a meaning beyond individual morality. I want to recall that classic insight about Eliot's fiction, its commitment to what Dorothea Brooke saw as being part of a world larger than self, belonging to a single, palpitating life. I want to suggest a new reading of that insight, that our sense of connectedness must come from a sense not of the ways we belong but of the ways we don't. A historical consciousness, at least in the nineteenth century in England, means feeling disconnected and realizing that, regardless of deserts, we won't reach the earthly home that sits at the far end of the vale of soul-making. Nor should we wish to. We wouldn't like it there. And that is our real education.

Once Eliot had linked the vision of a better world to valuing one gender more than the other, her idea of group progress carried its own negation, its moral claims canceled by its sexism. We know that there is no historical advance into the future if Gwendolen Harleth stays behind, no religion of humanity for a community that destroys Hetty Sorrel. If men try to escape repetition through a new Eden without Eve, they lose Eden and end up excluded along with her once again. Accepting that exclusion, identifying with that outsider, is the true break out of repetition into history. Art, at least the developing art of nineteenth-century British novels of education, does not imagine the recovery of paradise. Men and women, they are all Eves.

The pattern of development in Eliot's work that I have been discussing here illuminates an analogous direction in which feminist criticism about nineteenth-century British fiction may be moving. Eliot's narratives begin by being of Adam's party, with Hetty as an outsider, excluded from the main line of cultural progress. That exclusion, as Eliot's book tells us about Hetty and as feminist criticism has revealed about a woman's place in fiction, makes dangerous lunatics of us all. Eliot's novels moved from the depiction of woman as apart to woman as central because that is where human values lay. This also meant moving away from an earthly paradise. Gwendolen Harleth, culturally damaged and individually flawed as she is, remains the only human survivor in the community of *Daniel Deronda*, as Daniel accepts his true identity as a fantasy figure and sails away with Mirah to the dreamscape where they and Dinah and Adam and so many other figures belong.

The further insight we might take from *Adam Bede* is that insisting on a separate voice and thus a literature apart has been still to privilege Adam and, indirectly, to fall for the largest critical fiction of all, that there is a main voice of nineteenth-century British fiction that belongs to men. Our own growth as feminist critics may be from the crucial initial step of establishing the existence of a women's tradition as a thing apart toward acknowledging it as a major force directing the development of the British novel. Placing a feminine tradition as central must also include exploring the influence of women writers on men writers, and of men writers on women writers. It acknowledges that Jeanie and Effie Deans are influential relatives of Catherine Earnshaw, that Gwendolen Harleth is well known to Clara Middleton and Isabel Archer, that Hetty Sorrel is reborn and dreams and dies again in Tess. We have, at last, established a place for women in literature. But Eve's party is more extensive than we have imagined so far. We are now moving out from separatism to reclaim a larger place, a great feminine tradition that informs nineteenth-century British fiction. During that time, in that place, women characters are the voice of the novel, the imaginative center of the genre during its greatest growth. Inheriting the endurance of their long-talking predecessors, Moll Flanders and Clarissa Harlowe, these characters embody many of the issues and the methods of the British novel up to the modern age.

6

"Deeply a Woman, Dumbly a Poet": Language as Betrayal in Meredith's Later Fiction

> Ah! Meredith! Who can define him? His style is chaos illumined by flashes of lightning. As a writer he has mastered everything except language: as a novelist he can do everything, except tell a story: as an artist he is everything, except articulate.
>
> OSCAR WILDE

> He is an avowed feminist who sees in woman an oppressed class dominated through male self-interest, prevented from developing as human beings by a system which prostitutes them in and out of marriage and deliberately miseducates them.
>
> KATE MILLETT

George Meredith was famed in his own century for being a great mind, the philosopher of novelists or, as George Gissing so madly asserted, a Shakespeare in modern English.[1] In this century Meredith has been repudiated and dismissed for the pretentiousness and obscurantism of that philosophizing. As Ezra Pound put it, he's "chiefly a stink."[2]

Meredith's work remains somewhat neglected today, commented on by a small group of readers, alluded to whenever anyone discusses theories of comedy in fiction, but very far from resting in the glittering intellectual place Meredith had not been too modest to claim for it.[3] But perhaps Meredith, like Scott, has been done in by his own party, and masculine critical values, however dear both to Meredith and to his traditional readers, are not those on which Meredith's work should stand or fall.

Readings of Meredith's fiction in the last four decades follow what is now the classic approach to Victorian fiction. They look at such topics as the processes of the inner life, the inseparability of private and public lives, the destructive effects of both society and ego, the power of love and, *de rigueur* with Meredith, style and comedy.[4] But when the text is a Meredith novel written after *Beauchamp's Career* in 1876, most discussions scream of what is not being discussed. The coming of age of literary criticism in America has been so sublimely sure of the insignificance of gender as a critical tool as to be deaf to the voice of the feminine even in the face of its most explicit literary expressions.

Traditional critical focus on the dynamic tensions between self and society and on the narrative methods for exploring those tensions assumes that the self, whether portrayed as man or woman, is really everyman or, more exactly, is every exceptional, attractive, intelligent, sensitive, upper-class, white man or woman.[5] Thus hero or heroine both become the individual or the protagonist or the self, that familiar humanist subject, no functional difference worth mentioning between Nevil Beauchamp and Diana Warwick. This effectively means, at least for questions of interpretation, that, man or woman, they are all men. No need for the reader to ask further why so many of Meredith's heroes are, in fact, heroines, or why Meredith kills off Nevil but not Diana. Meredith's own biography, his marriage to Mary Peacock Nicolls, along with his pervasive literary theme that society impinges on the individual struggling to find self-fulfillment, these together are taken for granted as adequate for those who might want to explain Meredith's use of female lead characters.

Arabella Shore, that Victorian lady novelist and genteel but unheard literary critic, may be a truer guide to Meredith's work than Gissing or Pound or so many literary critics whose writing established the values according to which our tradition in fiction has been selected, interpreted, and handed down. After the extravagant Victorian praises and Modernist insults, academic readers of this century have not found a critical place for Meredith's work, have not been able to locate it evaluatively and historically. Perhaps they have not asked the right questions. And they have not asked them because they have not been particularly interested, either intellectually or aesthetically, in what Meredith and so many of his literary contemporaries considered, as Shore put it, "that most fruitful of subjects—the social relation of the sexes."[6] It doesn't matter, at least not centrally, whether or not Meredith's novels are philosophic, whether they contain a new theory of comedy, whether his dense style denotes genius or opacity, whether his novels show a great mind at work. The place to look for Meredith's significance, a place obviously irrelevant to Pound and to many an academic critic, as the astounding absence of discussions of feminist issues in the record of criticism on these novels explicitly concerned with feminist issues so profoundly shows, is in Meredith's presentation of women.[7]

This is not to say that Meredith wrote feminist novels.[8] He has always been one of the boys. Yet finally it was a feminist reader who first offered an explicit and complex evaluation of the extent, and the limitations, of Meredith's presentation of women. Kate Millett's 1971 breakthrough tribute to the Meredith of *The Egoist* declared him to be "an avowed feminist" who "not only knows how things are ordered in sexual politics, he knows why." Yet that tribute is still followed by a clear warning about Meredith's "tritely masculine attitude" in settling Clara with Vernon Whitford at the end of the book.[9] Millett's reading, capturing this double aspect of the function of women in Meredith's novels, remains a classic guide to approaching his work.

Meredith's fiction is often disturbing. It faces, with a self-consciousness and explicitness rare in nineteenth-century British fiction, the woman question or, as Meredith puts it in the famous "Prelude" of *The Egoist*, "human nature in the drawing-room of civilized men and women" (1:1). Yet Meredith's insights and sensitivities in his novels about the problems for women's development in a constricting society are not only gleaned from his own cruelties to his first wife, and fed on the good cooking of his more docile second wife, they are also continually ambushed within the novels by attitudes that damage those insights. Meredith's heroines are almost universally long-limbed, finely proportioned, delicate featured, and have good skin. They are often virtual goddesses, and at the same time can behave like the snake woman in that odd first novel, *The Shaving of Shagpat*, or fill the marriage bed with sobs, "like little gaping snakes,/Dreadfully venomous to him" (24:181).

But what is special about Meredith's work, and finally what is appealing and energizing about reading his novels, is that they assume that whether one is male or female matters, and not in the insignificant sense of being a matter of biology but in the significant sense of being a matter of culture. Knowing how it matters, whether and how it should, and what one's own sex has to do with one's attitude to the other sex, is everyone's duty and the only hope for our modern malaise. Meredith's novels virtually declare gender to be the central issue of our lives, both private and public, "the within and without of us." The relations between the sexes, then, are "the brainstuff of fiction," (16:17) the dignifying subject that makes philosophy out of art.

In the 1877 "The Idea of Comedy" Meredith writes of his heroines that "[c]omedy is an exhibition of their battle with men, and that of men with them" (23:15). He goes on to imply that their differences are cultural rather than essential and can be reversed through the "similarity of their impressions" of life. Jenni Calder's study of women and marriage in Victorian fiction followed Millett's lead in praising Meredith. Calder points to Meredith's uniqueness here by asking, "Was there any other novelist in the century whose most important theme concerned the 'mutual likeness' of men and women?"[10] Certainly, in the novels gender differences are not a matter of biology. But I would add that Meredith's belief in the "mutual likeness" of the sexes speaks of possibilities rather than actualities, it presumes equality of education and opportunity and position. The commitment to mutual likeness in the future requires that Meredith consider mutual difference now.

We cannot, then, infer that Meredith's characters, male or female, simply represent human nature, at least in the drawing room. But this is not only to say that Meredith's interest in gender is finally sociological, or even psychological. Although the differences between the sexes may have been entirely culturally induced, as Meredith appears to have believed, understanding that does not offer a direct road out of inequality. Indeed, there are facets of the inequality that may be good, that may, in our present cultural situation, be the best means of helping us, male and female, toward a better future. The exploration of gender in these books has more at stake than offering portraits of oppression and the struggle for liberation. It has more to teach than the need to right social wrong.

The constant spotlighting of women in Meredith's novels does not mean that the stories are about women finding a place for themselves without men, as do Gaskell's Ruth Denbigh, Charlotte Brontë's Lucy Snowe, and, later, Gissing's Rhoda Nunn. These heroines' experiences in love are essential to their education and are also, and necessarily, left behind. The three heroines' stories offer nicely reversed instances of that classic plot where the beloved (or passionate love itself) is a sacrifice to the male lead's growth, a female martyr to what, all too usually, is the hero's more important cause.

Carinthia Fleetwood's story may seem to repeat the pattern of events for the above three heroines. Meredith's final heroine does appear to prefer action to love and thus to be an exception in Meredith's canon. Carinthia rejects the battle of her amazing marriage for the more external experiences offered by war in Spain. But the critical problem with this reading is not only the point that at the very end of the novel Meredith marries Carinthia off to a good man. More significant, the whole ending of *The Amazing Marriage*, both Carinthia's superficially independent freedom-fighting (not alone anyway, but with her brother, and offstage as well) and her remarriage to a reliable man, is outside the frame of the story, an unreality tagged on to provide closure. Many of Meredith's heroines do reject marriage and attempt to shape their own lives. But that attempt consistently turns out to include relations with a man. I would say that Meredith's novels are always love stories because in them the story of whom we love or whom we move away from loving is a primary expression of the active relations of self and world.

Like Austen's fiction, which had a profound influence on Meredith as well as on so many other Victorian writers, Meredith's fiction assumes the precedence of love over profession. In both it matters what people do, though in Austen's work only men have professions, and in the more advanced, at least temporally advanced, Meredith novel both men and women struggle to find a suitable profession. But in Austen's *Mansfield Park* the question of Edmund Bertram's profession is represented entirely through the question of which woman he loves.[11] Will it be Mary Crawford or Fanny Bertram? Like Nevil Beauchamp, Edmund Bertram's career is dramatized as his relations with women. And in *Sense and Sensibility* Edward Ferrars, who has foolishly been raised so as to be unfit for a profession, finds his career and a useful and productive future through his relations with Elinor Dashwood. In both canons the greater and more significant struggle is to find a suitable mate. This task, whether or not it is successful, remains an abiding measure of character and our best hope for learning to understand ourselves and our culture.

This is as true for men as for women. In Austen's work, Mr. Darcy, Captain Wentworth, Henry Tilney, all depend for their moral and perceptual growth on their relations with the women they love. That growth is the major story of their lives. The same is true of Meredith's Nevil Beauchamp, Willoughby Patterne, Lord Fleetwood, and Victor Radnor, with the painful distinction that theirs are stories of failure. The consequences of that failure help to measure what has been at stake. Nevil Beauchamp dies, Victor Radnor goes insane and dies, Lord Fleetwood becomes a Catholic and dies, and Willoughby lives on frozen in his public frame, with a wife who has stopped loving him precisely because she has come to know him. The predecessors of these characters are Mary and Henry Crawford, Austen's finest egoists and failed romantics, rather than Edmund Bertram or Fanny Price.

Not for Meredith or for Austen the voice of that sophisticated male (or female) narrator in *Middlemarch*, who could contrast the love story of a man and a career with that of a man and a woman and find the former more intellectually appealing, the latter too frequently told. We recall, of course, that the narrator deceived himself (or herself), that the tale of Lydgate and Rosamond is inseparable from the story of Lydgate and his career. That narrative voice does end up telling a love story, but in quite a Meredithian way. That is to say, the story it tells is of blind and shallow love, selfishness and misunderstanding, a marriage gone wrong and lives pervasively and permanently blighted through the deceptions of conventional romance.

Meredith's novels, like Austen's, take as a primary and valued truth the simple point that women matter to men and men matter to women. One measure of stupidity in his work is a character who deceives himself or herself about the centrality of that truth. A more frequent measure, since so many of Meredith's characters are egoists, and that is to say romantics, is to know the centrality of love and to misplace it. I think of *The Tragic Comedians*, in which the whole story is two people in love, and love is self-love. Alvan and Clothilde, as odd mutations of Lovelace and Clarissa, he not dissolute and she not a paragon, but each reputed to be so, destroy each other in courtship, he literally killed in a duel, she having no further life to live. And the role of their respective reputations in their own blindess and mutual destruction is characteristic of the way in Meredith's novels public definitions always participate in the sabotage of self.

Depicting character through social relations while seeing the social world as inevitably impinging on self in destructive ways, and seeing character as also ambushed by his or her own ego result in love stories that are brilliantly gnarled and frequently disastrous. In fact, Meredith's happy endings usually don't fit, don't convince, and don't matter. Austen can use arbitrary playfulness to effect a happy ending for Emma—Mr. Woodhouse being brought to consent to his daughter's marriage because he wants a man around the house because there is a turkey robber in the neighborhood. This playfulness, in a Meredith novel, becomes a clanking *deus ex machina*, such as Carinthia Jane returning from Spain to marry the loyal husband bequeathed to her by her conveniently dying best friend. We prefer Clothilde's equally clanking fate, marrying the dying consumptive who killed her only love in a duel. As with *The Amazing Marriage*, the ironies that close *The Tragic Comedians* may also seem mere artifice. But at least in *The Tragic Comedians* the emotions do not violate all we have come to understand about the characters.

In Meredith's fiction the subject of relations between the sexes presumes, as it does in so many novels in the nineteenth century, that meaning lies in the active encounter of self and others, that experience matters, that character, in the famous words of *Middlemarch*'s narrator, "is a process, and an unfolding." Another way to say this is that Meredith writes novels of education, that his stories usually concern, to borrow Fanny Burney's phrase, a young person's entrance into the world. The interaction of self and society, loving another person, the obstacle of ego, these are the familiar territories within which Meredith's characters struggle and sometimes learn.

Yet it is a familiarity with a difference. Meredith's characters live in fragmented worlds, where self-expression is distortion and deception. Women can embody this dilemma with special success because of how acutely their social bonds, difficulties in being heard, and struggles for freedom dramatize the general problems of self-realization and particularly self-expression. The anecdote of Robert Louis Stevenson's about Meredith's witty reply to the reader who claimed that Willoughby Patterne was modeled on him, "No, my dear fellow, he is all of us," can illuminate Meredith's fiction if we extend the insight to understand that the "us" means women as well as men.[12]

But even extending Stevenson's remark, it still covers only half the point. If we are all Willoughby, he is not all we are. We need also to understand whom Clara Middleton is modeled on. As Percy Shelley knew, if the tyrants are in all of us, so are the victims. Meredith's troubled love stories turned increasingly to focus on his heroines. The female protagonists dramatize with wonderful piquancy the dilemma of the male novelist. The heroines of Meredith's novels are himself.

Donald David Stone has noted that in two important ways, "both as a Romantic outsider and as a disciple of Nature, Meredith identified with women's position.[13] But there is also a third, more particular identification. In Meredith's fiction the problems of self-realization are problems of self-expression. Clara Middleton struggles to free herself from Willoughby by providing her father with "the name for it!" (14:209), while Emma Dunstane in *Diana of the Crossways* is described as "deeply a woman, dumbly a poet" (493). The social and psychological difficulties of being a woman in these times are the difficulties of the artist as well.

But the artist portrays his situation as that of a woman not simply through feeling somehow apart from and muzzled by society. More essentially, Meredith's fiction dramatizes our creativity, our longing to grow, our energy to shape, as feminine.[14] Percy Shelley's classic response to Peacock in *A Defence of Poetry* that science and economics are inadequate, that "we want the poetry of life," and that "man, having enslaved the elements, remains himself a slave," lives again in Meredith's own tributes to the "creative faculty." Like Shelley, Meredith attacks a creed of progress based on factual and rational knowledge, for him specifically evolution, and for the same reasons, seeing it as tied to the traditional masculine values of conquest, assertiveness, and control.[15] Belief in these does make monkeys of us all, does feed the primitive ego that shrieks in Willoughby's polished soul. The point becomes pervasively important because we as a society suffer from a "modern malady," for which "Art is the specific," which science cannot cure, (*E*, 4).

Yet Meredith's medium is Victorian fiction, not romantic poetry. Instead of Shelley's embodied principle of love, the sublime Asia of *Prometheus Unbound*, Meredith invents real women. Shelley's feminine principle of creativity as love is humanized and particularized as Meredith's heroines. Like Byron's Haidee compared to the goddess, Aurora, they were "quite as fresh and fair," and "had all the advantage too of not being air."[16] Stone has discussed in impressive depth Meredith's debt to the romantics.[17] I want particularly to note here the importance of Shelley's influence in Meredith's use of women leads,[18] Shelley's commitment to our cultural need to put forward the feminine principle in place of the Orc cycle of egoism and aggression becomes both a concrete and a central thesis in Meredith's fiction. The radical premise of Meredith's later novels is that cultural progress depends, truly depends, on the advancement of women. Their repression is, quite literally, the repression of the major creative resource of nineteenth-century British culture.

A belief that relations between the sexes are a fundamental value along with a conviction that individual education and personal fulfillment are inevitably part of some cultural progress means that those of us whom society crushes must be free if any of us are to be free. Men and women must liberate women if either sex is to find happiness. A male novelist can embody his general hope for social progress in fictions whose subject is the woman question, fictions that light the path to love and fulfillment by presenting the cruel wars between men and women, by analyzing why men try to murder the women they love and end up dying themselves, by explaining why women must struggle to speak, their own tale to tell.

Meredith's novels explore the tension in us, as civilized men and women living inevitably in the public sphere, between repression and creativity. His novels more and more locate our creativity, and thus our hopes for a better future where we are kinder to each other and freer ourselves, in the emancipation of women. Meredith's analysis in fiction of the conditions and causes of a troubled present pointed him to articulate a solution that must involve better lives for women, both internally and publicly. The question of gender, as the differences of meaning culturally attached to the differences of sex, turns out to be the heart of our "modern malady." Dissolving those differences may turn out to be the cure for our hearts.

Eliot's last novel, *Daniel Deronda*, was published in 1876, the same year as another work that, though George Meredith's ninth published novel, became a new beginning for his fiction: *Beauchamp's Career*. As Arabella Shore pointed out in her 1879 appreciation, this political novel about the life of a young naval hero turned radical also offered a view on the question of "the position of women in the social system" by creating a "picture of this clear and ripening intellect, framed in so fair a form."[19] The portrait of Cecilia Halkett began what would be an impressive series of studies of heroines learning to think and feel outside accepted roles and also learning the self-consciousness to analyze their own minds and hearts.

Yet Cecilia is only a secondary character in this novel, sharing with that other woman, Meredith's brilliantly sad invention, the Frenchwoman, Renee, the function of being the hero's possible choice or a mate. The story is Nevil Beauchamp's, and in his struggles, his failure, and his final death we can begin to see, at least to guess, why Meredith's novels would move from a male to a female lead. Beauchamp dies because a Beauchamp who survives would have to be a woman. The next struggling hero in Meredith's full-length fiction is a heroine, Clara Middleton.

Nevil Beauchamp is an egoist, but he is hardly a hopeless egoist, and anyway, in Meredith's fiction egoism is not necessarily a hanging offense. But being a hero is. Calling *Beauchamp's Career* "a novel about heroism," Gillian Beer comments that "while never finally repudiating the concept of heroism, it demonstrates the near-impossibility of finding a significant function for the hero within English Victorian society."[20] Captain Beauchamp, the hero of naval battles, has a nature that inclines to individual and independent deeds of courage and at the same time a politics that is committed to the larger social group. In spite of Nevil's good sense as well as modesty in stopping Timothy Turbot, the party journalist, from writing puff articles about Nevil's brave conduct in the navy as a way to get him elected, Nevil is, in fact, a traditional hero. His sense of honor, his ardent temper, his physical courage, all place him as a bright young representative of a masculine heroic tradition. His uncle Everard recognizes him as such, and loves him as such. So does the narrator. So would Scott. So do we.

But it is precisely the tradition of masculine heroism that misdirects Nevil throughout the novel and kills him in the end as he dives to save two drowning children. The old values of chivalry, codes of honor, and personal bravery are presented in the novel as anachronistic, as ineffectual modes of dealing with the social and political problems of Victorian England. But the point I wish to stress is that these masculine heroics are the best masculine patterns of self-presentation the novel offers, and are embodied in the best male. The rigid codes of Sir Everard, unenlightened by any idealism, and the noble idealism of Dr. Shrapnel, ungrounded by flesh or fact, merely cancel each other out. Of the younger generation we might choose between Mr. Tuckman, the egoist rising to worldly success, and Captain Baskelett, the egoist corrupt even to his own class. Finally, in the last lines of the novel, we are left with only one male representative, the young urchin whom Beauchamp saved, the "abashed little creature, . . . the insignificant bit of mudbank life," to carry England into her future.

Nevil Beauchamp is an Edward Waverley or Harry Morton, transported to Victorian England. Like them, he grows beyond the old-fashioned martial values. And like them, Nevil tries to unite the codes of martial valor with selflessness and social commitment. But unlike them, he fails. However much we may feel that Nevil learned and grew from that boy who sent a challenge to a duel to the French Guard, however much we may blame his society for its indifference and admire and love him for his efforts, Nevil Beauchamp cannot rescue England after all. He fails not simply because of England's resistance and his own blindness but because he represents a tradition that, aesthetically as well as morally, is now bankrupt. The future of Beauchamp's world, unlike that of Waverley or Morton, demands more from the present than even the crucial ability to accept, forgive, and transform the past. For Meredith present culture is more damaged and more damaging than for Scott. It demands a different sort of radical reform.

The historical distance between romantic novelist and Victorian novelist is clearly measured through the subject of heroes. Both Scott and Meredith repudiate the traditionally masculine values of martial heroism. But Meredith repudiates much more. He also repudiates the classic heroic possibility of salvation by an individual, a single good man. Meredith will go on to write only novels without a hero—and with a heroine—because even a loving, gentle hero is ineffectual now. If such a hero in the Scott tradition does not die from still being heroic, like Nevil Beauchamp, he becomes Thackeray's patient William Dobbin, or all Meredith's dull waiting lovers who pine after and eventually receive his heroines. But that's about all they do. We have passed the point, at least in nineteenth-century British fiction, where a man can turn a country, where history can be represented, can be understood at all, as the shaping efforts of a few particular people. The whole masculine notion of rescue, of individual heroic endeavors for the sake of the country, is exactly what, for our country's sake, we must put by.

Beauchamp's Career develops the good hero possibility to its final, virtually pointless, conclusion. Once the possibility of salvation by a hero is revealed as false, both the ideas of cultural progress and of personal self-development are called into question as well. There are no heroic solutions for Britain, no grand gestures that will cure the country's ills. But the novel does locate some hope on the sidelines, in the only reform the story will define as progress, the growing mental freedom of women.

Of Beauchamp's three love possibilities, the French Countess, and here is Meredith's national chauvinism, is shipped back to France "dead silent" (12:154) and having "learnt something in the school of self-immolation" (12:297). But the other two women are, in fact England's best hope for a better future. Cecilia Halkett develops real independence of mind and radical opinions of her own. Yet we cannot read this as a simple transfer of the heroic gauntlet from Nevil to

Cecilia, male to female. Cecilia's chosen fate is to put her fortune at the service of her conservative husband, Blackburn Tuckham. It's hard to decide if this is Meredith's pessimism reappearing, or simply his difficulty in ending novels. In any case, the development of this "beautiful young woman, deficient only in words" (12:297), seems at least threatened, if not actually stopped, by her marriage.

That leaves Jenny Denham. The spiritual child of Dr. Shrapnel, Jenny has been carefully taught her radical idealism. But she combines it with her own practicality, which guarantees her, and her child, the effectual future denied to Beauchamp and Dr. Shrapnel. Yet Jenny barely appears in the novel, and when she does she's hardly a thrilling character. We are left feeling that the possibilities at the end of *Beauchamp's Career* are either closed off or don't imaginatively satisfy. What Meredith needed was a different narrative perspective from which to focus his concerns.

That new perspective begins with *The Egoist*, in which what starts as Willoughby Patterne's story clearly becomes Clara Middleton's as well. Clara combines Cecilia's vitality with Jenny's future. After *The Egoist* will come novel after novel that looks at that vitality and that future, England's future, through women leads. But if Meredith had found his subject, the female forms through which to dramatize and articulate his concerns, he had not found a happy resolution to the problem of self-fulfillment at his historical moment. Perhaps, indeed, women's lives were the right vehicle for his subject precisely because he did not envision progress either for individuals or for the culture. The stories he went on to write do not offer a cure for his heroines' maladies, or his, or ours. Instead, the novels offer, through an evolving narrative technique, an analysis of the diseases of his culture and their causes. The novels offer a gradually darkening vision of what to hope from the future, a vision that, as readers in that future, can pierce us still. I turn now to these novels, to look both at the conditions of the dilemma and at a specific narrative method through which we can trace Meredith's declining hopes, for women, for writers, for England.

In one of the most familiar and most discussed passages in George Meredith's fiction, Clara Middleton in *The Egoist* sees Vernon Whitford under "the double-blossom wild cherry-tree":

> From deeper to deeper heavens of white, her eyes perched and soared. Wonder lived in her. Happiness in the beauty of the tree pressed to supplant it, and was more mortal and narrower. Reflection came,

> contracting her vision and weighing her to earth. Her reflection was: "He must be good who loves to lie and sleep beneath this tree! (13:135)

The lyric beauty of the passage, the inevitable and contracting movement from vision through wonder and happiness to articulated reflection, the association of natural harmony with goodness, all these are recognized elements of the scene. But for my purposes the most notable element is that we are to take Clara's reflection as true. Vernon really is good.

Clara's discovery of him sleeping under a tree has given her an insight into his character. And that insight has been provided not by anything he has done or said, not, to put it in novelistic terms, by plot or dialogue, but simply by the sight of him, by an image. Moreover, that image appears when, and probably because, Vernon is asleep. In this central moment of self-presentation Vernon is silent, passive, even unconscious. Clara's knowledge that "he must be good" comes both accidently (she happened to come upon him) and without his being able to convey it or even to be aware of it.

The Egoist also offers other successful methods of seeing into characters, which is one reason it has been considered an optimistic novel.[21] It seems to promise that, great as the difficulties are, we can, in the end, and before it's too late, match our relations to each other with our perceptions of each other. And we can do this not simply because the author writes it that way but because life makes some sense after all. Apart from the rare and almost miraculous imagistic moments, characters can reliably get to know one another by the more familiar methods of their own efforts, of self-expression and of judgment about other people's acts and words. Moreover, there is harmony, expressed in that tentative but blissful ending, between the insights provided by the images and those that come from the traditional sources, the sources of what people say and what they do. Clara's reading of the meaning of the scene, her reading of Vernon's character, is correct. Vernon not only loves to sleep beneath the tree, he also pays for and teaches Crossjay, and argues for the boy's right to independence as well as his own.

Yet we need to qualify this harmony by noticing that Clara's knowledge of Willoughby Patterne is provided entirely by the familiar means of what he does and says. Willoughby gives himself away to her, not by being asleep but by continually telling and showing her, actively and with a vengeance, what he is like. That kind of relentless revealing of self slays imagination and, of course, love. There could be no scene of Willoughby asleep amid the white heavens of the cherry blossoms because he is not good. In Meredith's morally optimistic scheme those lyric moments occur only as affirmations. They are inherently images of goodness.

But what happens if there is no harmony, if the insights provided by those images, those sudden moments of intuitive trust, do not agree with, even contradict, the information provided by traditional modes? And what will it mean to try to understand others when the only paths to insight are those beyond our control? Shifting the problem from the watcher to the watched, what will it mean to live in the world when the ways we are aware of to express ourselves cannot be counted on to convey truth, when our goodness is conveyed by chance, perhaps without our being aware of it at all? To ask these questions puts us in the erratic world of Meredith's final novels. It puts us among the grotesque and damaging complacencies of language, and in sight of our own complicity with its destructive power.

If Clara's reflection while peeping under the wild cherry tree is encouraging, its implications are not. Meredith went on to face those implications in his late work, abandoning the aesthetic and thematic harmony that is most successfully represented in *The Egoist*, finding in its stead a vision more coherent at least in the consistency of its truths if not in their content. His late novels challenge the reliability of any intended words and acts, and thereby also challenge the very fictional patterns on which Meredith's own methods of writing had relied. Meredith's use of these imagistic moments, and their changed meaning according to the changing context in which they occur, provide us with a helpful key to explaining what happened to Meredith's fiction, how his ideas developed and why his later novels, as Percy Lubbock observed long ago, "differ very considerably in structure from the former."[22]

Meredith's late writings, particularly his last four novels, are seldom read now, and less often liked. One reason, as Lubbock also said, is that "the Meredith of 1859 was far surer of poised and sustained effect than the Meredith of thirty years later," as Meredith "charged his art with ever more complicated burdens."[23] I want to extend the point made not only by Lubbock but by many of Meredith's contemporaries, that the flaws in the later fiction result from Meredith's advances in thought rather than regressions in talent. Specifically, the change to a less organized presentation of plot and dialogue is the consequence of Meredith's methods of expressing in fiction his ideas of how people perceive each other, and how they define the feminine in themselves and their culture. Central among

Meredith's ideas was the conviction that language, as a cultural construct, oppresses and destroys women. These final writings offer at least an aesthetic escape from this dilemma. They offer the eloquence of silence.

The last four novels, *Diana of the Crossways*, *One of Our Conquerors*, *Lord Ormont and His Aminta*, and *The Amazing Marriage*, all depict relations between major characters that are so bizarre as to be surreal. Lord Ormont, a military hero, is married for many years to a wife he will not publicly acknowledge because he is offended by his country's treatment of him. For even longer Victor Radnor of *One of Our Conquerors* lives with and is not married to the woman he publicly proclaims as his wife. His legal wife, very much a presence, is reduced by hatred and hypochondria to spending afternoons in a chemist's shop, trying out other people's prescriptions. And *The Amazing Marriage*, aptly titled, may be the strangest of them all. Barbara Hardy has called it "a book where really creative and strongly affined people tear each other to bits, commit rape, are cold, are deeply revengeful, just give up."[24] What Hardy here names the element of the fabulous again carries Meredith's sense of the disjunctions between characters' felt connections and their words and acts. Such disjunctions, though appearing in most of Meredith's fiction, are at the center of these late works and in them are too fundamental, too pervasive, to be convincingly overcome.

The Amazing Marriage is Meredith's last novel. His vision, never that hopeful, had darkened considerably even in the ten years since the publication of *Diana* in 1885. His continuing themes of the isolated self and the difficulties of sustained connections between people had become more explicit, while his recurrent machinery for a happy ending—the loyal waiting hero, the self-sacrificing female friend, the haven far from the British public eye—were still used but reduced to minor elements and more obviously sentimentalized. In *Lord Ormont and His Aminta*, Matey, who knows everything about how to teach boys to be good and true, runs off with Aminta to start a school in Switzerland. Nataly and Victor Radnor's illegitimate daughter in *One of Our Conquerors* has her devoted Captain Fenellan to legitimize her at last. Captain Fenellan is a hero about whom, Meredith assures us, the young heroine comes to feel that "the nobleness in him . . . was personally worshipped" (456). We feel how much more strained and artificial this is then even Diana Warwick's boringly loving respect for

Redworth. In *The Amazing Marriage* Carinthia meets her lover when Rebecca Wythan, unlike Diana's also sickly but enduring friend, Emma Dunstane, is already on her deathbed. Both friends direct the heroine to the true hero. But Rebecca's wisdom is the more absurd, and thus may offer the more honest self-critique, since the hero she provides is her own husband and, in an apotheosis of womanly self-sacrifice, she provides him by dying herself.

In an essay that does not consider gender but that is, nonetheless, important for offering a unified approach to Meredith's later fiction, Joseph Kruppa calls *Diana of the Crossways* the bridge to the final novels. In it "Meredith focuses his basic problem, the relationship of consciousness to consciousness and a corresponding consideration of self and the world." [25] The problem of presenting self is one of communication and therefore an aesthetic as well as a perceptual question. It is the basis of much of Meredith's constant worry about whether "Art is the specific" (*E*, 3) for our modern malady of isolation, whether it can save us from cruelty and despair.

Moreover, the problem of self-presentation is also the basis of Meredith's essential subject, the one that directs all his portraits of human relations: trust and its loyal companion, betrayal. The novels examine almost obsessively the extent to which we can trust other people or be betrayed, and betrayed most often by their need for self-assertion (as we will betray them by ours). This concern is inseparable from an increasing suspicion of any intended form of communication, and reflects Meredith's central conviction of the ever-present and ever-distorting power of ego on our words and acts. The result in Meredith's last ten years of writing is chaotic and despairing novels with tidy, cheerful endings, a fragmented and imagistic art.

At the end of *The Amazing Marriage* we are told that Carinthia married her faithful Owain "because of his wooing her with dog's eyes instead of words" (510). This is a familiar motif in Meredith's fiction, and even within the earlier optimism of *The Egoist* language had been primarily an elaborate disguise for the truth. Yet we can measure the distance from the qualified hope of *The Egoist* to the deep and increasing pessimism of the last four novels by saying that *The Egoist* still trusts somewhat to plot and dialogue, the truth of actions and the truth of words. But once the harmony between traditional modes of knowing others and imagistic modes is broken, not only the traditional modes but also the images become suspect as devices for telling pretty lies, on the level of the writer if not of the characters. Clara sees

Vernon that morning through the grace of a benevolent author. But for Meredith that benevolence became too difficult, and ultimately too fictional, to sustain.

Many readers are surprised that the late novels, starting with *Diana*, should have been so well received by Meredith's own public whereas *The Egoist*, a much greater novel than the rest, was not.[26] But with all their flaws, the final works explore directly the kind of pessimistic vision that in *The Egoist* had been successfully kept blinded by the bright, white heaven of cherry blossoms and Alpine snows. In spite of our present indifference to the novels of Meredith's last ten years, understanding what happened to them and in them can help us in evaluating the general development of Meredith's work. It can also help in guiding our interpretations of the novels, such as *The Egoist*, that some readers may care more about, as well as guiding our more general understanding of Meredith's special contribution to what I might call the imaginative debate about gender in nineteenth-century British fiction. The patterns of the late novels emerge as variations on the first of them, the novel that established Meredith's reputation, *Diana of the Crossways*.

Like the other late novels, *Diana of the Crossways* is Meredith's vision of the difficulty of interpretation, of leading a life in which conscious actions are a significant representation of self. All gestures are public. And all gestures are distortions. This dilemma, so familiar in the later fiction, is made especially compelling in *Diana* by Meredith's inspired choice of a scandalous public figure for his main character. It may be true, as Stone surmises, that Meredith based his story on the life of an actual person because he believed in facts.[27] But the choice was brilliant because Caroline Norton was someone whose reality, through the Victorian choral powers of gossip and scandal, had already reached the stature of a myth. She was, as they say, notorious. And notoriety was exactly what Meredith's novel needed from her. Caroline Norton's reputation depended upon her being the granddaughter of Richard Brinsley Sheridan and a writer herself, the consort of Lord Melbourne and Sidney Herbert, an accused adulteress in a famous divorce suit, and, perhaps most centrally, rumored to have betrayed her would-be lover's political secret to the public press. Thus a woman's sexual fate and passion is entwined with literary heritage, with science, with politics, with the very future of the nation.

What Meredith's novel takes from Caroline Norton is not the real person but a created public figure. To paraphrase Mayor Daley's words, this figure is one of our friends of the female persuasion. Her gender, her very identity, her meaning for her society and his novel, is a cultural artifact. Only a woman could be notorious in such a way. And Meredith's presentation of this figure explicitly defines her in terms of her need for self-expression. She is a woman in search of an identity, a self that she can create herself, living in a public context that both denies her the right to an identity and simultaneously creates one for her. Such women are dangerous. We are all fated to make false gestures, Diana Merion more dramatically than most. Her attempts at self-expression end in betrayal, in fragmentation, in collapse.

The opening chapter of the novel successfully invokes the public historical nature of Diana Merion's story through the references to her provided by those historians of good society, the diarists of her time. She is someone people talked about. Her identity depends upon the watchers, the circling crowd. Meredith first brings his heroine into our presence at a "public ball," and the hall is surrounded on the outside by cheering patriots. Inside the hall, "[t]wo staring semi-circles had formed, one to front the Hero, the other the Beauty. These half moons imperceptibly dissolved to replenish, and became a fixed obstruction. 'Yes, they look,' Diana made answer. . . . She was getting used to it" (33). By the end of the evening Diana, along with Mr. Redworth, Sir Lukin, and Emma Dunstane, is part of Lord Larrian's train, as all become the object of a massive, multiplying Irish cheer. This image of Diana as a center of a gazing and obstructing crowd is an accurate depiction of her relations with society, and it recurs throughout the novel. She is, as Lady Pennon tells her, "too famous not to have your troops of watchers" (348), just as she has that small band of adorers. The difficulty and the vitality of such a state is caught in Diana's defiant remark, "Gossip is a beast of prey that does not wait for the death of the creature it devours. They are welcome to my shadow, if the liberty I claim casts one, and it feeds them" (348).

The liberty Diana claims does cast a shadow. Meredith not only uses the details of Caroline Norton's life but carefully interweaves her notorious personal history with the public history of her times. At the service of his heroine, Meredith collects some of the major issues and events of the age. Mr. Redworth, Diana's finally successful lover, is the entrepreneur of railroads, an early participant in the new industrialism, whereas Mr. Warwick, the undeserving husband whom Diana refuses to live with, fails in his railway ventures. Redworth also stands against the duelling instincts of Mr. Sullivan-Smith and Sir Lukin Dunstane, those two gallants of a bygone age. Percy Dacier,

Diana's would-be lover, as the young statesman involved in the deliberations preceding repeal of the Corn Laws, must come to terms with the shift in government responsibility to a more democratic electorate with the extension of the franchise. The issue of Irish home rule permeates the story, as the three-quarters-Irish heroine fights for her own independence. Diana's career as a novelist invokes the debates between a new realism and old romance. And, of course, Diana herself is a bluestocking, an emotional rebel, a wife who lives apart from the protection of her husband and supports herself.

In a story involving political, aesthetic, economic, and social struggles for change, Diana Merion is the paradigm of that change. This does not mean that Meredith is writing an historical novel, however much he was concerned with a partisan expression of the issues of his time. Instead, he brings to imaginative life "the flecked heroine of Reality" (399). Reality, of course, here means the givens of her historical time and place. Diana is a created character, both in Meredith's novel and in her life. She is a woman whose gender, the boundaries of her meaning, has been established by her culture. The facts of England's history as well as Caroline Norton's are part of her public character. And Diana's crime is that she wants to rearrange the boundaries that define gender, wants to recreate herself.

Diana Merion's presentation through the inevitably transforming mediators of gossip and history means that she is doomed to being misunderstood. Jan Gordon has commented about Diana that "the central dialectic of the novel" is "the private or insulated 'self' and a 'self' as exteriorized, communal history."[28] But the dialectic is never resolved. As experienced readers of novels of education, we look for a glimpse behind the famous reputation of Diana Merion, for the "real" events, so that by the end of the opening chapter we hope for an informed private history of the feelings and dreams that animated the public facts and created the myth. Indeed, we require that this story provide a version of inner movements and motives large enough to account for the events and the reputation that became their expression. But our expectations are thwarted. Our sense of the life of an individual (or a country) as linear and progressive, whether in history or in fiction, is denied.

Meredith will allow a private view of Diana, but only to show its frustrations as well. In the second chapter of the novel Meredith introduces a legitimate and convincing source of private knowledge about Diana through her most intimate friend, Emma Dunstane. Yet in spite of all the advantages of lifelong intimacy and influence, Emma

Dunstane is repeatedly unable to see into her friend. Gillian Beer has noticed that "*Diana of the Crossways* shows how spectators misunderstand the real nature of relationships; but Meredith does not suggest that they are fully understood by those involved and he shows that any relationship is always in a state of flux. Within the sustained friendship of the two women there are unspoken periods of estrangement."[29] The letters between them, aiming at tones of frankness and sincerity, are often masks. And a major fact of the plot is the secret of Sir Lukin Dunstane's attept to seduce his wife's friend, a secret that Emma can never know.

Yet Emma's moments of distance do not constitute an imaginative or intuitive failure. In the terms of the novel she understands as much as any person can about another. And that, finally, is the point. For Meredith, connections between people, lines of understanding, are piecemeal and discontinuous even at best. The view from the crowd is an obstruction. Yet it is also true that private knowledge can obstruct as well. We are taught the life-giving possibilities of loyalty and affection, but we are also shown the effort, the obstacles, and the failures of vision involved. Diana, who wears a mask for society, also veils herself to her friend. It is not through the private sources of friendship, any more than the recorders of scandal and public history, that we will get to know Diana.

Meredith creates a portrait of a character struggling to find external expression for her qualities, to realize her inner life outside her own dreams, while existing in a milieu that can manipulate, transform, and murder those dreams. In her own defense or to protect those she loves, Diana's gestures too often turn out to be nothing more than disguise. She presses Redworth for an analysis of the League and sends it to Percy as her own. She entertains Percy in conversation sparkling with an apparent spontaneity, which is in fact the product of deliberation and self-control. The novel is full of moments, most obviously when Diana braves the vultures of society, but also, I want to stress, with Emma, Percy, and Redworth, when her presentation of herself is false.

Diana's inability to express her nature through her actions is complicated in the traditional way of novels of education by various kinds of self-deceptions. But it is complicated in a more central way by Meredith's sense of the dubious and distorted truth of any representation of ourselves. The dilemma, of course, is that such a representation is the only self-realization possible. Expression needs a witness. But Meredith calls any public understanding into question by his hostile descriptions of society, by Diana's frequent falseness to her friends and to herself, and, most importantly, by his belief that even her sincere attempts to present herself are somehow misconstrued. Women particularly cannot control their meaning for others or freely express themselves. Society, which means other women as well as men, will rearrange the meaning anyway. Such inappropriate responses as Mrs. Crambone Wathin's anger about Diana's joke or Mr. Sullivan Smith's warlike gallantry about her Irish beauty are both versions of how cultural definitions bind women. The forms through which the culture answers Diana's gestures toward an individual public meaning feel, to borrow Meredith's phrase for Percy Dacier's analogic imagination, like being "seized by the grotesque" (221).

Meredith ends *The Amazing Marriage* with the claim that in life "[c]haracter must ever be a mystery, only to be explained in some degree by conduct; and that is very dependent upon accident" (511). This important idea of character, forming almost the final words to Meredith's final novel, turns us back again to Clara Middeton's accidental encounter with Vernon Whitford under the cherry tree almost twenty years before. The image that in *The Egoist* had provided but one of the means by which a character can judge that another is good has, from Diana on, become virtually the sole means. Moreover, Meredith's use of such images has changed. In the late novels they no longer provide a lyric reassurance of natural and moral harmony but rather an isolated testimonial to goodness in a context that judges that testimony as suspect and probably false. Accepting the information of those images becomes a matter of trust. To borrow Stone's apt phrase, "life, in the elderly novelist's view, is inexpressible as well as incomprehensible." [30] One result is that the moments that explain the mystery of character are virtually revelations. And, as such, they are rare, unpredictable, and a matter of faith.

Beer has remarked about Diana that the "movement of the work is seismographic, tracking deep emotional stirrings and eruptions which on the surface may seem disconnected." [31] This description can be applied generally to Meredith's late narrative method, a method somewhat changed from such earlier, more unified plots as *The Ordeal of Richard Feverel*, *The Egoist*, and even *Beauchamp's Career*. It is also a fitting description of the process of love for Percy Dacier and Redworth. Percy is cold, with a limited possibility of emotion. Yet both men come to care about Diana not through the slow and intimate process of getting to know her but through certain intense moments that live as images in their memories. For Redworth, the passionate man, it is virtually love at first sight. He meets Diana at the Irish ball and, "in the maelstrom of a happiness resembling tempest" (34), is immediately lost in the dream of how to transform his life so as to provide for her. He acts on that dream by staking his safe fortune on new investments in railroads.

What Meredith is depicting here is not a convention of romance but his belief that there is a level of reality in which connections between people consist of these sudden moments that catch their imaginations. The significance of the images, no more than hinted at in *The Egoist*, becomes clear. Only in these moments can we know each other. Such, for Redworth, was his first sight of Diana at the Irish ball. Another was Diana laying and lighting a fire when he had ridden to the Crossways to prevent her first attempt at flight. In the first glow "[h]e could have imagined a Madonna on an old black Spanish canvas" (104). In Diana's mysteriousness and grace in that simple act Redworth finds a conviction of her innocent heart, and he carries the picture and the trust through her relations with Dacier. Against the gossip Redworth holds onto and believes the illumination of his images: "The girl at the Dublin Ball, the woman at the fire grate of The Crossways, both in one were his Diana" (335).

Percy Dacier too has his images, and if he has not the depth of heart for a love at first sight or the imagination for a perfect trust, he is at last moved to homage by Diana's having "Character." What Percy means by this turns out to consist of a pastiche of these images: "Since the day when he beheld her by the bedside of his dead uncle, and that one on the French sea-sands, and again at Copsley, ghostly white out of her wrestle with death, bleeding holy sweat of brow for her friend, the print of her features had been on him as an index of depth of character" (332). Percy too has found in momentary visions, in "the print of her features," the certitude of reality. And Percy's failing is not in trusting these images but in his inability to sustain a belief in their reality and truth against the damning social judgments, the public definitions, of her character.

The particular visions of Diana that haunt her lovers are vivid for the reader as well. When we think back on the plot of Diana it is a series of special moments that we recall. These are illuminations of great intensity, presented in the novel almost as pictorial stills. To the images her lovers hold we might add that summer day when Diana visits Copsley with Lord Dannisburgh, the lyric dawn at Rovio, the somnambulant drive to the newspaper office, and Diana as a figure of cold, dying in London of a guilty heart. These moments, along with the tentative insights other characters can offer, are the only means Meredith gives of knowing his heroine. Like her lovers and friends, we are forced to trust these moments as true revelations of character against what Meredith presents as the questionable indices of behavior, dialogue, public definitions, and coherent patterns of events.

Recognizing how Meredith uses these images helps to explain a scene that has troubled many readers, the climactic midnight encounter between Diana and Percy when he arrives after a dinner party to reveal his successful political news and demand a "trifle of recompense" (364). He wants an embrace as a payment of a debt owed simply as a tribute to himself. When Diana refuses, "for very wrath of blood—not jealousy: he had none of any man, with her; and not passion; the little he had was a fitful gust—he punished her coldness by taking what hastily could be gathered" (365–66).

Percy lets go of his images of Diana, those sources of truth and feeling, and chooses to live by public definitions of personality. Diana demands, "Have you forgotten who I am?" (364). Percy has forgotten. Later he will briefly remember some of the images: "the hour at Rovio was rather pretty, and the scene at Copsley touching: other times also, short glimpses of the woman, were taking" (400). But he calls up those memories only finally to efface them. It is the essential betrayal, the ego's self-assertion at the expense of understanding, at the expense of another's self. To Percy that night Diana has become what society would make of her, his mistress. He tells her that "you know we are one. The world has given you to me, me to you. Why should we be asunder? There's no reason in it" (366). But they are only "one," of course, if only one of them exists. Against such a murderous definition of reason Diana replies with simple accuracy: "But still I wish to burn a little incense in honour of myself, or else I cannot live" (367).

Diana tells Percy that her error was to trust him. And she is right. Trust, in Meredith's scheme, means the willingness to believe that the self of another will not find nourishment by feeding on you. Trust is the basis of communication and affection, the difficult way out of egoism. Trust replaces those traditional modes of evaluation, discernment and judgment. It is nourished by those accidental images, necessarily accidental, we now see, because the gestures we can choose to make are necessarily colored by our insatiable ego. And ego, as Blake so intensely taught us, is a social animal. Though Percy can still claim that "Trust me you may," (366) we know, as does Diana, that he has betrayed her. And she too will assert her ego, will fight to feel she lives, by betraying him. Her revenge is utterly appropriate. She tries to destroy his reputation, that public self he has preferred to truth and has chosen to accept the definitions of. She offers up his political secret, the secret that, for Percy, set self so egoistically above the crowd, to the morning papers for all the world to share. Their connection ends with Percy's recognition that "I can never trust you again" (390).

When Percy, in demanding that Diana admit that they are "one," offers as his reason, "Just to let me feel I live!" (364), we recognize that life has become a devourer, that we are back to the masculine will to power in Willoughby Patterne's primitive letter "I." We need to distinguish between that "I," competitive and aggressive, with its self-definition depending on subsuming others, and the "I" Diana wishes to burn a little incense in honor of. For there are really two definitions of self operating in the novel. We can call them, with Blake, the false selfhood of Satanic ego or the divine self. And we can also see, through the eyes of recent feminist theorists, that the distinction is between what culture has traditionally valued as masculine and what I am calling the feminine heroic. Is identity a matter of nature, a fixed essence, somehow sturdy and firm, resistent to time? Or does self create and recreate self, "rewrite" self, as what Teresa de Lauretis describes as "a multiple, shifting, and self-contradictory identity, a subject that is not divided in, but rather at odds with, language"?[32] Meredith's novels portray the struggle between these conflicting notions of identity, not only in understanding ourselves but in understanding others. And the outcome is not encouraging.

In the three novels that follow *Diana* we see Percy's masculine "I" again, and his failed trust, in Victor Radnor's love for Nataly, Lord Ormont's for his Aminta, and Lord Fleetwood's for Carinthia Jane. These late works offer the same pattern as *Diana*, the juxtaposition of random images that are our only source of truth with those traditional modes of knowing that distort and destroy. *Lord Ormont and His Aminta*, the simplest of the final novels, introduces its imagistic moment at the very beginning, when Matey Weyburn (as well as all his school chums) is entranced when a girl from the neighboring school looks at him: "The look was like the fall of light on the hills from the first of morning" (18:4). Matey's trust in the goodness of that look, like Redworth's in his image of Diana, lasts the rest of his life. Lord Ormont loses faith in his images and thus, though he has been the one to marry Aminta, loses his wife.

One of Our Conquerors, though marred by an unusually gnarled style, even for Meredith, is an especially compelling study of the failure to believe in our better knowledge of each other and of the ways that those familiar, culturally provided, forms of knowledge, words, and actions, erode our better feelings and shatter our images of each other. Nataly has spent her life with Victor and has sacrificed conscience and reputation to that end. We watch her as she comes to understand him, to see how he has changed from the young lover who so entranced her, to see the difference between his self-presentation and his feelings, between what he is and what he says and does. And as she understands, as she recognizes his egoism twenty years too late, she sacrifices self-esteem as well. Both Victor and Nataly let go of their images of each other. And the horror here is precisely that they are right, that the images are no longer true, that both characters have been changed from what they were by the devouring power of self.

The Amazing Marriage may be the most starkly dramatic of Meredith's late novels in its portrayal of the essential opposition between our trust in images or in other forms of judgment to guide our understanding of the identity of others and of ourselves. Lord Fleetwood accidentally sees Carinthia one morning in the forest outside Baden, soon dances with her and proposes. He goes through with the marriage but for almost all the rest of the novel repudiates his bride as a reckless and uncharacteristic mistake. Carinthia, on the other hand, trusting deeply in their harmony in that initial dance, begins by loving him and slowly, over the long years of rejection, learns from his behavior to withdraw that love. He, not trusting to his first vision of her or to the dance, begins the marriage by not loving her and just as slowly, in spite of his behavior, learns that he does. At last, and too late, Lord Fleetwood comes to believe "that the woman to aid and make him man and be the star in human form to him, was miraculously revealed on the day of his walk through the foreign pine forest, and his proposal to her at the ducal ball was an inspiration of his Good Genius" (19:508). Percy Dacier and Lord Fleetwood are alike in their shared denial of what has been "miraculously revealed" to them. The distance between them, a matter of circumstance rather than character, lies in the degree to which that denial damages their lives. Dacier marries a cold woman. But for Fleetwood, fate holds a hair shirt, a false religion, and an early death. The price of denial has surely increased.

In *The Egoist* Clara Middleton, unable to find the words to tell her father why she should be released from her engagement to Willoughby, finally escapes through the help of society. In this earlier novel the harmony between those chance images and the traditional sources of getting to know other people is not the only harmony. There is also, however tentatively and temporarily, the harmony between Clara's vision and that of the society that surrounds her. At the end of the novel Willoughby has gone too far. He has violated the rules, has proposed to Laetitia and been overheard. Clara is saved. And saved ultimately not simply by her own efforts but by everyone's, as one by one the visitors at Patterne Hall join with her that morning in the garden till together they rout the egoist and extricate the lady.

But the heroines of the late novels are not so supported. The disjunction between the sudden images of Diana Warwick and public interpretations is paralleled by the irreconcilable differences between her views and those of the representatives of good society. All four late heroines are hunted by Dame Gossip, a fate Clara merely fears. Moreover, the late heroines, all married, are not like Clara, an ingenue gifted with the innocent power of harmonizing, of "dressing to suit the season and the sky" (18:201). Meredith's distrust has extended even to the cherry tree, to the natural as well as the social world. Thus the struggle between men and women can no longer be resolved, as it was with Clara and Willoughby, by a journey in which the heroine's delicacy and, more importantly, her innocence remain intact. Diana's journey to the newspaper office is a journey into the crude realism of a London night that even her maid is "femininely injured by the notice of" (373). Clara, we recall, never gets closer to the sullying freedom of London than the waiting room of a country train station.

Many readers have found Diana's night journey too sullying and have found inappropriate the cruelty of her revenge. Meredith himself must have been aware of the problem, for he has Diana reveal her lover's secret while virtually in a trance. Walter Wright has pointed out that this device allows Meredith to avoid showing Diana's feelings, and thus "the execution of the scene is wanting."[33] Stone comments that Meredith "may be able to persuade the reader that Diana's most vividly irrational act . . . is not beyond the realm of possibility, but he cannot expect the reader to applaud the act for its rational heroism."[34]

But the terrible point, I think, is that "the flecked heroine of Reality" (16:399) does not move in a landscape of rationality or of heroism. Indeed, both are merely weapons in a more fundamental social pattern, Percy's fight for "proofs of his commandership" (375) over Diana. In that fight stealing a kiss is as serious as revealing a state secret, because Meredith has given both the power to destroy. It is the masculine world, the world of men in politics and women who cannot vote, that judges the latter as more important. Meredith exposes the self-centeredness of that judgment. But he also exposes, with an explicitness absent from *The Egoist*, the cost to the heroine of opposing it. Diana responds to her sensation of "feminine danger" (437), her sense of a public definition virtually killing her own power to define herself, by striking back. But there are no simple moral victories. We see, at least for that time in London, how Diana's energy for independence in this hostile masculine culture drains her. And we also see how it brings out the ultimately self-destructive values she has internalized from that masculine culture: her need for self-assertion even at another's expense, her cruelty, and her egoism.

Meredith turns away from this stark portrait of a heroine as "a singular mixture of good and bad; anything but the feminine ideal of man," (16:400), to end with that familiar masculine portrait of the feminine ideal. Even the flecked heroine has proven to be too thoroughly trapped by her public reality, and the price of self-expression, for her and for her creator, too sadly high. Meredith chooses that Diana will live, will become strong again by a retreat to the redemptive sunsets of rural Copsley, and marry Redworth. They are united by a kiss powerful enough to dissolve ego, a kiss that like "a big storm-wave caught her from shore and whirled her to mid-sea, out of every sensibility but the swimming one of her loss of self in the man" (483). We are reminded of the last pages of *The Portrait of a Lady*, and that other kiss "like white lightning, a flash that spread, and spread again, and stayed." Henry James ends his novel by setting aside the kiss, along with the convenient, and false, romantic conclusiveness it implies. Meredith uses his to clothe the truths his novel has bared.

Meredith's happy endings become more obviously sentimental and more bizarre as Meredith, like Percy Dacier, finds the images that would justify those endings too difficult to believe. A schoolboy's love at first sight for the vision of Browny's smile is given the blessing of another chance as Aminta and Matey Weyburn run off to a second childhood in their school in Switzerland. Carinthia runs off from her amazing marriage to the preposterous and noble world of battles in Spain and, at the last, to a union so distant as to be barely recorded with her loyal lover. Among these fantasy endings perhaps the least wrenching is that of *One of Our Conquerors*, in which "the snow-heights" (17:511) of happiness come to the second generation rather than the first.

As the late novels present with increasing intensity the disjunction between the public truths and those contained in momentary images, the happy endings, the unions that presumably emerge from the images, look more and more like sideshow tricks, like, to borrow a phrase from Sylvia Plath, the miraculous comeback in broad daylight. Our response is suspicion and doubt. For these unions, depending as they do on the presumed innocence of those so united, instead reveal to us how damaged as well as how isolated from each other the members of the happy couple can be.

The light of the extravagant and arbitrary conclusions to these late works in turn shines back to *The Egoist*, showing us the falseness built in to the more integrated optimism of its ending as well. For if Clara's innocence is credible as she peeps into the cherry tree bower, is it still so after she has urged Laetitia to see Willoughby's sincere generosity? And how little should we fault Clara for her willingness to sacrifice her friend? The snowy land of happy endings cannot be found in any world we recognize or can inhabit. And who trusts Vernon anyway, Willoughby's cousin and his vengeful choice for Clara? But even if we still want to believe that blissful image of Clara and Vernon sitting by Lake Constance between the Swiss and Tyrol Alps, an image that invokes sentimental novels and wild cherry trees, it is too late to find the ending of Diana, or any of the other three final novels, anything but a "facile thematic conclusion."[35] All we need acknowledge about this ending—from the author who claimed he couldn't decide whether to marry off Diana or kill her instead—is that ours is a judgment that Meredith created and probably shared.

For Diana, of course, is right: "The moment we begin to speak, the guilty creature is running for cover. . . . I am sensible of evasion when I open my lips" (428). Like Meredith, and the rest of us, she is doomed by her own participation in the politics of language. Percy's attack on Diana exemplifies the attack of a masculine culture on its women. Though it includes a physical dimension, the kiss as a form of rape, that dimension functions only as a typical expression of a more significant truth. The essence of Percy's attack is the attempt to destroy Diana through language, through the sheer verbal act of naming her, and thus publicly and privately controlling her definition of her self. Diana's vengeful response is also a matter of language, simply to speak, to tell a secret, to make public what was private, to say what had been unsaid. And at least one measure of the power of language as event is that the telling causes a political scandal and almost literally kills her.

Or perhaps what Diana almost dies of is the recognition that she does play the same game as Percy, that they are somewhat alike. Meredith really cannot absolve her of the evil, the egoism, of her revenge on Percy, not by nature walks or country sunsets or Redworth's faith in the purity of her soul. Diana, no more than any of the rest of us, cannot regress to the innocence of some presocial self. The implications of Clara Middleton's struggle are explicit at last. Clara has been educated by her struggle with Willoughby. And she has been tarnished, she has fed the self at another's expense, for she has been part of the press to make Laetitia marry Willoughby. The cultural definitions of gender are in us all.

But Diana—and, I think, Nataly Radnor and Carinthia Fleetwood—who are also corrupted by their culture and therefore by themselves, see their corruption with an insight that was spared to Clara. Meredith has dramatized their problems of self-expression more honestly than he had presented Clara's simply by refusing to allow them to be rescued by society and thus refusing them, and us, and himself, the fiction that language can be a rescuer rather than a destroyer. There is no Crossjay, no lucky overhearing, no gathering together of concerned and effectual friends. Indeed, it is the telling of a secret, the very narrative device that blesses Clara, that will damn Diana.

The late heroines are all betrayed, through the needs of others for self-assertion and ultimately through their own needs as well. In a culture dominated by the masculine values of aggression and competition, neither tyrant nor victim can win, as the victim internalizes tyranny. Because each of these characters (though finding both admirers and supporters) must finally struggle alone, the drama of their attempts at self-expression becomes a fight for independence in which victory requires some kind of damage to self. To remain pure is also to fail, to fall victim to Willoughby's "devouring exclamation" of "Mine! She is mine!" (14:214). And in the struggle even the speechless images of truth must lose some of their goodness as they too are used as fictions to clothe that bared ego and thus happily conclude the tale.

Meredith's late fiction has moved from a precarious but still positive belief in the harmony between traditional and imagistic ways of knowing and of being, a harmony that connects us to both civilization and nature, to a belief only in the imagistic mode. Then comes a mistrust of even that as the images are used to support socially and aesthetically conventional endings in which no one can believe. The aesthetic result of this loss of harmony is a loss of coherence, novels in which plot and dialogue, those classic modes of presenting character in action, can hardly be trusted at all. Meredith's important narrative discovery was the use of images not only to supplement traditional tools of judgment but more and more to conflict with and, indeed, replace them. But in the late novels the discovery extends to a sense that this image-making is itself not natural but artificial, not an escape from culture but another form of its trap.

The implications, of course, are extremely pessimistic about the future of women and the future of the culture. In Meredith's late novels the present in England is shown as a time and place where truth occurs randomly and in silence, where women can trust men and men can trust women only through imagistic moments of raw faith, and where even those moments turn out to have a significance created by convention to sustain the inequities and repressions of traditional romance. We must conclude that the accumulation of past and present can only create a future without any connections or communications we can rely on. Writing will also be a lie. Even the images of silence cannot sustain the truth and beauty Meredith no longer believed in. And finally, the novels can define only the problem, not the solution. They cannot depict successful ways for England to break free from its culturally inherited oppression of women, or for English writers to break free from their culturally inherited constrictions of language in defining the self. The two are intertwined. If *Emma* joyfully heralded the identification of artist and woman, Meredith's fiction traces the destructive social and literary consequences of that identification for a culture committed to trap, train, and silence its women and its artists as well.

The need to evolve a new stylistic approach to contain changing insights has always been characteristic of the history of the novel. But it is fair to say that late Victorian novelists were writing at an historical moment when that need was felt with special intensity. That intensity was nourished by the public political debate about and the literary interest, by men as well as women, in the questions of woman's nature and rights. Many of the younger male writers—Wilde, Stevenson, Gissing, Arthur Symons—turned to Meredith's obscure experiments in celebrating feminine heroic values, in revealing the sources of women's oppression, and in attempting to envision at least a fictive life for his heroines. They saw Meredith "as the opponent of mid-Victorian attitudes and the apostle of modernism."[36] Perhaps the very fact that the novels did not successfully image the flecked heroines of reality, or relations between men and women, or public forms of self-expression and self-fulfillment, perhaps the very breakdown of Meredith's narrative attempts to do so, highlight both the pervasiveness of the problem and its centrality.

Meredith's novels, for all their insights, finally could offer little to the novelists who followed in the way of directly useful literary innovations, and little in the way of hope.[37] But Meredith was not the only major Victorian novelist concerned, at least imaginatively, with the significance of the condition of women for the condition of England. There was, of course, Thomas Hardy. Certainly, his influence has been great. But so, too, is his cultural pessimism. After the frightening depictions of the culture's vision of women and feminine values in *Tess of the D'Urbervilles* and *Jude the Obscure*, and after the public's apparent indifference to, and even annoyance about, those warnings, Hardy abandoned fiction. The apostle of modernism and, not accidentally, also the creator of more optimistic portraits of the future of the feminine, if not the future of the culture, turned out to be Henry James.

7

The Feminine Heroic Tradition and Henry James

> I have to cast my lot with those
> Who age after age, perversely
> with no extraordinary power,
> reconstitute the world.
>
> ADRIENNE RICH

Henry James was to write again and again about women, to center his books almost continuously in the consciousnesses of little girls, of adolescent girls, of young ladies. He belongs with Austen and Eliot as a consistent creator of some of the most complex, appealing and famous heroines in British fiction.[1] First came *Watch and Ward*, offering a self-conscious confrontation with literary history through its use of the Pygmalion myth in the story of a man trying to shape his young female ward. Following this initial effort, James's first two major novels, novels that established the "Americano-European legend," were focused on a man.[2] It was only after *Roderick Hudson* and *The American*, in a short, brilliant, and impressively successful tale, that James invented the character who would provide the sketch for his great novels: the American girl. *Daisy Miller* was followed by three short novels, and then, when he was thirty-seven, came the book and the character that would establish James as one of the masters of English and American fiction.

The Portrait of a Lady has a unique place in a discussion of nineteenth-century heroines as the climactic work of a particular literary tradition. With his familiar self-awareness, James, in his "Preface" to the New York edition, refers to such a tradition and puts his heroine in the company of Shakespeare's and Eliot's frail vessels.[3] But we see the selectivity of that self-awareness when James locates his development of and original contribution to this tradition in the formal innovation of placing "the centre of the subject in the young woman's own consciousness," of pressing "least hard, in short, on the consciousness of your heroine's satellites, especially the male," and thus depending "upon her and her little concerns wholly to see you through."[4] As Arnold Kettle reminded us thirty years ago, and as most Jamesian readers seem to have forgotten yet again since then, James's claimed innovation in form is precisely the narrative technique of *Emma*.[5] The predecessor James does not mention in the "Preface," a formal innovator in his own genre as well as a rather more direct ancestor than Shakespeare in this business of making heroines, a writer whose novels seventy years earlier brought to greatness the very tradition James claims as his original innovation, that of depending on "the heroine and her little concerns wholly to see you through," is, of course, Austen.

I do not excuse James for preferring the artistic company of the greatest English writer to the lady novelist he so diminishingly described as a "brown thrush" singing on a garden bough who keeps her readers in an "arrested spring."[6] Nor do I excuse the thirty years of Jamesian commentators since Kettle's essay who have also refused to pay the tribute of critical analysis to James's enormous and quite obvious borrowings from Austen, preferring to credit in detail the presumably mightier pens of Hawthorne and Hardy, Balzac and Flaubert.[7] James's undeniable debt to Austen has always been given lip service to, first by himself. His own acknowledgment also includes the cunning attempt at denial implicit in this artist of consciousness choosing to base his tribute to her on her unconscious artistry, as if Austen's own commitment to consciousness in her novels did not extend to her use of the novel form.[8] When we turn to look at *The Portrait* as the development of a tradition, we must not be guided by the claims and the silences of either James or his male commentators. We must look somewhere else than in the assertions of its "Preface" for defining the special achievement of *The Portrait* in the use of the heroine.[9]

The initial singularity of *The Portrait* is how vividly it stands out among James's early writings. It is an early James novel, and the common critical opinion is that the best novels are the three from James's last phase, all written more than twenty years after *The Portrait* and all considered notably more advanced, stylistically, structurally, and emotionally. In spite of all this, *The Portrait* has always been granted an inherent power and significance beyond its allotted place in the canon. It does not stay put as an early, repressed, female version of *The Ambassadors* or a sort of Ur *The Wings of the Dove* or *The Golden Bowl*. And what makes *The Portrait* so irrepressibly larger than its execution in comparison with the later big three is precisely the success of its portrait of that "mere slim shade of an intelligent but presumptuous girl" (8). Isabel Archer is not only the first of James's major heroines. She is also one of the most memorable creations in our fiction, a heroine who has imparted a special fineness to the novel in which she appears. As Richard Chase put it, the girl from Albany remains "among the most complex, the most fully realized, and the most humanly fascinating of James's characters."[10]

A good part of Isabel's fascination is precisely the company she keeps, not only James's own cast of creations but, at least as vividly, those past heroines this memorable character, in her eager love of life, her intelligent blindness and fear of commitment, her situation and her difficult fate, so evocatively recollects for us. Isabel's story is haunted again and again with the unheard voices of those other heroines and the "ghostlier demarcations" of their creators, all melodies that inform the book.[11] To consider Isabel outside that visionary company of heroines is to rest content with a view of history as a quite dead past and a quite new present. It is to rest content, as does Emily Brontë's Mr. Lockwood, with seeing only the now-deserted moors.

The echoes of these ghostly heroines are especially powerful, their recollected presences especially intense, because, unlike James's other novels, the plot of *The Portrait* is such a direct borrowing from and transformation of previous plots. It is a novel peculiarly suited to, even requiring, a critical reading that attends to questions of tradition and individuality. The very narrative simplicity that James asserted as its innovation and that distinguishes it from *The Wings of the Dove* and *The Golden Bowl*, refers back to its predecessors with a direct intensity the more muted and complex transformations of the late novels do not have. Listening to those past voices as they reverberate in this modern novel can help to create a frame of meaning within which to interpret *The Portrait*, particularly to discuss the vexed problem of how to judge Isabel's final flight back to Rome.

There can be many literary big sisters for Isabel Archer. Her family ties extend from Hester Prynne to Anna Karenina to Emma Bovary. But when, among the sisterhood who inspired her conception, I choose, in Austen's phrase, not simply good company but the best, I place Isabel most specifically with Austen's own Elizabeth Bennet and Emma Woodhouse and with Eliot's Dorothea Brooke and Gwendolen Harleth.[12] *The Portrait* quite self-consciously draws on the classic pattern of these nineteenth-century British novels of education: the heroine is a young, attractive, intelligent, sensitive gentlewoman affronting her destiny; the plot is a *rite du passage* from innocence to experience; the action of the novel is a perceptual process that inevitably involves self-revelation; the education is to be open to experience, to use imagination and feeling to reach outside oneself rather than to insulate oneself; the epistemological assumptions include the changing nature of truth, its relativity, its historicity; and the values of the book, both the true and the good, are located in sympathy and involvement rather than in objectivity and detachment.

Since there is not, after all, a paradigmatic novel of education, a single normative model, but only many novels of education, each with its own form, how does *The Portrait* extend and modify the British tradition composed of these novels from which it so extensively and originally borrows? Within this beautiful and highly evolved narrative pattern, what makes Isabel unique? And how does delineating both her representative qualities and her originality reach back to illuminate the portraits of her ancestors as well?

In her love of freedom and hidden understanding of that freedom as a way of distancing herself from involvement, Isabel's character reaches all the way back to the beginning of the century, to the novels that first elaborated the pattern and thereby so profoundly influenced the course of nineteenth-century British fiction. Of all the heroines who live again in Isabel Archer, her original model is surely one of the most familiar and irrepressible heroines in British fiction, Austen's Elizabeth Bennet. With the intellectual energy and the great charm that look forward to Isabel, Elizabeth, too, thinks of herself as different from and freer than the common fate and at the same time proceeds in quite a common way to blind herself. She believes that her superior intelligence and perceptiveness are precisely what make her an exception, and the self-deception in that belief makes her exceptionally vulnerable to the deceptions played upon her. Freedom as both these heroines conceive of it is an isolation that both protects and confers distinction. Elizabeth and Isabel, both brainy, both believe they can choose their brains over their hearts. Both believe that intellectual freedom makes them different from other women, allows them a destiny somehow larger and less predictable than the tidy conclusiveness of a good match, whether that conclusiveness be embodied in its grotesque form as Mr. Collins or in all its alluring shapeliness as Lord Warburton.

But these heroines' ideas of freedom will neither protect nor distinguish nor bless. Wanting "to see, but not to feel," (*PL*: 134) making choices without heart, turns out to mean making heartless, and stupid, choices. It turns out to mean being trapped, relinquishing the very modes of perceiving that might lead them to see. As Austen had elaborated in 1811, in her first published novel, there is no sense without sensibility. Both heroines must learn that the dichotomy itself is false. And at least one charm for me of both heroines and both novels is that their education does not mean learning to choose their hearts over their brains.

Elizabeth and Isabel do not escape from the common fate, the fate of people, of women. That is the fate of living inevitably within the frame of all the social and temporal and psychological givens we both find and make if we would dwell in Blake's realms of day. This does not at all mean that the givens themselves are either inevitable or part of a natural order of things. It does mean that consciousness of the cultural constructs, external and internalized, that shape these heroines' lives, is itself a value and perhaps even the most productive beginning to the process of remaking those constructs. Do we want to read Isabel Archer's return to her miserable marriage or Elizabeth Bennet's happy marriage to that exceptionally good catch, Fitzwilliam Darcy, as representations, intentional or not, of the social trap, of how women are shrunk by cultures and by authors into fitting a domestic role? To do so would mean to define education ironically and to dismiss textual signs of the heroines' growth.

Elizabeth Bennet is using her quick intelligence and her laughter as perceptual tools better at the end of her story than at the beginning, when her insights stayed on surfaces and her humor tended to the snappy punchline. And Isabel Archer, in those last days at Gardencourt, puts herself first at the mercy of love's sweetness and then of its passion. In both instances she shows a depth of response she was incapable of when she first walked that smooth lawn. Not to believe that each heroine's life can be better for what she has learned must mean to challenge the novel's premise, or to argue that the novel challenges its own premise: that to see better brings a chance to live better; that perceiving is a form of doing; that consciousness, education, matters; that life can be a matter of art, and event a matter of mind.

For both young women the measure of their blindness is their misjudgment of a man or, more precisely, their willful susceptibility to a bad man. Elizabeth is drawn to Mr. Wickham in part as a response to his singling her out and in part because of his external charm, though Austen locates that charm in a simple red uniform rather than a Florentine villa on a hill. More fundamentally, Elizabeth is drawn to Wickham because she can, like Isabel with Gilbert Osmond, and for similar reasons, make a convenience of him. What Elizabeth uses him for I could almost describe as simply to fill a blank. As will be true of Isabel with Osmond, her relations with Wickham appear to represent a vital connection: two clever, handsome, charming people finding each other interesting and engaging beyond the common way. They make, as we say, a nice couple, a point Austen develops even more outrageously in Emma Woodhouse's appropriate and meaningless flirtation with Highbury's best, that dashing and visibly unattached bachelor, Frank Churchill.

Conveniently, the relation is no relation at all. The man offers and in turn expects only surface, the gestures are empty of real involvement, no part of self is actually committed or owed. And that, in a Jamesian sense, is the beauty of it all. As many readers have suggested, Isabel too selects her wrong man for convenient reasons, to save herself from emotional engagement, from sexual passion, from private and public responsibility for her money and her self. She likes the look of her life with Osmond, at least initially, and she likes the presumed freedom it gives her as well.

Isabel's most significant differences from her Austen predecessor are located not in her character but in her circumstances and her fate. In the course of her *rite du passage* Elizabeth trades in the red uniform for the harmonious rooms and grounds of Pemberley and a better man, whereas Isabel travels from the Florentine villa to a Roman palace owned by the same man. One clear reason for the difference is that there is no Ralph Touchett in *Pride and Prejudice*. Elizabeth moves from the wrong man to the right man, whereas Isabel does not. But that is not a sign of the earlier heroine's greater innocence or moral superiority. No one in the novel, and certainly not her creator, comes forward to present Elizabeth Bennet with the fortune necessary to complete her real charm for Mr. Wickham. He wanders off, looking for the heroine with money. Elizabeth will be given the fortune, of course, but only because it comes along with the right man.

Such fortuitousness in one's choice is exactly what Osmond, that passive fortune hunter, could initially have claimed about his marriage to Isabel, since he would never have married her for her money if he did not also love her in his way. Moreover, in the work of both Austen and James, it is foolish to marry without money. But the distinguishing point is that Elizabeth, like Eleanor Dashwood and Anne Elliot and Isabel Archer, would marry with enough to live on simply, because money is just an aid. Gilbert Osmond requires a fortune to create a style of life with Isabel, to create an Isabel who fits the aesthetic and social demands of his imagination.

In the sense of not having money, Elizabeth is the more blessed of the two heroines, and the less tried. Perhaps Elizabeth is better than Isabel. Perhaps, if Austen had somehow made her rich and Wickham had therefore persisted in a suit, as he certainly would have, she would have known not to marry him, she would have been able to bear the weight of having her own fortune, she would not have deluded herself so far as to visualize a full future with the man. I tend to believe so. But the point must be that Elizabeth is not so tried. Before Elizabeth has any understanding of Wickham's character, before Mr. Darcy has written to her the factual information that she really does need in order to see through Wickham's façade, he draws off himself, in pursuit, indeed, of a lady with money.

Isabel, less blessed, is early given the large fortune that will lure the hunters, a drawback Ralph smoothly dismisses as "appreciable" but "small" (162). Moreover, Isabel has to learn quite on her own to understand Osmond's character, and only then, and long after her marriage to him, does the Countess Gemini tell her the secret facts of Osmond's history. Elizabeth's pensive scene in the lane at Hunsford is triggered by Mr. Darcy's letter. Isabel's narratively similar meditative vigil has no such informational catalyst. To whatever degree we may decide to place greater blame on James's heroine than on Austen's, the difference in their circumstances effectively minimizes the difference in their culpability. An education in self-awareness in nineteenth-century British fiction always has its price. And the price continually goes up. Isabel's, in Lambert Strether's phrase, is exceptionally dear.

Another way to say this is that Isabel's mistakes in perception are irretrievable, whereas Elizabeth's are not. This is not because the perceptual mistakes in themselves are significantly worse. Is Isabel more culpable with Osmond than Elizabeth with Wickham? Maybe, though I think it would be a fine line. But is Isabel more culpable than that arch-egoist, Emma Woodhouse? Austen's heroines, whatever their degree of blindness, do not act on that blindness in ways that cannot be recalled. But whom should readers credit for that restraint, the character or the text? When Austen's heroines do things that need to be recalled, I want to point out who does the recalling. Emma breaks the real romance between Harriet Smith and Farmer Martin. At the end of the novel their romance is reinstated, more or less as it was, though not in any way that can credit Emma. As with Wickham's turning away from Elizabeth, the plot, which is to say her author, does it for her. Considered in the light of Austen's flawed heroines who end happily, Isabel's fate cannot be accounted for simply as a matter of character.

In spite of James's insult about Austen's work being songs of an arrested spring, her heroines are hardly singular in being both flawed and blessed. This is also true of the more somber midcentury portraits of Eliot's heroines, particularly Dorothea Brooke and Gwendolen Harleth, the two previous heroines to whom critics have been attentive in discussing sources for *The Portrait*.[13] Is Isabel with Osmond any worse than Dorothea with Casaubon? Again, maybe. Someone, not I, could plausibly argue that Dorothea's blindnesses are a little nobler than Isabel's, that the fault lies more in her culture's sexism, that she wants to expand herself and the only route open is through a man. This is certainly true, and it also seems to me only part of the truth. Nor can I see what are the routes her fictional social context allows to Isabel that are not to do with fulfilling oneself through a man (as in the presumably splendid opportunity of Lord Warburton) and are roads not taken. Ralph Touchett can do no more than hope that Isabel will break out of that predictable female fulfillment in some way even he can't imagine. Nor can I. At least not within James's story. Though the forms of fulfillment offered in the novel are not those of traditional marriage, they all include, for either sex, some sort of love relations. And that point is an important element in the novel's claims.

The Portrait is littered with publicly and professionally successful men—Mr. Touchett, Lord Warburton, Caspar Goodwood—whose lives are defined by the failures of their personal relations. The one independently professional woman, Henrietta Stackpole, ends by choosing to marry. Isabel feels this to be a regrettable confession of being "human and feminine," instead of being "a light keen flame, a disembodied voice" (470). But we should surely suspect Isabel's judgment by then, and particularly suspect any such sign of human distancing as a preference for a "disembodied voice." We are prevented from also reading Henrietta's decision as some sort of sad commentary, a defeat for the feisty journalist, by the basic point that her professionalism throughout is portrayed as a matter of surfaces. That's hardly a valuable kind of flame. And her marriage, in which Henrietta will continue as a journalist anyway, will probably not make her life worse, and also not better.

Henrietta's significance simply cannot be located in some kind of tension between career and marriage, no matter how significant that tension may be in her readers' lives. Her success, true in the beginning of the novel and in the end, is located neither in her career nor in her prospective marriage. It is located in her friendship, in her generous and continuing love for Isabel. Her friendship is what moves us about Henrietta, rescues her intelligence from superficiality and her role from that of social commentary or ficelle.[14] When she judges Henrietta's engagement, Isabel has still to make that last visit to Gardencourt, to learn the superiority of "common passions" (470) over a light keen flame and a disembodied voice. Given the Jamesian universe, no reader can justifiably argue that Isabel should have been conceived as having some form of professional possibilities or, more to the point, that such possibilities could have brought her essential good. Within the novel there is no approved alternative for either sex to self-fulfillment through other people. There are simply good and bad, mostly bad, forms of human connection.

The book does represent Isabel as reaching self-fulfillment, in her friendship with Ralph. The fragility and the transience of this achievement are obvious, presented literally as a deathbed scene. In those last moments with Ralph, Isabel knows a deep and vitalizing connection with another person, a bond I might as well call true love, and presented in this novel as happening not in romantic union but in friendship, the one form of our relations to others and our expressions of self that *The Portrait* continually celebrates.

Yet after Isabel's moment of truth and pain and joy, the moment that makes possible her following brief moment of sexual passion, Isabel will go back to Rome. I believe Dorothea Brooke is kept unfulfilled by her literary historical context and did deserve to be free of Casaubon. I want her to be released from the lifelong consequences of her forgivable mistake. But then, I believe the same of Isabel. I want her released as well. In spite of her having more ego and less selfless idealism than Dorothea, Isabel deserves just as much to be excused from the permanent consequences of her mistakes. Dorothea is released and finds a new future in that lightning kiss of Will Ladislaw, but only by the heavenly intervention of her author. Isabel, without such a gift, turns away from her evocatively similar lightning kiss and refuses to do the releasing herself.

Why doesn't James reach out and kill off Osmond? There is already a happy tradition of such disposals. But perhaps that is the crucial point. The reason cannot be that Isabel doesn't deserve such luck. For these rescues of heroines, these deaths of villains, are precisely a matter of luck rather than of deserts. Isabel is no worse than her sisters, than Elizabeth Bennet and Emma Woodhouse, who never actualize their mistakes in permanent forms and so don't have to be rescued. She is probably even better than Gwendolen Harleth, who steals the rightful place of a friendless woman and her children to marry a man for money and power, then wishes him dead and watches him drown. Yet Grandcourt does, conveniently, drown.

How good, once these heroines have outgrown the blindnesses that cause their mistakes, to be rid of the horrible consequences of those mistakes. Eliot even did it once for a hero, before heroines became the central characters of her novels. Having Hetty Sorrel seduced and then transported offered a vivid means of rescuing Adam Bede from the disastrous marriage he chose so blindly.

As with Eliot's heroines, Meredith's also make bitter and permanent mistakes, learn apparently too late, and then are magically relieved of those supposedly inevitable consequences. I think of *The Egoist*, published only two years before *The Portrait*. Its subject, cast in the terms of breaking an engagement, is how one escapes the apparently inescapable. As the haunting example of Constantia Durham shows, Clara Middleton finally won't run, any more than will Isabel. Yet unlike Isabel, Clara does get free of her binding commitment to the wrong man. The release comes not from her efforts alone, which, indeed, are failing, but by the plot device of an overhearing along with the combined efforts of a whole social group. Meredith's later heroines, Diana Warwick and Carinthia Fleetwood, do marry the wrong man, who again conveniently dies. Like Dorothea and Isabel, Diana at the end of her story is also swept away by the kiss of true passion. But following Dorothea rather than Isabel, Diana finds her future there. It will be a place of love and private happiness, but not of struggles for self-realization among the killing exigencies of public authorship. In Millamant's unforgettable phrase, Diana will dwindle into a wife.

It cannot be a random fact that as the century goes on the heroines of British fiction commit themselves more to actions based on their failures of perception, and thus the cost of their failures gets higher. Austen's heroines, in their deepest moments of stupidity, never get engaged to the wrong man, let alone marry him.[15] They never do anything irretrievable. Indeed, they don't do much of anything at all. Perceptions and misperceptions are themselves the action of the novels rather than being realized in events that are also the action. Austen's first published novel, *Sense and Sensibility*, distinguishes sharply between action as perceiving and action as doing, and the distinction is arguably the major lesson of the book. Eliot's and Meredith's heroines often do go all the way, as it were, and commit the irretrievable. But their authors simply lean over and retrieve it for them. The engagements are off, the husband is dead, the future is there. The difference, simply, is that James does not.[16]

I am not arguing that Isabel, having made her bed, must lie in it. She had long since lain in Osmond's bed, as their predictably dead child proves, while her similarly culpable predecessors often enough leapt gaily from theirs. And we certainly don't believe that the passionate experience at last of Caspar's kiss will impart any new glow to her marriage bed. I am arguing that the continuing struggle to interpret the ending of *The Portrait* is brightened by placing the novel within the tradition of heroic heroines; which is, after all, where James himself, with some hedging, placed it, and where it certainly fits. The structural light of the stories of Elizabeth Bennet, and Emma Woodhouse, Margaret Hale, Dorothea Brooke, and Gwendolen Harleth, and Clara Middleton does brighten the darker path of Isabel Archer.

The whole tradition is one of heroines holding themselves to the consequences, refusing to become, like Meredith's Constantia Durham, one of those who "ran." Again and again these heroines accept and even affirm the consequences of their blindness, refuse to escape, insist on offering their futures to pay for the follies of their past. Elizabeth Bennet teaches herself that her willful mistreatment of Mr. Darcy and her part in her family's relations with Mr. Wickham must cost her Mr. Darcy's good opinion, when, in fact, it hasn't. Emma, having spent Manichean months convincing Harriet Smith of her expanded prospects, sees their imminent realization in Mr. Knightley's about-to-be-declared affection for Harriet, and yet brings herself "to take another turn" (429) around the garden with him, to allow what she believes will fulfill Harriet's hopes and end her own. Dorothea Brooke, responsible to the point of near martyrdom, not only would never leave Mr. Casaubon but has actually brought herself to the point of making an even more imprisoning commitment to him after his death, to fulfill some unknown duty in regard to his endless and meaningless scholarly notes. Gwendolen Harleth is rare in being blessedly short on self-sacrifice. But even she remains frozen in her imprisoning marriage to Grandcourt. It is morally quite in keeping, even absolutely normal, for Isabel to choose to return to Rome. What is not normal is for her creator to let her go through with it.

Why doesn't James release his charming and deserving heroine from the dreadful consequences of her wrong choices? Is he simply being mean, punitive, or despairing?[17] After all, there are many heroines in late Victorian fiction who do leave their husbands. Unfortunately, this does not usually turn out to mean that they can walk away from their terrible fates. Some we may feel are simply punished by their conservative authors, as is that notorious adulteress, Lady Isabel Vane, in *East Lynne*. But many of these heroines who have escaped the wrong men continue to lead interestingly difficult lives. Meredith's Constantia Durham, it is true, simply gets to marry her handsome, soldier rescuer, but she had only run from an engagement. In Meredith's late novels the initial blind act effectively cannot be retrieved by running, because the heroines are still married. These novels explore the ways in which the literal escape turns out not to be an escape at all. The new-found freedom of these heroines carries with it all the painful social and emotional consequences of their departures. Diana Warwick and Carinthia Fleetwood leave their spouses for a life of chastity and frustrated efforts of self-development, hardly for forbidden fruits or for an honorable new life in the arms of another man. It is their author who finally arranges that honor for them. These endings are so implausible and also so unappealing as to offer an implicit testimony to the hopelessness of these heroines freeing themselves from their mistaken pasts on their own.

Hardy, who along with Meredith is more or less James's contemporary in writing novels, also created some of the most memorable heroines in British fiction. And, like James, Hardy will not play *deus ex machina* to his flawed creations. Sue Bridehead follows the common pattern of escaped wife who cannot really escape, with the horrifying difference from Meredith's heroines that her author does not, at last, conveniently erase her husband. Sue's break for freedom puts her back in the same prison again. And the consequence, for part of the point is that there are always consequences, is that her spirit is broken as well. Neither Sue nor Tess is released from the man who would define her fate. In relation to this pattern we appreciate the elegance of the plot variation Hardy offers in *Tess of the D'Urbervilles*. He has his creature do for herself what other authors had done for their heroines: kill off that tenacious bond to a mistaken past. And we also see the horrible logic of consequences in having that murder effectively be a suicide.

These novelists are not engaged in imaginatively penalizing bolting wives or shoring up the sanctity of the marriage tie. Neither, on the liberal side, do I think they are centrally concerned with the social injustices for women in a world that presses women into marriage as the one available fate but prohibits access to divorce. These novelists are engaged in arguing the sacredness of a continuity that allows progress, a future better than the past, only by transforming rather than repudiating that past. To run, in Meredith's metaphor, is to step outside history. It is to say that one's life doesn't matter, in the sense that one's past doesn't matter. It is to say, in the words of a recently popular bumper sticker, that today is the first day of the rest of your life. What happens to the definition of character as developing self if the choices a character made yesterday do not generate consequences that affect what a character can be today? For these novelists, probably before the day you were born and certainly the day on which their novel begins, is the first day of the rest of your life.

Constantia Durham is Meredith's symbol for pure act. She does not literally appear in his novel precisely because she ran, and therefore she has no story to tell. Mere act has defined her. She exists only as a tantalizing temptation in the true heroine's mind. Clara Middleton's fascination with Constantia is the fascination of inner with outer, of motive and judgment with the world of event. As Meredith said, internal history is the brainstuff of fiction. And neither he nor Hardy nor James, neither Austen nor Scott nor Gaskell nor any nineteenth-century British novelist I can think of, celebrates pure act any more than they celebrate a fixed self. For them Yeats is right, you cannot tell the dancer from the dance.

Isabel cannot choose to ignore her marriage without thereby choosing to ignore the whole dynamic of self and circumstances that has composed her present identity. To be disturbed that Isabel doesn't run off with Caspar is like wondering how Meredith could write *The Egoist*, how he could ever organize such an ado about the simple act of breaking an engagement. Why doesn't Clara Middleton just tell Willoughby Patterne that the engagement is off, and leave? That why is, of course, the very story the novel tells. Not to run does not mean just accepting the situation. What else it can mean is the subject of *The Egoist*, so many of Meredith's other novels, and *The Portrait* as well.

Caspar Goodwood claims to Isabel that "[w]e can do absolutely as we please; to whom under the sun do we owe anything? What is it that holds us?" (489). I imagine that this is what Captain Oxford, Constantia's rescuer, said to her, the very questions he asked.[18] Nineteenth-century British novels have a strong tradition of making fun of handsome rescuers, heroes or villains. Perhaps its earliest example may be the original Willoughby in *Sense and Sensibility*, the benevolent Pygmalion who first appears in his hunting jacket in the rain to carry Marianne Dashwood home, and is referred to ever after by her younger sister as "Marianne's Preserver."

By 1880–81 and *The Portrait of a Lady*, readers should recognize the sweet tones of the would-be savior not simply as a reference to Milton but generally as an invocation of old romance, an invocation of the sexiest, the most seductive, the falsest, story we tell ourselves, the story of freedom from the givens of our lives. These romancers, these rescuers, are either liars or fools. The answer to Caspar's questions is that what holds him and Isabel is their own past lives, everything they've been and done. They owe everything, and the debt is to themselves. They cannot be rescued from their own pasts, any more than will Jude or Sue or Tess. There are no instant transformations, no new worlds.

With all Caspar's goodness, with all the strength of his deep love for Isabel, he is still part of the same old continuum that contains his opposite in Gilbert Osmond. Both are moments in the Orc cycle, Caspar as the sexual desires of youth, Gilbert as the acquisitive desires of age. Both finally are involved in the masculine-labeled values of aggression, competitiveness, and control. The good guy is the same as the bad, which is why a conventional love story can no longer be told. Who will rescue us from our rescuers? For Isabel to run off with Caspar is to make them the Miltonic version of Pygmalion and Galatea. It is to accept that these two are Adam and Eve and "The world's all before us" (489). It is to believe that history doesn't exist because it is only something that's about to begin. It is also, and this may be its original literary sin, to make Isabel's whole story, and therefore James's novel, insignificant. With James's work we are not yet at the kind of narrative that can contentedly assert its own irrelevance.

If Isabel does not betray her past, if she moves, as she does, to the music of the whole dance of internal history that makes up her present out of her past, the dynamic encounter with experience that has shaped her present self, what external form, what mere act, might represent that continuing affirmation and progress toward the future? Starting for Rome.

The dissatisfaction of many readers with this ending is caught in Kettle's classic description of Isabel's return as a choice of death over life, a turning her face to the wall, a "final sacrificial tribute to her own ruined conception of freedom." [19] The power of Kettle's analysis lies in suggesting that to see the ending as a renunciation of life, given Isabel's vital appeal throughout the novel and her moving dignity at the end, is effectively to argue that not just Isabel but the novel, which is to say, James, honors ruined ideals over real futures, argues for death over life. Readers are then left with some kind of absolute opposition between an "idealized sensibility" and "actual living" (689) or, in Tony Tanner's eloquent phrase, "the birth of a conscience out of the spoiling of a life." [20] And Kettle is right. To argue for the tragedy, or sense of the loss, of the ending is implicitly to argue for the novel's glorification of that loss. This is a serious criticism, one that points to why the question of how we interpret the novel's ending is so important. To idealize loss is to argue, and with the force of Jamesian eloquence, for hopelessness and ultimately for passivity.

The basic opposition between being "too valuable" and living "only to suffer" (466), between the greater possibilities of self and the lesser actualities of one's fate, which has delineated the boundaries of traditional responses to *The Portrait*'s ending, has simply recurred in a new form in many feminist readings of the novel. The initial dualism translates easily into the fate of a woman in a male society. As Virginia Fowler puts it, "the American girl treated in realistic fiction can have but a muted triumph because the powers of her femininity are inevitably limited by the world the fiction forces her to inhabit." [21] In other words, there has always been an inescapable political dimension to readings of the ending of *The Portrait*, regardless of how that dimension has traditionally been ignored. To say that the book idealizes loss is also to imply, consciously or unconsciously, approvingly or critically, that the book accepts both the final passivity of women and the hopelessness of their finding fulfillment in their historical place and time.

The point must surely invoke for us all the spectre of Isabel's great midcentury predecessor, Dorothea Brooke. But Dorothea's resolution, as we know, was the kiss and the man. And the kiss and the man are intertwined with our sense that Dorothea is a latter-day St. Theresa, that if fulfillment means no more than the romance of a happy marriage to Will Ladislaw and an incalculable and diffuse good influence, then there is little self-realization possible for Dorothea amid the actualities of her time and place. But Isabel explicitly rejects that resolution, does not accept that form of influence, that means of making a difference, of effecting the actualities of life. Isabel holds out for something better. She may or may not get it, but surely remembering Dorothea is enough to make us consider that Isabel isn't renouncing that much when she runs from the kiss and may be right to take a difference chance.

Five years before *The Portrait* another Eliot novel, her last, created an ending for its heroine that illuminated in new ways the narrative possibilities for future closures. Eliot simply provided Gwendolen Harleth with the barest necessities, the absolute minimum, what I might now define as the required elements for a happy ending in their most purified form. She left Gwendolen with the twin gifts of life and of knowledge. Those final gifts are the ones James gives Isabel as well. Echoing Gwendolen's cry of "I shall live. I mean to live," is Isabel's intimation of herself "in distant years, still in the attitude of a woman who had her life to live" (466). We are told that the "quick vague shadow of a long future" lies "deeper in her soul than any appetite for renunciation." Isabel goes back to Rome as a heroine who really has been educated, has embraced life, as much with Ralph as with Caspar, has reached depths of feeling that the brittle and repressed young woman from Albany who married Osmond was incapable of. Isabel's future, like Gwendolen's, is unknown. What is known, all that can be known, is that a future exists. And that the heroine who faces it is more insightful and less vulnerable than before.

Osmond, of course, remains. Isabel's crucial difference from Gwendolen may be that Eliot had gotten rid of Grandcourt. It is undeniable that life has gotten more tenuous, the future darker, for Isabel. But there is no need for readers to romanticize that fact. Osmond remains not as the tragic answer, not as death embraced at last, not even as the fate of woman in a man's world; just as the continuing problem. Isabel's life is not spoiled, unless life means only circumstance, unless a changed conscience and a changed vision cannot change circumstance, unless only acts by gods and men and authors can. And to believe that, to borrow Kettle's own language, may be the ultimate self-indulgence of the intelligentsia. Isabel is more than a victim. *The Portrait* does embody the horrible bonds for women in a world of seemingly inevitable and permanent marriages and men's rules. But that world is the given on the lawn at Gardencourt at the opening of the book. The rest of the novel does more than explore that world's power. It suggests that world's boundaries as well.

In the end Isabel is freed, because she has freed herself, of the only significant chain binding her to Osmond, and that is not the chain of his physical existence as her husband. She is freed of her own complicity in the values he embodies. As readers have long noted, Isabel was capable of marrying Osmond not simply because he and Madame Merle had "made a convenience" (475) of her but also because Isabel was a willing victim, one who had her own uses for Osmond as he had his for her. Isabel too wanted a detached soul, a life offering an objective correlative to her inner superiority, and, perhaps most important, a life without emotional vulnerability. She had, indeed, internalized the masculine values of her culture.[22]

Isabel frees herself of this satanic and sexist cycle of tyrant and victim through the trip to Gardencourt. She chooses to honor over "the observance of a magnificent form" (446) the debts of heart she owes to Ralph Touchett. At Gardencourt she first moves past her pride, the satan of ego, to the deep connection with another that comes from "the only knowledge which was not pure anguish—the knowledge that they were looking at the truth together" (478). Then, finally, Isabel lets go of her last maidenly self-definition. She allows her protected self, that eidolon of selfhood, that "pale virgin shrouded in snow," to drown in sexual passion, in the full sensation of Caspar's kiss.

Does experiencing the kiss require running off with the man? And does not to do so mean renunciation? Would Isabel have married Caspar if James had disposed of Osmond? James, as well as the rest of us, had before him the example of the heroine who kissed while the elements raged, and married the man. Surely one clear historical message of reading *The Portrait* within its literary tradition of heroic heroines is that the days are over when a heroine can end her adventures by being settled with a good, loving man, and have such an ending produce satisfaction or credulity. It is the very lesson Meredith should have learned with *Diana* and didn't. An emancipated point of the ending of *The Portrait* is that one can lose one's sensual virginity to a man and still not stay with him. A kiss is just a kiss, even when it is a great kiss, even when it is the single great kiss of one's life. It establishes neither an obligation nor a resolution. Passion is not a final answer.

And if the kiss cannot light its own path and so conclude the tale, there remains only Rome. For these two encompass all the possibilities: one to leap out of circumstances, the other to continue within them. The circumstances, the characters, in Isabel's life are not created as markers along some Bunyanesque educative path, fading into invisibility once our heroic heroine has walked past. As her connections to them evolve, so also must her separations from them. As readers we have perhaps become too used to the convenient vanishings through which many fictions dispose of characters who have outlived their use. But if, unlike Eliot, James does not kill off Osmond, and if, unlike Tess, Isabel does not kill him herself, he is still there, the unfinished business of her life.

There can be no vague going off somewhere alone for Isabel, no sudden opening of a new and unknown direction. That would also be to deny her past, all that made the self she now is, the consciousness she now has, and she might as well do the denying with Caspar. To run from him is, with beautiful Jamesian ingenuity, to run from all forms of flight.

And why should we presume that when Isabel goes back to Rome she will take up her place as victim again? Why should we conclude that, because Osmond does not die, "in James there is no second chance"?[23] Perhaps what Isabel returns to is precisely a second chance, but understood in a fresh way from what it had meant to James's, and Isabel's, predecessors. Isabel has gained a new power at Gardencourt. Without her participation Osmond cannot play the tyrant, no matter how long he makes a scene. Isabel's new freedom, so different from the old, means an engaged rather than a detached self. It means knowing, in Ralph's words, that "life is better; for in life there's love" (477). Isabel does rid herself of the masculinist values of detachment and selfhood, but she does not literally rid herself of the man. Each reader must decide what that inner liberation is worth; what its power can be.

I suggest that James's refusal to kill off Osmond, far from being despairing or retributive, gives his heroine the opportunity for emancipation in a way that both her own earlier chance and the seemingly kinder and more optimistic fates of Dorothea and even Gwendolen do not. Gwendolen's story does foreshadow Isabel's, but even Gwendolen remains, in the end, in a more protected state. Isabel goes to meet her enemy. It may be preferable to have one's enemy dead. But when that enemy is the masculine values of a culture, I find a deep charm in a heroine who chooses to confront them, a deep credibility in an ending that insists that they cannot be escaped. Those values, precisely because they are cultural and relative, are also pervasive. Osmond is everywhere. Understanding that is entwined with getting beyond him, with getting him out of oneself. It may be that Isabel's return to Rome is the one significant act that can tell us that she is her own woman, that, at least for the moment, she is free at last.

Placing Isabel Archer within a literary tradition of nineteenth-century British heroines helps to explain the special intensity of her story. James was able to make such an ado about that "mere slim shade" of a girl in part because, again and again, an ado had already been so magnificently made. In building his own architectural structure, James adds on to an already well-constructed, indeed, a sophisticated and refined, literary inheritance. So that part of the sophistication of his edifice, part of its complexity and sense of proportion, must be credited to those predecessors who had long since solved some of the basic structural problems, and long since created some of the refinements, of the particular subject of a "certain young woman affronting her destiny" (8).

Once we see that certain young woman as, if not quite a multitude, at least a small crowd, we gain a literary frame of meaning and value within which to interpret James's own inspired version. As I have been arguing, one clear effect is that Isabel looks less culpable when she is seen amid so many other heroines who are also self-deceived. Her flaws look a little less hers alone and more everyone's, while her story's ending looks more positive alongside those more upbeat, conventionally happy but unconvincing endings of Eliot and Meredith, in which the heroine kisses and keeps the man. Against their false sense of closure, of the adventures of life being over and problems formally rather than substantively solved, Isabel's open future, however ominous, allows for hope.

Isabel's identity with her predecessors and her originality both need to operate in interpreting *The Portrait*. But there remains the underlying question of biology. These characters are all women. I can say that Isabel is a heroine rather than a hero because she is modeled on heroines, on Gwendolen Harleth and Elizabeth Bennet. That answer is not tautological or evasive. It carries historical truth, partly captured by James's stress in his "Preface" to the novel on the apparent discrepancy between women's lives and "how inordinately" they "insist on mattering" (9). This is the same point Eliot made with her frail vessels. Women's lives—and the implicit qualification here is: unlike men's lives—don't have big public destinies but are still centrally important, maybe even more important than those public destinies.

As Anne Elliot said, "men have had every advantage of us in telling their own story" (*Persuasion*:234). Women's lives are the history that doesn't get told in histories, in "all stories, prose and verse." They therefore need to be told in the internal histories of novels, not because of some schoolroom principle of evenhandedness but because women's lives can carry the values out of which cultural history, as progress rather than repetition, can actually be made. We need Austen's and Gaskell's and Meredith's characters. We need the frail vessels and the presumptuous girls and, most of all, we need the novels that recount their histories. These novels tell the women's stories because, they would claim, within these stories, rescued from nonexistence by these novels, are whatever hopes for humane progress our culture has.

There are, as James says, millions of these heroines. A small group is of heroic stature and most are "much smaller female fry" (9). Their private histories, when told, become representative and general, as testimonials to a culture's desires and possibilities. Not only does the story of a certain young woman carry the story of millions of young women. The stories of one sex carry the conditions of both. The literary tradition is composed primarily of heroines because the premise of that tradition is to defend relational values, values traditionally, but not necessarily, associated with the feminine rather than the masculine. As *Cousin Phillis* suggests, it is more important to understand the obligations of flirtation than to build railroads in Canada. Failure in one can slow down travel, failure in the other can break a heart. And success? Which form of success would measure our cultural progress? Or, in one of Austen's many versions, asking a neglected girl to dance is a more socially constructive heroism than rescuing her on horseback from a band of gypsies. And, as the above example reminds us, the heroine, learning and carrying what are culturally defined as feminine values, is usually a woman. But this is not a matter of biological or cultural determinism. The heroine, like her author, doesn't have to be a woman. She can also be a man.

The heroine in *The Portrait* is normative in being a woman, whereas the reality that traps Isabel, the cultural givens she must expel from within in order to fight from without, are masculine. Thus the earthly powers who try to determine her future are primarily, but not only, men. Mr. Touchett's money, Ralph's benevolent artistic hand, Osmond's objectifying greed, and Goodwood's passion—these are the powers that conspire to shape Isabel's destiny. But Madame Merle is there, too, Isabel's most active enemy. Madame Merle is in essence a henchwoman, Osmond's voluntary helpmate, her many talents long since coopted by the competitive world of power and detachment. Not her own woman, she is patriarchal society itself. For more than twenty years after writing *The Portrait* James continued to explore the same gender-associated tensions and the same drama. In one of the last of those later works the familiar Jamesian heroine appears as a man.

In an evaluation that has been echoed by many of his readers, James thought *The Ambassadors* "quite the best, 'all round,' of my productions."[24] Its long slow analysis of the intelligent heart of Lewis Lambert Strether, his combination of memory and desire, along with the interfusing of observation and experience, of seeing and living, that characterizes his trip to Europe; these elements compose a brilliant portrait. The master novelist of fifty-seven wrote the story of the might-have-been artist of fifty-five who had missed his life, who "had failed, as he considered, in everything."[25]

Strether's mission in Paris brings him one of the great gifts that art can offer its creations, the gift of a second chance. That gift is rare enough, even in works of fiction. Strether's opportunity echoes the plot of *Persuasion.* The story of Captain Wentworth and Anne Elliot is also structured as a repetition that leads to an improvement, with Captain Wentworth's sea adventures looking forward to the world of Woollett while life with Anne shows some of the charms of Paris. Unlike this early nineteenth-century couple, Strether will, in the course of taking his chance, lose "everything" (1:75). But he will also be able to say, "Of course I'm youth—youth for the trip to Europe" (2:50). Strether is old again when he buys his ticket home, and he goes back to the loss of what he had seen as his remaining possibilities, back to "a great difference" (2:325). But part of that difference in his relations to Mrs. Newsome and to Woollett, a wonderful part for Strether and his readers, is that "I do what I didn't before—I *see* her" (2:323).

The Ambassadors is one of the finer representations of that central interest and recurrent genre in English fiction, the novel of education. "I do what I didn't before—I *see*" can stand as a summary statement of a procession of famous characters who dance behind the elderly lead of *The Ambassadors*, from Elizabeth Bennet and Emma Woodhouse to Adam Bede and Dorothea Brooke and Gwendolen Harleth, to Clara Middleton, and to Strether's own youthful self, Isabel Archer. What distinguishes the stories of these figures is that the action of the novel is their education, that experience is observation, that to live is to learn to see. So Bilham translates Strether's injunction to "live all you can" (1:217) as "*really* to see, for it must have been that only you meant" (1:278).

The point had been sharply made at the beginning of the century, through Mary Crawford in *Mansfield Park*. Mary appears "really" to live, unlike Fanny Price, the weak heroine who watches others but neither rides well nor dances or walks without fatigue. Yet Mary does not learn how to see, and therefore she does not "do" anything, she does not live all she can. At the end of the novel Mary remains in a repetitive cycle of meaningless encounters, whereas the little seer flourishes in the life her vision has opened to her.

The question of what constitutes the action of a novel and thus what constitutes human experience, what it might mean to "live all you can," is inherent in the working out of any plot. So too is the artist's suspicion of any definition of action as mere event, a point frequently made in novels. We see it in such touches as the invisible Constantia Durham, and it has been comically immortalized in *Mansfield Park*, in Maria Bertram's belief that "good horsemanship has a great deal to do with the mind" (69). In the history of British fiction it is Austen who, for the novelists who came after her, so fully identifies to do with to see, experience with perception. When Lambert Strether cries that "I do what I didn't before—I *see*," he articulates a tradition that goes directly back to the revelations of Austen's heroines: Catherine Morland's repudiation of her gothic fancies at Northanger Abbey, Elizabeth Bennet's new vision of Mr. Wickham and herself in the lane at Hunsford, Emma Woodhouse's avowal to look into her own heart. In other words, Strether occupies the place in his novel's structure that so often in James's work and originally in Austen's is filled by a heroine.

The point is important here because it can direct us, as critics of James's fiction have not up to now been directed, to see that one essential question to bring to *The Ambassadors* is why it has a hero rather than a heroine. A bias toward the male sex may be why past readers have not asked the question, indeed have seemed to assume, implicitly and perhaps unconsciously, that it is simply natural that James's lead is a man. I am arguing that in the historical light of literary tradition, of the specific narrative structure James takes up and transforms, we could more accurately call it unnatural.

Certainly, James identified with his hero. We can only be grateful for the knowledge and insight James's great biographer, Leon Edel, brought to explaining the motives and reach of that identification.[26] But Edel's similar knowledge and insight also revealed the profundity of James's personal identification with Isabel Archer.[27] For a male artist to put himself into his creations does not at all imply that he must put himself there as a man. To assume that when he does so his work is less psychically mediated, more directly a representation of his own deepest vision, is, in other words, less repressed, is itself a critical fiction. And whether we apply that fictive assumption to male or female authors and their creatures, we should be wary of elevating it to a psychological truth.

As much of this book argues, nineteenth-century British fiction is rich in moments when a male writer represents the central self of his novel as a heroine. Years before *The Ambassadors*, Constance Fenimore Woolson challenged James on this precise issue: How did you ever dare write a portrait of a lady? Fancy any woman attempting the portrait of a gentleman! Wouldn't there be a storm of ridicule! Every clerk on the Maumee river would know more about it than a George Eliot."[28] But James, as well as Fenimore, sides with Eliot rather than with the clerks on the Maumee River. For him an observant woman can write on any subject of her choice. And so, he need hardly have said, can a man. Imaginative artists can, in the words of Henry Tilney, Austen's male voice in *Northanger Abbey*, "guess for ourselves" (151). As James understood it eighty years later, the artist can guess the unseen from the seen.[29]

In James's fiction as well as in the novels of the other writers I have been discussing, feminine and masculine are not bounded by biology. Nor are their meaning monolithic or fixed. To see them as such is continually represented in these novels as social repression and historical stupidity. Indeed, the very openness of these terms is the basis for much of the imaginative richness of nineteenth-century British fiction. What feminine and masculine might mean, how their meanings are shaped by and in turn give shape to the culture we live in, how the tensions between masculine and feminine play out in individual lives; these are some of the favored topics in James's work. The literary, if not the psychological, choice of Lewis Lambert Strether does need to be accounted for.

Critical attention to this question of gender, so generally ignored in discussions of *The Ambassadors*, can give a new and, I believe, a fuller view of that old problem, Strether's final decision to go home. Strether's story ends when he rejects Maria Gostrey's implied proposal of marriage as making him "wrong" (2:326), and leaves her to go back to Woollett. This renunciation is at the center of what remains a major dispute in interpreting *The Ambassadors*: what Strether learns and whether he learns at all. Is to see to live, and does Strether see too little and/or too late? In this novel of education, is Strether educated? If not, does the fault lie in himself or in his creator? Ian Watt and Larry Holland accept Strether's education but see it as qualified. Watt stresses the novels' humor, which both shrinks and endears the hero.[30] Holland makes an either-and-or claim for Strether's renunciation, as both "genuine tribute to his experience" and "substitute for the payment that might be made in the life of the emotions."[31] F. W. Dupee, accepting James's own description of "poor convenient, amusing, unforgettable, impossible Gostrey," argues ingenuously that when Strether refuses her "he is not 'renouncing' . . . , he is only conceding frankly to the actualities of his mind, heart, and time of life."[32]

Other critics, perhaps looking back through the haunted eyes of May Bartram's sacrificial spectatorship of John Marcher in "The Beast in the Jungle," which James wrote immediately after *The Ambassadors*, have read the ending more negatively. For F. O. Matthiessen the burden of the novel is that "Strether has awakened to a wholly new sense of life. Yet he does nothing at all to fulfill that sense." We feel "his relative emptiness."[33] Garis and Knoepflmacher argue explicitly that Strether is not educated.[34] And Maxwell Geismer explains Strether's failure as James's own "superstition that sexual love . . . was not a source of life and pleasure, but was a hideous devouring and destructive process."[35]

This nosegay of traditional critical choices, for all its eloquent color and intelligent variety, is wrapped around with a single ribbon, probably blue: silence on the subject of gender. That silence is not true to the novel's stated motifs, any more than to its represented concerns. To decide the meaning of Strether's renunciation requires also deciding whether he should renounce Maria Gostrey, which in turn requires deciding her value as well as her function in the novel. To do that, of course, is to decide the meaning of Paris, and therefore of Woollett.

Woollett may represent bourgeois business life, but it is also, in Strether's words, "a society of women" (2:83). And Paris, where lives the imagination, the spirit, and the body, is also where Maria Gostrey rightly tells Strether that "you owe more to women than any man I ever saw. We do seem to keep you going" (2:135).

What do such moments mean? We can hardly conclude that for James there are just bad women and good women, and together they delineate life's alternatives. Looking at the plot of *The Ambassadors*, the dynamic tensions among Mrs. Newsome and Strether and Maria Gostrey, among Mrs. Newsome and Chad Newsome and Marie de Vionnet, must we not grant that the book takes up once again what Arabella Shore gracefully termed "[t]hat most fruitful of subjects—the social relation of the sexes"?[36] It is surely time that readers take up the subject as well.[37] Unlike James, and his interpreters, Lambert Strether exists in a controlled context, accessible to the reader, of male–female relations that both expressly and implicitly play out more subtle relations between masculine and feminine values. Attending to the context of those relations, tracing the interplay of those values, what can we decide Strether walks away from when he walks away from Paris and Maria Gostrey?

When I ask why James's heroine is a man, I am effectively asking what difference it makes that he is not a woman. The most immediate thought, that men, at least in nineteenth-century England and America, have different life choices than women, have professions, business commitments, public involvements, notably does not operate in *The Ambassadors*. Or rather, it operates as precisely not the point, as the very perspective *The Ambassadors* rises up to testify against. Before the story even begins James has taken Lambert Strether out of his familiar work and out of his work world. That world looms threateningly from offstage for the rest of the story. However we wish to define what Strether is doing in Paris, and thus what *The Ambassadors* is about, we cannot, we must not, define his enterprise as a matter of business.

Yet that is how Waymarsh, described by the verbal master who had not known great financial success, as a man who "had held his tongue and had made a large income" (1:28), believes it should be defined. Waymarsh's relation to Strether, in its small way, offers yet another of those debates about the nature of reality that so pervade James's work and nineteenth-century British novels. James's major borrowings from and adaptation of a British literary tradition are not limited to the powerful influences of Austen and Eliot. The structure of *The Ambassadors* owes a particular debt to yet another English woman novelist, this debt not even acknowledged at all. The particular opposition between Waymarsh's way of seeing and the novel's echoes directly back to the work of Gaskell and through it to the work of Scott. We can read *The Ambassadors* as yet another taking up and transforming of the imaginative alternatives that Scott and Gaskell used continuously, and that Gaskell was to capture quite explicitly, and with great dramatic power, in her most influential work, as the two towns of Drumble and Cranford. *Cranford* is a primary model for the special form the interplay of masculine/feminine roles and values takes in *The Ambassadors*. That model can help us to see why the perennially young heroine would turn up as an aging hero, and why that hero would turn away from love and marriage.

In this century Gaskell's novella, along with the rest of her fiction, is hardly read at all. Her work has generally been assumed to be of little critical importance, intellectually and historically, and is virtually inconceivable as a significant influence on what is of critical importance, the masterpieces of "The Master." For influences on *The Ambassadors* critics, directed, of course, by James, have turned to other masters, Hawthorne, of course, but perferably masters from the continent, to Goethe and Maupassant, and primarily to Balzac.[38]

But James has left some intimations that can take us beyond Balzac. We can at least glean that *Cranford* was in James's thoughts during that formative time before writing his novel, when he first moved away from London to the different world of Lamb House, Rye. That world would provide the harmonious context for what would be James's greatest period of literary productiveness. He expresses his early impressions in a letter to Grace Norton on Christmas day, 1898 describing his new life in Rye. Offering a sample of what "the local" is like, James recounts meeting "good old little Mrs. Davies, straight out of *Cranford*," with "her little archaically-sculptured wooden door-canopy of the last century" and her "rosy maidservant almost as fluttered as herself and quite as much out of *Cranford*."[39]

Edel suggests that on moving out of London to Rye, James from the first "spoke of himself as if he were a character in one of Balzac's scenes de la vie en province."[40] But the letter Edel quotes to support this, about the "compensations on strictly domestic lines" of life "in a small country town," is that very letter to Grace Norton that describes Mrs. Davies, and her maidservant and the door of her house in Rye, as out of *Cranford*. I stress here how Edel tranforms the actual allusion to Gaskell somehow into an intimation of Balzac. The point is important because of our general sense that James's move to Rye and his sense of its contrast to the London life he had left created a tension between kinds of values that he would draw on in writing his final three novels.

The move in late June 1898 from London to Sussex may have invoked images from the French provinces of Balzac. But it did explicitly invoke images from what was one of England's most familiar and most beloved literary depictions of life in a small country town. And not the least of the reasons for the enormous popularity of Gaskell's novella is that it encapsulated in the image of Cranford a world of values that generations of Victorian readers and writers saw as preferable to and in danger from the commercial and aggressive and masculine tendencies of the age. *Cranford*'s power is that it is the past speaking to the present, not, I would stress, speaking so much about the past as about the future. It does not read peaceably, as nostalgic tribute, but stirringly, as prophetic challenge. If Mrs. Davies lives in Cranford, so too must Henry James. His move to Lamb House, Rye, and its awakened associations with Gaskell's novella, provided not only the physical but also the literary and imaginative setting from which James was to construct the first major work of his final phase.

Mary Smith, the narrator of *Cranford*, is a visitor to Cranford from her home in Drumble. She is an observer and chronicler who participates vicariously in the affairs of the town and writes long letters home. Mary Smith does not actively engage in life in Cranford, though she does help out, and she never moves to the center of the story. Yet while in Cranford Mary lives under the surprising spiritual guidance of the gentle Miss Matty Jenkins. And through Miss Matty, as well as through her own willingness to see, Mary grows in understanding and sympathy. Her opening tones of kindly irony deepen into those of greater affection and respect. Cranford gives Mary imaginative life and through her sympathetic recording she in turn brings it to imaginative life for the reader as well.

James's novel opens with Strether in a situation similar to that of the narrator of *Cranford*. For what else, structurally and conceptually, is Paris but James's updated, sophisticated, cosmopolitan, sexy version of Gaskell's Cranford? Like Mary Smith, Lambert Strether has come from Drumble to Cranford, from Woollett to Paris. And both characters at the end of their stories will be returning or have already returned home, though as changed people, who, in Kate Croy's famous words, "shall never be again" as they were. Like Drumble,

Woollett is that other world of commercial, competitive, and aggressive values that the entire story, in its unfolding of character and events and motifs, speaks against. And as with Drumble, we never visit Woollett, a good deal for the same reasons. It is masculine and it is unreal.

The masculinity of Drumble, the domain of that delusional arch-realist, Mr. Smith, is rather easy to see, as is the femininity of Cranford, that society of Amazons. Less easy to see, but nonetheless definitive, may be the masculinity of Woollett and the femininity of Paris. For unlike Drumble, at least what we are given to know of Drumble, Woollett is the domain of a woman. Indeed, thinking of Mamie Pocock and Sarah Pocock and Mrs. Newsome, along with Jim Pocock, who doesn't count, Strether calls Woollett a "society of women" (2:83). And it is. But readers who have thereby assumed that Woollett is a feminine world, the deadly realm of devouring mothers, that dreaded and unnatural kingdom, a matriarchy, have missed the point.[41]

Mrs. Newsome is the invalid mother who defines Woollett society and initiates Strether's mission to bring her son back within its borders. In spite of physical weakness, she is a woman with that unyielding hardness toward a changing reality that was long since characterized, by Scott as well as Gaskell, as the blindness of the masculine heroic perspective. If Strether has too much imagination, Mrs. Newsome has too little. She cannot see that Chad is improved, can never have the "real revelation" (2:202) that Chad's life "has been affected so beautifully" (2:204), because she cannot conceive of change at all. "Wonderful" (1:56) in her firmness but actually too weak to travel to Paris and to appear in the book, Mrs. Newsome stands against the basic premise of *The Ambassadors* and of the entire genre of novels of education: the premise that character can grow, that experience can be a vale of soul-making.

In the very strength of her certainty and her fixity, Mrs. Newsome has heroic stature. She doesn't exist in the novel, except as the projection of Strether's idolatry, because existence is only for those who can come to Paris. But the powerful and dangerous perspective she so exhaustingly embodies makes her a fit opponent for Strether, and of fitting allure. We must not visit Woollett in part because we must not see Mrs. Newsome; feeling her, like Shelley's west wind, only through her effects, those dead leaves of ambassadors she blows across the sea.

But precisely what Mrs. Newsome lacks is the power of creativity or renewal. Along with Mr. Smith and so many of her other predecessors in fiction, Mrs. Newsome is the false prophet of progress. For her the future means expanding the "big brave bouncing business" (1:59), means more money, means progress defined as a most important product. Yet at the same time, in the immortally foolish words of Austen's Marianne Dashwood, Mrs. Newsome believes that "at my time of life opinions are tolerably fixed" (*SS*, 93). James's unmet character follows in the tradition of those creations of Austen and Scott and Gaskell who close themselves to the flow of time. All stand against a future different from the past and thus against the redemptive possibilities of personal history.

Gaskell's Mr. Smith lives again or, to be precise, does not live again, as James's Mrs. Newsome. More extensively, Mrs. Newsome belongs in the long literary tradition of dominating and limited businessmen. She is directly the progeny of the similarly invisible Mr. Smith, but also of Mr. Bradshaw in *Ruth* or that modern doctor, Mr. Gibson in *Wives and Daughters*. More remote ancestors, but perhaps the original members of the clan, might be some of Scott's law-abiding fathers. I think of that community pillar, Reverend Staunton in *The Heart of Midlothian*, along with his alter ego, another wayward son. And recollecting the fate of George Staunton/Geordie Robertson only lengthens the shadow over Chad Newsome's unknown future.

Unlike most of her literary ancestors, Mrs. Newsome is not literally a man. Yet she does embody the masculine heroic tradition. Once again, recollecting *Cranford* can illuminate *The Ambassadors*. Very much in the same way as Cranford's Miss Elizabeth Jenkins with her dead father, Mrs. Newsome has taken up the values, the place, the very identity of both her dead father and her dead husband. The society of women had been established by, been directed by, a man. If Sarah Pocock is effectively nothing more than her mother's ambassador in Paris, Mrs. Newsome is her husband's ambassador in life. And what was he but a different and no better version of her father?

Mrs. Newsome's identity has long been fixed as daughter who passed into wife. We know her only by her husband's name. Her fundamental role in Woollett is to continue her husband's business, and explicitly not as inheritor but as temporary custodian. Mrs. Newsome is entrusted with the cultural imperative of passing on the business to the rightful inheritor, who is, of course, the son. If Woollett were a matriarchy, it would be Sarah Pocock who took her mother's place. The matriarchy of Woollett simply carries on the patriarchy, with the society of women as keepers, as purifiers, of the shrine.[42]

Mrs. Newsome truly is a devouring mother, or reaches out to be. The interplay of traditional masculine and feminine values in the novel defines such a maternal role as what happens when women internalize masculine values, when they live vicariously through their husbands or their fathers. Mrs. Newsome has embraced the heroic tradition of aggression and stern certainty. If that embrace has lent her worldly power, it has also literally withered her, and it has surely rendered her own embrace the more damaging. We share Strether's suspicion that as her husband he would become "out of the question" (2:82). Mrs. Newsome is a portrait of woman as killing other. The novel's insight is that this is what happens to women as well as to men who give up self in the service of the masculine heroic tradition. Mrs. Newsome stands as a kind of latter-day Fergus McIver, with Strether as the apparently passive new hero, engaged in a kind of internal activity his more forceful opponent is incapable of.

In dealing with Sarah Pocock in Paris, Strether faces the representative of a ghost (the absent mother) who herself represents ghosts (the dead husband and father). We can see why Strether feels that, in Sarah, Mrs. Newsome "was reaching him somehow, by the lengthened arm of the spirit" (2:198). We also need to see that her spirit, no more than that of *Cranford*'s Elizabeth Jenkyns, is not her own. Both women, the former early killed off and the latter never introduced, are the haunted remains of their male lineage. Possessed themselves, they in turn would possess the living. Both Miss Matty Jenkyns and Strether speak of looking behind them, as it were, for the unseen presence there. *The Ambassadors* is not such a departure from that most famous of ghost stories that James had written just two summers earlier, *The Turn of the Screw*.

Strether is accurate in saying that in the years before his coming to Paris he had not lived, because he had lived in Drumble, lived a ghostly life as yet another reincarnation of the Newsome spirit, another priest of the shrine. Like Mr. Smith, like the hierarchy of Mamie and Sarah and Mrs. Newsome and Mr. Newsome and ultimately Mrs. Newsome's father, Strether had supported the Drumble version of reality. One reason for Strether's memory of his first trip to Paris so long ago, when he had glimpsed, in the lemon-colored covers of the books, a different version, is to allow for something in this ambassador that distinguishes him from the rest. That something will allow him to become more than an ambassador, to see Paris and to guess for himself. We don't finally know why Strether, any more than Mary Smith, should have been blessed with that possibility of vision.

Perhaps because they are both artists manque, writers of sorts. But we do know that Strether's having that possibility is why he has a story to tell.

When *The Ambassadors* begins, the man from Drumble has as his real business not the world of business, though it is in the service of that world that he has been sent. Strether's true business in Paris is the task of discrimination, of seeing and understanding others and himself, of learning the truth and also learning generosity and love. This is, of course, the classic business of many nineteenth-century British heroines, of Mary Smith but more fulsomely of heroines ranging from Emma Woodhouse, handsome, clever, and rich, to Lucy Snowe, plain and struggling to make her living. Writers' choices of such leading characters had from Austen's work at the beginning of the century represented a commitment to time and to change, and a fascination with the self's relations to private and public history.

This tradition shapes the subject of *The Ambassadors*. The novel offers conscious tribute to its literary inheritance by choosing as its central measure of whether a character has been educated precisely the ability to recognize that a character has been educated. To grow means to see that Chad Newsome has grown. At the same time, James rearranges the usual pattern of gender roles in the work of his major predecessors, for it is Sarah Pocock (representing Mrs. Newsome) who can never develop because she can never bring herself to see Chad's "fortunate development" (11:205), whereas it is Strether who can and does. There seems to me a blindness to the novel's deliberate relation to its heritage as well as a critical legerdemain in arguing that Strether has not been educated, has not improved. For he does see that Chad has developed, sees it as an initial revelation but then slowly expands that revelation as its implications change his entire perspective. We may persuasively claim that Strether does not see all. We may claim that to see is not the same as to live. But we, no less than the characters in the book in their relation to Chad, are called upon to bear witness to a "fortunate development." That development is presented as a growth into femininity.

As if to emphasize the feminine quality of Strether's perceptual journey into truth and life, James from the outset provides him with a female guide. Strether senses that Maria Gostrey "knew things he didn't" (1:11). Though recognizing her deeper knowledge "was a concession that in general he found not easy to make to women, he made it now as good-humouredly as if it lifted a burden" (1:11). Would that we could all, at last, concede the point as cheerfully as Strether. For it does lift a burden, the weight of not hearing, not seeing, not atttending to the kind of truths that women, including women writers, can tell. Maria's knowledge is not about how to run factories or reviews, how to gather and keep public power. She has the "more thoroughly civilized" (1:9) power that all James's fiction honors, to "see into the life of things." And that kind of power, whether it appears in Maria Gostrey or Ralph Touchett, whether in Cranford or in Paris, whether in Salem, Massachusetts, or Lamb House, Rye, is characterized within the fictions in which it appears as feminine.

Strether's receptivity is a response to Maria's own. She appears in the book simply to take care of him, and does not develop any other function. One of the proofs of her intelligence and value, for Strether and for the reader, is her attitude of intense responsiveness, of "looking really interested in the point he had made" (1:15). Able to "have no reserves about everything" (1:6), Maria offers Strether freedom of feeling, of mind, of expression. As he tells her, "the kind of freedom *you* deal in is dear" (1:43). His homely phrase speaks not only of what such freedom can cost, which is "everything," but of how lovingly he values it.

Maria is a woman quite other than the Mrs. Newsome who, thinking him fully one of her creatures, made the fatal judgment of sending him out alone into life. Maria helps Strether to see, undermines his position of being "quite sure" by reminding him that one never does know, "does one?—beforehand. One can only judge on the facts" (1:54). Strether early learns to recognize that he came to Paris "exactly to see for myself" (1:109). But when Strether asks, "[h]aven't we seen enough?," it is Maria who reminds him that "wasn't what you came out for to find out *all*?" (1:189). All turns out to be the sexual—and not only sexual but literally adulterous and psychically incestuous—nature of Chad's and Marie de Vionnet's "virtuous attachment." As Strether does find out, as he sees himself in the presence of new facts less and less met by old reasons, his relation to Maria can never be "quite the same" (2:48). Yet the "extraordinary" difference has, of course, been built in from the beginning, as "the very conditions of perception, the terms of thought" (2:49). Maria's purpose with Strether was precisely to guide him to being able to see for himself without a guide.

Maria's characteristic relation to Strether, as a person using her power to teach him to develop his own power and be able to go off on his own, is entwined with Maria's other effect on Strether, one that marks her as the embodiment of a feminine perspective. The identification as feminine of the whole complex of values captured in the phrase, "really to see," is fixed early in the novel when Strether and Maria dine out in London before the theatre. Maria Gostrey's femininity and its particular definition in this novel as perceptual openness is symbolized by the red velvet ribbon she wears. I think of another red ribbon worn a few years before by Hardy's Tess Durbeyfield, and the contrastingly hopeless fate of the feminine it signified.

Strether is drawn to Maria Gostrey's red ribbon, effected because he is, for the hour anyway, "so given over to uncontrolled perceptions" (1:50). Strether takes that ribbon "as a starting-point for fresh backward, fresh forward, fresh lateral flights" (1:51) of thought. The red ribbon stimulates a long flow of thought, as "all sorts of things" (1:52) come over Strether. This is the scene in which Strether most explicitly contrasts Maria with Mrs. Newsome, who would wear a black dress "never in any degree 'cut down'" (1:50). Mrs. Newsome never wore a red ribbon around her throat and, if she had, "would it ever have served so to carry on and complicate, as he now almost felt, his vision?" (1:50). The red ribbon does serve so because it means the daring of free thought as well as of low necklines, it means a tribute to really seeing that this novel, borrowing from a major literary tradition, defines as feminine. Mrs. Newsome's black high-necked ruff, invoking Queen Elizabeth, is the stiffness, the closure, of a masculine heroic stance.

Still fresh from Woollett, Strether asks himself, "what, certainly, had a man conscious of a man's work in the world to do with red velvet bands?" (1:51). The conventional answer, the regrettable answer, for a man or a woman at a man's work in the world, is nothing. Red ribbons are not serious, at least not in Drumble, they are not the important business of life. One might think of them, at best, as Jim Pocock thinks of Paris, wicked but thrilling. Yet of Maria's band, Strether had "caught himself in the act—frivolous, no doubt, idiotic, and above all unexpected—of liking it" (1:51). Mrs. Newsome, we recall, "doesn't admit surprises" (2:239). For the point is that a man, or a woman, at a woman's work in the world has everything to do with the unexpectedness of red velvet bands.

To see that Maria Gostrey stands as representative of and guide to a way of looking at life traditionally undervalued and characterized as feminine, as opposed to the masculine viewpoint of Woollett borne onward by the Newsome women, does not by itself illuminate Maria's meaning for Strether or his relations to her. Those relations are shiftingly portrayed. Initially, James writes that for a spectator it would not "have been altogether insupposable that . . . they might have been brother and sister" (1:10). Maria herself early tells Strether that "we're beaten brothers in arms" (1:45). Waymarsh and the Newsome ladies have suspected them of being would-be lovers, while generations of critics with similar suspicions, or perhaps simply projections, and encouraged by Maria's own half-spoken proposal, have wanted them to solidify their relation in the union of husband and wife. Maria's image in the middle of the book, of Strether toddling by himself, places them as parent and child. And very near the end the pair are described as "a kindly uncle" and "an intelligent niece" (2:291). Certainly the links between Strether and Maria do change as he outgrows his need to depend on her vision, as he develops his ability to see for himself. But with such a richness of familial ties, the two must surely be some sort of relatives. Perhaps the point of all the proffered variety is that we need not fix their relations in a specific and literal tie.

Yet Maria's red velvet band speaks not only of the daring of a feminine perspective, of the risk and the beauty of being open to experience. In speaking of such things it, like Keats's urn, speaks inevitably of sex as well. But Maria is not a clay vase or a maiden loth. She is a living woman and, moreover, willing and unattached. And her student observer and spiritual relative is an appreciative, deserving, needy, and ultimately unattached man. Why then should James end his novel with these two people who could be lovers forever frozen in their Attic attitudes? Where, even, is Caspar Goodwood's single kiss?

The feminine perspective that stands against the masculine view in *The Ambassadors* is ultimately sexual, as Maria's red ribbon, as the evocative choice of Paris, as the play on a virtuous attachment, and as the climax of Maria and Chad forgetting themselves in a boat all show. But need Strether's slow coming to recognition and affirmation of that sexuality mean literal sexual fulfillment with Maria? To believe so is to end the novel according to the conventions of a love story rather than to the inner logic of its own themes. It is to wish that the character of Maria Gostrey and her relations to Strether had been written differently, to wish that *The Ambassadors* were a different novel. Near the beginning of his time in Paris, Strether, thinking he will soon marry Mrs. Newsome, feels in the position of a father to Chad and asks himself what sort of father he should be. The answer to that question is not a father at all, not in the way both Chad's parents have been. The answer is a kind of mother. And before Strether becomes a feminine parent to Chad, he needs one himself.

Fiction is full of immaculate conceptions, one of the most delightful being Miss Matty Jenkins's unassuming procreation of Mary Smith. Fiction, though not Cranford, is also full of incest. Paris has already provided Chad Newsome with a parent to replace his patriarchal mother. Mme. de Vionnet has guided Chad by developing his sensibility, his intelligence, and his morality far beyond what Woollett would have wanted or could have done. She has opened Chad to feminine values, including the final values of being able to let him go. And she has also educated him sexually. To see the sexuality in Chad's and Marie's virtuous attachment does not mean that Strether should take up incest himself. The very range of definitions of Maria's relations to him, as sister, brother, niece, or mother, mean that sexual love between them would be incestuous. And if James cannot carry the point alone, surely Freud, for all his cultural limitations, has convinced us that one can learn of sexuality from one's mother without actually making love to her, indeed that spiritual health may lie in moving away from such an alluring fruition. Strether's multiple familial ties with Maria connect them to each other in ways that preclude pruning their story down to a literally sexual affair.

To regret that Strether does not choose to stay with Maria is like asking that Mary Smith settle permanently in Cranford. It is like asking that Lucy Snowe be allowed to marry M. Paul, or being glad that Clara Middleton gets to sit in alpine purity with Vernon Whitford, or that Diana Warwick settles into her sunset with Redworth. Such endings when they occur are an emotional relief, the valiant steamer in port at last, and when they don't occur leave a residue of pain. But they are, nonetheless, sentimental. For all her amused wit at Strether's blindness and her own kind intelligence, Maria Gostrey is someone for Strether to outgrow. She does have a minor role, is not developed beyond being a seer, and is given no imaginative life of her own. Whatever Maria's endless engagements outside Strether may be, neither the novel nor Strether, nor the reader, is interested in them at all. Maria's lesser role in the novel is both imaginatively and literally of lesser significance. Her changing yet continuous familial relations to Strether highlight the appropriateness of that lesser role and that union passed by.

When Isabel Archer turns from Caspar Goodwood's kiss we can speak of sexual passion experienced and put aside. But at the end of *The Ambassadors* Maria represents something else. Her language invokes not a paradise for lovers but the Bide-A-Wee home. Maria makes Strether "the offer of exquisite service, of lightened care, for the rest of his days. . . . It built him softly round, it roofed him warmly over, it rested, all so firm, on selection" (22:325–26). Maria does not offer Strether passion. She offers him the reward of a job well done. To accept that offer would be to fall back to the traditional notions of fictional endings and of female characters as rewards. It would be to convert a helper into a helpmate and at the same time to domesticate the eroticism of life. Staying with Maria, with Paris as virtually a final resting place, represents not sexual fulfillment but sexual denial.

But Strether has just begun to live, just begun to see and to feel for himself. He may be an aging intellectual, but unlike many American intellectuals and academic critics Strether is not looking for the aesthetic and physical comforts of an early retirement with a younger woman in a charmingly decorated domestic retreat. The challenges and the stimulation do lie in Woollett, as they lay in Rome for Isabel Archer, which is to say that they lie in the courage to encounter those whose fixed visions generally shape our culture and stand against the unpredictable, changing, and sensual quality of truth. Strether says he renounced Maria because he wants to be right. But both he and she also know that the substantive motive, and the right motive, is that he does not want "consideration and comfort and security" (1:71). He does not want, by Maria's own early definition, to marry so as to be protected "from life" (1:71).

There is a special quality to the familiar Jamesian renunciation as it ends *The Ambassadors*, one that we need not account for as either a failure of the novelist's art or a betrayal of his loyal heroine or a limitation of his hero. Ignoring the continuing play of masculine and feminine values in the novel, readers may see only a charming and lonesome older man turning away from the comforts offered by an agreeable and sensual woman. The wastefulness of the sight may lead them to look for someone to blame. But it would cost Strether more, be more restrictive to his newly flourishing imagination and senses, to stay with Maria than to go. He has learned to see as she sees, which is to say that he has both become responsive to the visions of others and he sees with his own eyes. It would be imaginatively as well as structurally inappropriate to reward that beginning so immediately with the completion signified by the "ancient peace" (2:320) of Maria Gostrey's nest.

Like Chad, Strether has been feminized. The feminization of Lambert Strether is essentially his growth into "the common, unattainable art of taking things as they came" (1:83). But notably unlike Chad, and so many conventional feminine creatures in British fictions, Strether's new openness to experience, his flexibility, do not simply mean that "he's formed to please" (2:325). Strether's education has taken him far enough to be past being taken up by a new guide, as well as past needing or wanting to be taken care of by the old one. This statue, having come to life at last, is not required to pay for its new ability to breathe by becoming the reward of its Pygmalion. Like his older/younger sisters, Gwendolen Harleth and Isabel Archer, Strether chooses, against the closure of a "modest retreat" (2:322), a dark future of which he can say, "I shall see what I can make of it" (2:325).

The Ambassadors, in its fashion, does have a happy ending. We can reach what it celebrates by suspending our familiar critical and social expectations, by freshening our own skills at taking things as they come. *The Ambassadors* is not a love story, not a failed love story. It is not about the growth in understanding and intimacy between a man and a woman as one (or both) also grows in self-understanding. Instead, it is a story of growth into femininity, about a man becoming more like a woman. So the measure of happiness, the reward, is not to marry a heroine but to become one. The poles between Mrs. Newsome and Maria Gostrey delineate Strether's opposing choices. And the identities and differences in the Parisien choice that make up the continuum from Maria Gostrey to Marie de Vionnet also remind us that the feminine, like Paris, is neither a uniform nor an ideal grouping of meanings and values. It will not save us, though it will offer the best hope we have of understanding and creating our world. In James's novel both Woollett and the complex range of choices that make up Paris are all embodied as women because the point is not that one chooses women but that one may choose a vision the novel locates as feminine, a vision that many women have closed their eyes to, a vision that many men do see.

The other men besides Strether in James's Paris provide a range of possible attitudes. Waymarsh is unsusceptible to the vision Paris offers or, more accurately, unable to acknowledge ever being susceptible. Strether is right that "almost any acceptance of Paris might give one's authority away" (1:89). Waymarsh, guarding his authority, betrays not Strether but himself. He, rather than Strether, is the truly repressed character in the book. The opposite of Waymarsh is probably little Bilham. As for Austen's Jane Bennet, for little Bilham a feminine understanding just comes naturally, which is why he is both so charming and so limited, why for all his intuitions he could never understand enough. Chad Newsome, however, has needed to be educated to his fine appreciation of Paris. The difficulty with Chad is that he has needed to be so thoroughly taught. Mme. de Vionnet has made him and, as he says, "I owe her everything" (2:312). Without her, what could he have been, and more important, what more could he become? There may always be another teacher in Chad's development.

Strether has needed a teacher as well. But, and in this he is surely endearing as well as familiar, he has not had the benefit of either a perfect nature or a perfect nurture. Strether's special achievement is that, with a little help, which is, after all, as much as most of us can expect, he has worked at educating himself. Because Strether is a man, one without exceptional blessings or opportunities, one who has followed main-traveled roads, his education into the receptive and thoughtful vision that the voice of Drumble/Woollett usually consigns to loose women and little American artists, will hopefully become harder to distort or ignore.

The female world of Paris—Maria Gostrey, Marie de Vionnet, Miss Barrace—all cheer Strether on to become, as Maria Gostrey says of Bilham, "one of *us*" (1:125). Miss Barrace tells Strether that "we ladies" do, "among us all, want you rather far on" (2:175). "We take such an interest in you. We feel that you'll come up to the scratch" (2:179). Strether, of course, does, justifying the ladies' faith in him as "the hero of the drama" (2:179), with all that role entails.

The Ambassadors fulfills the logic of so many of the novels that preceded it, including some of James's own, by adding an aging American hero as one of the youngest members of that visionary company of heroines in British fiction. By telling a story of how one of them becomes "one of us," and thereby distinguishing gender values from literal sex, James's novel argues once again for the universal value of the perspective that western culture has so often tried to devalue by defining as merely feminine. Readers of James's novel have generally subverted that argument, have held on to biology, by ignoring the novel's masculine–feminine dynamics. But critics, as well as characters, who offer visions that deny the central significance of feminine values in interpreting our literary inheritance and prophesying our cultural future, who refuse to become "one of us," may only meet the fate of Waymarsh, of becoming insignificant themselves.

Notes

Chapter 1

1. Nancy K. Miller, *The Heroine's Text: Readings in the French and English Novel, 1722–1782* (New York: Columbia University Press, 1980); and Roy Roussel, *The Conversation of the Sexes* (New York: Oxford University Press, 1986).

2. Lee Edwards, *Psyche as Hero: Female Heroism and Fictional Form* (Middletown, Conn.: Wesleyan University Press, 1984).

3. Tony Tanner, *Adultery in the Novel: Contract and Transgression* (Baltimore: The John Hopkins University Press, 1979); John Lucas, *The Literature of Change: Studies in the Nineteenth-Century Novel*, 2nd ed. (New York: Barnes and Noble, 1980); and Jenni Calder, *Women and Marriage in Victorian Fiction* (New York: Oxford University Press, 1976).

4. Rachel M. Brownstein, *Becoming a Heroine: Reading About Women in Novels* (1982; reprint New York: Penguin, 1984).

5. Carolyn G. Heilbrun, *Toward A Recognition of Androgyny* (1973; reprint New York: Harper and Row, 1974).

6. James, I would say, does less well at creating a hero than a heroine until he conceives of the hero in much the same ways as he had been conceiving of the heroines.

7. Paul Smith, *Discerning the Subject* (Minneapolis: University of Minnesota Press, 1988), xxix, xxxi. I am indebted to this useful book for much of the following discussion.

8. Andreas Huyssen, "Mapping the Postmodern," *New German Critique* 33 (Fall 1984):44.

9. Jane Flax, "Postmodernism and Gender Relations in Feminist Theory," *Signs* 12, 4 (Summer 1987):627.

10. Smith, *Discerning the Subject*, 158; Nancy K. Miller, "Changing the Subject," *Feminist Studies/Critical Studies*, ed. Teresa de Lauretis (Bloomington: Indiana University Press, 1986), 102–20.

11. For an overview of feminist criticism in the last decade, see Elaine Showalter's "Introduction: The Feminist Critical Revolution," in *The New Feminist Criticism: Essays on Women, Literature and Theory*, ed. Elaine Showalter (New York: Pantheon Books, 1985), 3-17.

12. Some representative books would be Hazel Mews, *Frail Vessels: Women's Role in Women's Novels from Fanny Burney to George Eliot* (London: Athlone Press, 1969); Francoise Bosch, *Relative Creatures: Victorian Women in Society and the Novel*

(New York: Schocken, 1974); and even Leslie Fiedler's discussion of Clarissa Harlowe and the gothic in *Love and Death in the American Novel*, 2nd ed. (New York: Delta, 1967). An important example using American fiction is some of the sections of Judith Fetterley, *The Resisting Reader: A Feminist Approach to American Fiction* (Bloomington: Indiana University Press, 1978).

13. I am indebted for this observation to Barbara Page, Professor of English and currently Director of the Women's Studies Program at Vassar College.

14. Some familiar studies are Sandra M. Gilbert and Susan Gubar, *The Madwoman in the Attic: The Woman Writer and the Nineteenth-Century Literary Imagination* (New Haven: Yale University Press, 1979); Elaine Showalter, *A Literature of their Own: British Women Novelists from Brontë to Lessing* (Princeton: Princeton University Press, 1977); Ellen Moers, *Literary Women: The Great Writers* (New York: Anchor Books, 1977); Patricia Meyer Spacks, *The Female Imagination* (1972; reprint New York: Avon, 1976); Pauline Nestor, *Female Friendships and Communities: Charlotte Brontë, George Eliot, Elizabeth Gaskell* (Oxford: Clarendon Press, 1985); and Margaret Homans, *Bearing the Word: Language and Female Experience in Nineteenth-Century Women's Writing* (Chicago: University of Chicago Press, 1986).

15. Miller, "Changing the Subject," 106.

16. An analogous and, I would argue, significantly related point has recently been made by Evelyn Fox Keller and Helene Moglen in their article, "Competition and Feminism: Conflicts for Academic Women," *Signs* 12 (Spring 1987):511. They conclude that "while the romance of women's culture has been extremely helpful in baring some of the roots of masculinist liberal capitalism, its own mythology of difference and separatism has worked to obstruct the recognition of fundamental interconnection that is essential to dialogic engagement."

17. *The George Eliot Letters*, ed. Gordon S. Haight (New Haven: Yale University Press, 1954), 5:170, 175.

18. There are several references indicating Gaskell's familiarity with Scott's novels in *The Letters of Mrs. Gaskell*, ed. J. A. V. Chapple and Arthur Pollard (Manchester: Manchester University Press, 1966).

19. Nancy Armstrong, "The Rise of Feminine Authority in the Novel," *Novel* 15, 2 (Winter 1982):138.

20. This choice comes partly from the fact that Austen was the novelist whose work first so completely filled my imagination and absorbed my critical interest. It is a given of Austen studies that there isn't much biographical information, and there probably never will be. A new source was added in 1983, George Tucker's *A Goodly Heritage: A History of Jane Austen's Family* (Manchester: Carcanet New Press, 1983), but it was not about Austen herself. Austen lovers learn to accept the absence of information. We also learn to suspect those would-be biographers who project a life, or even a state of mind, from the work, and to feel acutely the arbitrariness of these projections, since they so seldom agree with our own. A psychologically oriented work of criticism like Gilbert and Gubar's *The Madwoman in the Attic* is much stronger on Charlotte Brontë's fiction than on Austen's. Discussions of the former can rely on, and can partly be evaluated by, much more information outside the texts.

21. Lillian Robinson, "Treason Our Text: Feminist Challenges to the Literary Canon," in *The New Feminist Criticism*, 116. A similar concern, but about the study of works of theory rather than literature, may motivate Alice Jardine's new study of modern French male (and, briefly, female) writings in theory, *Gynesis: Configurations of Woman and Modernity* (Ithaca: Cornell University Press, 1985).

22. Armstrong, "The Rise of Feminine Authority in the Novel," 138.

23. For a helpful discussion of critical directions, see John Kucich, "Narrative Theory as History: A Review of Problems in Victorian Fiction studies," *Victorian Studies* 28, 4 (Summer 1985):657–75.

24. Judith Lowder Newton pointed out in 1981 that one problem with feminist studies that use this pattern of doubleness is that they write as if the pattern were "unchanging or transhistorical." *Women, Power, and Subversion: Social Strategies in British Fiction, 1778–1860* (Athens: University of Georgia Press, 1981), 12. That charge has been elaborated in Kucich's "Narrative Theory as History."

25. This is the critical problem with Mary Poovey's fine study, *The Proper Lady and the Woman Writer: Ideology as Style in the Works of Mary Wollstonecraft, Mary Shelley, and Jane Austen* (Chicago: University of Chicago Press, 1984).

26. There are, certainly, studies that do attend to the public impact of women's novels. See, for example, Joseph A. Kestner, *Protest and Reform: The British Social Narrative by Women, 1827–1867* (Madison: University of Wisconsin Press, 1985). See also Nancy Armstrong's excellent study, *Desire and Domestic Fiction: A Political History of the Novel* (New York: Oxford University Press, 1987). Another kind of writing, Victorian women's travel writings, also suggests the public power of women's voices. See my "Introduction to Victorian Women's Travel Writings About Southeast Asia." *Genre* 20 (Summer 1987):189–207.

27. Tracing a particular historical example of the political power of fiction is central to the argument of Armstrong's *Desire and Domestic Fiction*.

28. Heilbrun, *Toward a Recognition of Androgyny*, 50.

29. Ibid., 91.

30. Carolyn Heilbrun and Catharine Stimpson, "Theories of Feminist Criticism: A Dialogue," *Feminist Literary Criticism: Explorations in Theory*, ed. Josephine Donovan (Lexington: University Press of Kentucky, 1975), 65.

31. It should be clear that I mean something quite different by the terms *feminine* and *feminize* than does Ann Douglas in her fascinating study, *The Feminization of American Culture*, (1977; reprint New York: Avon, 1978). She uses the term in its negative connotation as it evolved in American culture, as something sentimental and weak.

32. I am indebted here to Catharine Stimpson for her categorizing of critics as minimalists and maximalists depending on the extent to which they believe there are fundamental sex differences, as well as for her listing of four kinds of maximalists depending on what they see as causing sex differences. Clearly, I am in the minimalist group. See "Our 'Wild Patience': Our Energetic Deeds, Our Energizing Future. An Overview of Women's Studies Today," a paper delivered at Vassar College, May 1986.

33. Flax, "Postmodern and Gender Relations," 637.

34. Miller, *The Heroine's Text*, x.

35. Perhaps not never, when I recall the recent shout of praise from male critics for the profound philosophic content and great aesthetic genius of what looks from my feminist perspective to be a massive sex fantasy, an enormously elongated hymn to the power of the penis: *Gravity's Rainbow*.

36. See, for example, Martin Battestin's "Introduction" to the Riverside edition of *Joseph Andrews* (Boston: Houghton Mifflin, 1961); Ian Watt on Richardson and Fielding, in *The Rise of the Novel: Studies in Defoe, Richardson and Fielding* (Berkeley: University of California Press, 1967); and Walter Allen, *The English Novel: A Short Critical History* (New York: Dutton, 1954).

37. Ellen Moers is refreshing in her view that Richardson's preference for the company of intelligent women is "another proof of the good sense that characterizes everything else we know about the man." *Literary Women: The Great Writers* (New York: Anchor Books, 1977), 175. I can only agree.

38. See Leon Edel's classic discussion of "An Obscure Hurt," in *The Life of Henry James* (New York: J. B. Lippincott Co., 1953), 1:167–83.

39. The links between some nineteenth-century heroines, particularly those of Austen, Eliot, and James, have often been mentioned. See, among many, George Levine, *The Realistic Imagination: English Fiction from Frankenstein to Lady Chatterley* (Chicago: University of Chicago Press, 1981), 78; and Normal Page, "The Great Tradition Revisited," in *Jane Austen's Achievement* (New York: Barnes and Nobel, 1987), 44–63.

40. Gillian Beer, *Darwin's Plots* (London: Routledge and Kegan, Paul, 1983).

41. Ibid., 10.

42. This point seems, to me at least, to be very close to what Heilbrun, in *Toward a Recognition of Androgyny*, means by adnrogyny, if not generally then specifically in the nineteenth-century novels she discusses.

43. *The Novels of Jane Austen*, ed. R. W. Chapman, 3rd ed. (Oxford: Oxford University Press, 1933), *Persuasion*, 5. All further references to Jane Austen's works are to the volumes in this edition.

44. *Wives and Daughters*, in *The Works of Mrs. Gaskell* (London: Smith, Elder and Co., 1906), 154.

Chapter 2

1. For a useful discussion of the kinds of fiction being written at the beginning of the nineteenth century, see Neal Frank Doubleday, *Variety of Attempt: British and American Fiction in the Early Nineteenth Century* (Lincoln: University of Nebraska Press, 1976).

2. For a comprehensive study of Edgeworth and her writings, see Marilyn Butler, *Maria Edgeworth: A Literary Biography* (Oxford: Clarendon Press, 1972).

3. Edgeworth also put male leads in the observer role, such as Lord Colambre in *The Absentee*. Her most famous observer, and a long way from a conventional hero, is Thady Quirk in *Castle Rackrent*.

4. There have been many fine studies of Austen's use of eighteenth-century literary conventions. Among the first, see Henrietta Ten Harmsel, *Jane Austen: A Study in Fictional Conventions* (The Hague: Mouton & Co., 1964), and Frank Bradbrook, *Jane Austen and Her Predecessors* (Cambridge: Cambridge University Press, 1966). For a recent, and excellent work, see Judith Wilt, *Ghosts of the Gothic: Austen, Eliot, & Lawrence* (Princeton: Princeton University Press, 1980).

5. They may seem to do so in *Mansfield Park*, but Fanny Price slowly moves to a better level of seeing and feeling than her childhood mentor. She loves Edmund Bertram, but she learns to see his mistakes and his weaknesses, as he learns to recognize her insights and strength.

6. *The Portrait of a Lady*, Norton Critical Edition, ed. Robert D. Bamberg (New York: W. W. Norton and Company, 1975), 175. All further references to the novel are to this edition.

7. Hardy's vision is at least as dark.

8. Graham Greene, *Collected Essays*, reprinted in the Norton Critical Edition of *The Portrait of a Lady*, 671.

9. Tony Tanner, "The Fearful Self: Henry James's *The Portrait of a Lady*," *Critical Quarterly* 6 (Autumn, 1965):205–19; and William Gass, "The High Brutality of Good Intentions," *Accent* 18 (Winter, 1958), reprinted in the Norton Critical Edition of *Portrait*, 707.

10. Gass, "The High Brutality of Good Intentions," 707.

11. This may be, as Judith Lowder Newton argues, a means of undercutting our "sense of male control." *Women Power, and Subversion: Social Strategies in British Fiction, 1778–1860*. (Athens: University of Georgia Press, 1981), 67. I would agree. I would also say that the point is not so much to discredit male power and men as it is to humanize men by replacing conventional heroic behavior with feminine heroic behavior for women and men.

12. The wise cynic who doesn't understand the real lessons of life will reappear in Austen's fiction. Henry Tilney's most notable heirs are probably Mr. Bennet and Mary Crawford, neither of whom, unlike Henry, learn.

13. Compare, for example Ian Watt's attitude to Catherine's being educated in "the norms of the mature, rational" male world, in "Serious Reflections on *The Rise of the Novel*," *Novel: A Forum on Fiction* 1 (1968):218, with Judith Wilt's description of Henry Tilney as a "threatening" lover with a formidable "psychological advantage over his heroine," in *Ghosts of the Gothic*, 146, or with Sandra Gilbert and Susan Gubar's view of the novel as a parody because Austen herself can only rebel in hidden ways against "an inherited literary structure that idealizes feminine submission," in *The Madwoman in the Attic: The Woman Writer and the Nineteenth-Century Literary Imagination* (New Haven: Yale University Press, 1979), 144. I am suggesting that Austen's "rebellion" is not at all hidden. She begins by mocking the old structures, but her real achievement is to invent new ones.

14. This point was made in 1937, in R. P. Utter's and G. B. Needham's useful study, *Pamela's Daughters* (New York: Macmillan). Ian Watt also discusses this "new sexual ideology" in *The Rise of the Novel: Studies in Defoe, Richardson and Fielding* (Berkeley: University of California Press, 1967), 161. It is difficult to say when in the eighteenth century this vision of the heroine as vulnerable virgin arose. Certainly, it became highly popular with *Pamela*, but fiction before Richardson also used this convention.

15. Nancy K. Miller, *The Heroine's Text: Readings in the French and English Novel, 1722–1782* (New York: Columbia University Press, 1980), xi.

16. The constancy of sex in eighteenth-century novels has been noted by many readers, some of whom have guided my own reading in the field. See J. M. S. Tompkins, *The Popular Novel in England 1770–1800* (Lincoln: University of Nebraska Press, 1961); John J. Richetti, *Popular Fiction Before Richardson: Narrative Patterns 1700–1739* (Oxford: Clarendon Press, 1969); Ruth Perry, *Women, Letters and the Novel* (New York: AMS Press, 1980); and Jerry C. Beasley, *Novels of the 1740s* (Athens: University of Georgia Press, 1982).

17. For an excellent bibliography, as well as helpful discussions of seventeenth-century novels, see Paul Salzman, *English Prose Fiction 1558–1700: A Critical History* (Oxford: Clarendon Press, 1985).

18. For an excellent discussion of the gothic, including its characteristic heroines, see William Patrick Day, *In the Circles of Fear and Desire: A Study of Gothic Fantasy* (Chicago: University of Chicago Press, 1985).

19. Poovey, discussing the connections between sentimental novels and the sexual definitions of women offered by bourgeois ideology, argues eloquently that "Wollstonecraft was repeatedly crippled by this collusion between sexuality and sentimentality." That crippling effect is certainly visible in *Maria.* Mary Poovey, *The Proper Lady and the Woman Writer: Ideology as Style in the Works of Mary Wollstonecraft, Mary Shelley, and Jane Austen* (Chicago: University of Chicago Press, 1984), 110.

20. Poovey, *The Proper Lady*, 161.

21. See particularly her chapter, "Romantic Love and Sexual Fantasy in Epistolary Fiction," in *Women, Letters, and the Novel*, 137–67.

22. Poovey, *The Proper Lady*, 19.

23. See Marlene Legates's discussion of the myth of the ideal woman and the aggressive male in "The Cult of Womanhood in Eighteenth-Century Thought," *Eighteenth-Century Studies* 10 (Fall 1976):21–39.

24. Newton, *Women, Power, and Subversion*, 23.

25. Patricia Meyer Spacks, "Female Changelessness: Or, What Do Women Want?," *Studies in the Novel* 19, 3 (Fall 1986):282.

26. Tompkins, *The Popular Novel in England*, 135.

27. On the connections between social and literary attitudes to eighteenth-century fallen women, see the excellent article by Susan Staves, "British Seduced Maidens, *Eighteenth-Century Studies* 14 (1980–81):109–34.

28. For excellent readings see Margaret Doody, *A Natural Passion: A Study of the Novels of Samuel Richardson* (Oxford: Clarendon Press, 1974); Leo Braudy, "Penetration and Impenetrability in *Clarissa*," *New Approaches to Eighteenth-Century Literature*, ed. Phillip Harth (New York: Columbia University Press, 1974); and Terry Eagleton, *The Rape of Clarissa: Writing, Sexuality and Class Struggle in Samuel Richardson* (Oxford: Basil Blackwell, 1982).

29. William Warner, *Reading Clarissa: The Struggles of Interpretation* (New Haven: Yale University Press, 1979) and Terry Castle, *Clarissa's Ciphers: Meaning and Disruption in Richardson's "Clarissa"* (Ithaca: Cornell University Press, 1982). Warner's reading, as Castle so eloquently points out, contradicts its own deconstructive position by its apparently unrecognized patriarchal bias against Clarissa and for Lovelace.

30. One of the more deviously, and charmingly, phrased of these claims against Austen is Angus Wilson's resolution of the apparent contradiction of this passionless spinster liking Richardson's fiction. What she liked, we are told, was "Richardson's Grandisonian care for minutiae and mistrust of worldliness; while foreigners preferred Clarissa, Lovelace, and passion." Quoted by Marvin Mudrick, amid his own appealing and convincing argument for the passion and the sexuality in Austen's fiction, in "Jane Austen's Drawing-Room," *Jane Austen Bicentenary Essays*, ed. John Halperin (Cambridge: Cambridge University Press, 1975), 248.

31. The portrait of Austen as a detached rationalist has reigned for so long in traditional readings of her work that it has the status of a truism. It seems hardly fair to give selective citations. Yet I suppose I could say that one of the more extreme versions of what virtually everyone was claiming, that Austen chose to be antipassion, was Marvin Mudrick's *Jane Austen: Irony as Defense and Discovery* (1952; reprint Berkeley: University of California Press, 1968). At the same time, Mudrick's "Jane Austen's Drawing-Room," published only seven years later, is one of the very few essays effectively arguing for Austen's passion, certainly in *Pride and Prejudice* and, most fully, in *Persuasion.*

32. A. Walton Litz has argued that in *Mansfield Park* Austen turns away from,

indeed, rejects, the liberal tone and ideas of *Pride and Prejudice*. *Jane Austen: A Study of Her Artistic Development* (New York: Oxford University Press, 1965), 112–31.

33. Quoted by John Halperin, "Introduction: Jane Austen's Nineteenth-Century Critics: Walter Scott to Henry James," *Jane Austen Bicentenary Essays*, 8.

34. Quoted by Marvin Mudrick in "Jane Austen's Drawing-Room," in *Bicentenary Essays*, 252. Moore's answer seems to be that the burning human heart went to France and Russia.

35. Susan Kneedler, "Feminist Hope in the Novels of Jane Austen," unpublished dissertation, May 1987, University of Southern California, 105.

36. Mary Chandler, "'A Pair of Fine Eyes': Jane Austen's Treatment of Sex," *Studies in the Novel* 7 (Spring 1975):94.

37. In this sense Mary Chandler is right that Austen's novels are "very much about sex," right in part because she supports her claims by discussing such evocative activities in the novels as dancing and walking. "'A Pair of Fine Eyes': Jane Austen's Treatment of Sex," 88. Perhaps the finest discussion of dancing in Austen's fiction is Stuart Tave's, in *Some Words of Jane Austen* (Chicago: University of Chicago Press, 1973).

38. This was probably started by Virginia Woolf, who suggested that in *Persuasion* Austen "is beginning to discover that the world is larger, more mysterious, and more romantic than she had supposed." *The Common Reader* (1925; reprint New York: Harcourt, Brace and World, 1953), 147. But Woolf, in her defense, could not have known the use critics would make of that remark. And *Persuasion* does offer some passionately suggestive moments of proximity (at least in Anne Elliot's mind), as when Captain Wentworth lifts the tired Anne into his sister's buggy or when he lifts her nephew off her back.

39. I am indebted throughout this discussion to Rich's classic article, "Compulsory Heterosexuality and Lesbian Existence," *The Signs Reader: Women, Gender and Scholarship*, ed. Elizabeth Abel and Emily K. Abel (Chicago: University of Chicago Press, 1983), 139–68.

40. There are many critics, the masculine traditionalists long before some feminists, who see Marianne as a voice of freedom and feeling who is silenced by her socially conservative author. See, for example, Mudrick, *Irony as Defense and Discovery*, 75, or Tony Tanner's "Introduction," in *Sense and Sensibility* (Baltimore: Penguin, 1969).

41. See my discussion of Charlotte Lucas in *In The Meantime: Character and Perception in Jane Austen's Fiction* (Chicago: University of Chicago Press, 1980), 92–97.

42. This explains the well-recognized point that Austen does not provide much physical description of her heroines. When she does provide descriptions, as with Harriet Smith and Jane Fairfax, these function as ways characters who do rely on fixed conventions can misjudge others. Emma makes Harriet the ingenue lead in her fantasies a good deal because of Harriet's blonde blue-eyed looks, while the stories of Jane's shady love for her friend's husband come partly from her dark beauty.

43. It shocks me that many feminist readers see Marianne's change from Willoughby to Brandon as a giving up of freedom or a reduction of herself. Willoughby, after all, is a silly shallow man with weak principles and a pretty face. He's a cliché of romantic convention. Colonel Brandon, in spite of his stolid loyalty, in spite of his flannel waistcoat and taste for sentimental convention, shows the inner strength to be true to his principles and to his affections. Which of these characters, as a husband and friend, would be more willing to see and to honor the needs and desires of a woman

independently of his own? Which of them is capable of imagining that someone else even has an inner life independent of his own? And which of the two would struggle harder to honor that separateness?

44. See Joseph M. Duffy, Jr., "Moral Integrity and Moral Anarchy in *Mansfield Park*," *English Literary History* 23 (1956):71–91. A contemporary version of this argument is found in Jane McDonnell, "'A Little Spirit of Independence': Sexual Politics and the Bildungsroman in *Mansfield Park*," *Novel: A Forum on Fiction* 17 (Spring 1984):212.

45. Thus Mary Poovey, in a usually complex reading of Austen's fiction, in discussing *Mansfield Park* invokes the tired dichotomy traditionally called upon to interpret Austen's work. She discusses the book as a contest, unadmitted by it, between feelings and principles, with Austen, of course, on the side of principles. Within this opposition, Poovey concludes that "Austen cannot acknowledge that the society she is so anxious to defend can either accommodate Maria's passion or punish it, remorselessly, forever." *The Proper Lady*, 221.

46. Lionel Trilling, in his superb but mistaken reading of *Mansfield Park* as "antivital," insightfully remarked of Maria and Henry's affair that "it is not sexuality that is being condemned, but precisely that form of asexuality that incurred D. H. Lawrence's greatest scorn—that is, sexuality as a game, or as a drama, sexuality as an expression of mere will or mere personality, as a sign of power, or prestige, or autonomy: as, in short, an impersonation and an insincerity." "*Mansfield Park*," *The Opposing Self* (New York: Viking Press, Inc., 1955), 220–21.

47. Avrom Fleishman made a similar point about *Mansfield Park*. He noted that "Jane Austen sees her characters as free, and this makes her hate them momentarily when they willfully neglect their possibilities of self-realization." *A Reading of Mansfield Park: An Essay in Critical Synthesis* (Baltimore: Johns Hopkins Press, 1967), 55.

48. The difference I am highlighting between the two works have a great deal to do with the fact that one is written by an Englishwoman, the other by an American.

49. Kneedler, "Feminist Hope in the Novels of Jane Austen," 105.

50. See my own discussion of how Mary Crawford, contra Gilbert's and Gubar's sense of her as an "unrepentant, imaginative, and assertive girl" . . . who refuses " to submit to the categories of her culture," (*The Madwoman in the Attic*, 168) is trapped by the conventions of her culture and fails to grow out of them (*In the Meantime*, 134–48). Janet Todd offers yet another variation of that too familiar, and masculine, critical dualism about freedom and convention in Austen's fiction, when she defines Mary Crawford as "the subversive female threat" and Fanny Price as "the patriarchal woman." *Women's Friendship in Literature* (New York: Columbia University Press, 1980), 271.

51. Kneedler, "Feminist Hope in the Novels of Jane Austen," 109. Kneedler's discussion is particularly valuable in its analysis of how, in the novel, "new emblems of sexuality are created which serve to remove the violence from ideas of the erotic," (105). Whereas I have focused more on the kind of sexuality that is not in Austen's fiction, Kneedler focuses more on the kind that is.

52. See Marianne Hirsh's excellent discussion of the links between *The Mill on the Floss* and *The Awakening* as female variations on the *kunstlerroman*, in "Spiritual Bildung: The Beautiful Soul as Paradigm," *The Voyage in: Fictions of Female Development*, eds. Elizabeth Abel, Marianne Hirsh, and Elizabeth Langland (Hanover: University Press of New England, 1983).

53. But I can think of one who has believed at least as much in women's power and worth, and that is Richardson.

54. Wayne Booth, *The Rhetoric of Fiction* (Chicago: University of Chicago Press, 1961), 245.

55. For an extreme version see Leroy W. Smith's chapter, "*Emma*: The Flight from Womanhood," in *Jane Austen and the Drama of Woman* (New York: St. Martin's Press, 1983), 129–55.

56. For one among many traditional views, see A. Walton Litz, *Jane Austen: A Study of Her Artistic Development* (New York: Oxford University Press, 1965), 132–49. A similar interpretation appears even in studies more sensitive to the issue of gender. Reading Mr. Knightley as the wise guide appears in Judith Wilt's generally superb discussion of the relations of Austen's work to its gothic predecessors, *Ghosts of the Gothic*, 154. And Gilbert and Gubar, in *The Madwoman in the Attic*, argue that Austen punishes Emma by initiating her into the female "secondary role of service and silence," 160.

57. See P. J. M. Scott, *Jane Austen: A Reassessment* (New York: Barnes and Noble Books, 1983).

58. Henry James, *The Ambassadors* (New York: Charles Scribner's Sons, 1909), 172.

59. "Introduction," *Emma* (Boston: Houghton Mifflin, 1957) x, xvii.

60. One result is that some later readers have provided their own framework for Trilling's remarks, finding them examples of Trilling's own critical sexism. Ellen Moers is hardly alone in criticizing what she called "the disgrace of that paragraph." *Literary Women* (Garden City: Anchor Books, 1977), 241. And Carolyn Heilbrun has offered a chilling portrait of Trilling as her professor in *Reinventing Womanhood* (New York: W. W. Norton and Company, 1979), 125–37. Whatever Trilling's own attitudes toward women, in fiction or not, his comments on Emma seem to me both accurate in terms of the history of the novel before Austen and impressively conscious of the problematic depiction of women in fiction.

61. For an excellent reading of *Frankenstein* as a drama about birth, see Moers' now classic discussion in *Literary Women*, 137–51.

62. Many critics point to the convergence of the artist and the feminine in literature by the end of the nineteenth century. See Tony Tanner's discussion of Isabel Archer's education as "becoming an artist," in "The Fearful Self: Henry James's *The Portrait of a Lady*," *Critical Quarterly* 7 (Autumn 1965); or Susan Gubar, "The Birth of the Artist as Heroine: (Re)production, the *Kunstlerroman* Tradition, and the Fiction of Katherine Mansfield," *The Representation of Women in Fiction*, eds. Carolyn G. Heilbrun and Margaret R. Higonnet (Baltimore: Johns Hopkins University Press, 1983), 19–59. And Nancy K. Miller suggests that the first artist heroine is Mme. de Stael's Corinne, in *The Heroine's Text*, 156.

Chapter 3

1. Unsigned review (January 1838) and "Some Words About Sir Walter Scott" (September 1871), quoted in *Scott: The Critical Heritage*, ed. John O. Hayden (New York: Barnes and Noble, 1970), 371, 458.

2. Unsigned review (April 1858), Hayden (ed.), *The Critical Heritage*, 414, 408.

3. Georg Lukacs, *The Historical Novel*, trans. Hannah and Stanley Mitchell (London: Merton Press, 1962); David Daiches, "Scott's Achievement as a Novelist," *Nineteenth-Century Fiction* 6 (1951):81–95, 153–173; Francis R. Hart, *Scott's Novels: The Plotting of Historic Survival* (Charlottesville: University of Virginia Press, 1966); Avrom Fleishman, *The English Historical Novel: Walter Scott to Virginia Woolf* (Baltimore: Johns Hopkins Press, 1971); and David Brown, *Walter Scott and the Historical Imagination* (London: Routledge and Kegan Paul, 1979).

4. *Life on the Mississippi: The Complete Travel Books of Mark Twain*, ed. Charles Neider (Garden City: Doubleday and Co., 1967) 2:576.

5. John G. Lockhart, *Memoirs of the Life of Sir Walter Scott, Bart* (New York: Charles Francis, 1841) 7:29.

6. Fleishman, *The English Historical Novel*, 100.

7. Judith Wilt, in a superb recent book, *Secret Leaves: The Novels of Walter Scott* (Chicago: University of Chicago Press, 1985), suggests that *The Heart of Midlothian* has been seen as special because of the "consoling presence at its center of a quartet of women," 116. I hope so.

8. *Waverley Novels* (Edinburgh: Adam and Charles Black, 1871) 1:423. In the absence of a standard text, all further references to Scott's novels are to this edition.

9. Ernest Baker, *The History of the English Novel: Edgeworth, Austen, Scott* (London: H. V. and G. Witherby, 1942), 147.

10. Alexander Welsh, *The Hero of the Waverley Novels* (New Haven: Yale University Press, 1963); Marion Cusac, *Narrative Structure in the Novels of Sir Walter Scott* (The Hague: Mouton, 1969).

11. George Levine, *The Realistic Imagination: English Fiction from Frankenstein to Lady Chatterley* (Chicago: University of Chicago Press, 1981), 84.

12. Ibid., 103.

13. This is a common assumption, appearing in Daiches, Hart, Levine, and others. A strong example is Robert C. Gordon, *Under Which King: A Study of the Scottish Waverley Novels* (Edinburgh: Oliver and Boyd, 1969).

14. Fleishman, *The English Historical Novel*, 39.

15. Ibid., 43.

16. "Scott's Redgauntlet," *From Jane Austen to Joseph Conrad*, eds. Robert C. Rathburn and Martin Steinmann, Jr. (Minneapolis: University of Minnesota Press, 1958), 46; Welsh, *The Hero of the Waverley Novels*, 68.

17. *The Works of Joseph Conrad* (London: William Heinemann, 1921), 12:163–64.

18. Scott has encouraged a simplistic approach, in such comments as his famous remark that "[t]he tale of Waverley was put together with so little care, that I cannot boast of having sketched any distinct plan of the work," in the 1829 "General Preface," *Waverley* (London: Archibald Constable, 1895). For an excellent discussion of the prefaces, see "Conclusion, with Prefaces" in Wilt, *Secret Leaves*.

19. I am probably most indebted to Albert G. Guerard, *Conrad the Novelist* (Cambridge: Harvard University Press, 1958) and Ian Watt, *Conrad in the Nineteenth Century* (Berkeley: University of California Press, 1979).

20. Levine, *The Realistic Imagination*, 114.

21. Graham McMaster, *Scott and Society* (Cambridge: Press Syndicate of the University of Cambridge, 1981), 149.

22. Wilt, *Secret Leaves*, 117.

23. Myra Jehlen, "Archimedes and the Paradox of Feminist Criticism," *Signs* 6 (1981):596.

24. See, for example, Margaret Doody, *A Natural Passion: A Study of the Novels of Samuel Richardson* (Oxford: Clarendon Press, 1974); Leo Braudy, "Penetration and Impenetrability in *Clarissa*," *New Approaches to Eighteenth-Century Literature*, ed. Phillip Harth (New York: Columbia University Press, 1974); Ramona Denton, "Anna Howe and Richardson's Ambivalent Artistry," *Philological Quarterly* 58 (1979):53–62; and Susan Staves, "British Seduced Maidens," *Eighteenth-Century Studies* 14 (1980–81):109–34.

25. Lukacs, *The Historical Novel*, 52.

26. Daiches, "Introduction," *The Heart of Midlothian* (New York: Rinehart, 1948), viii; Fleishman, *The English Historical Novel*, 79.

27. Wilt does discuss gender in *The Heart of Midlothian*, in *Secret Leaves*. She offers interpretations tantalizingly similar to (Jeanie seems "Edward Waverley in drag," 134), and finally different from, my own.

28. Welsh, *The Hero of the Waverley Novels*, 142–47.

29. Hart, *Scott's Novels*, 199.

30. Harry E. Shaw, in *The Forms of Historical Fiction: Sir Walter Scott and His Successors* (Ithaca: Cornell University Press, 1983), does place Jeanie against George Staunton, whom Shaw describes as historically "ineffectual," 238.

31. I agree with Shaw that *The Heart of Midlothian* is not a bildungsroman, in *The Forms of Historical Fiction*, 229. It is the readers, and not Jeanie, who may be educated by Jeanie's visit to that parsonage.

32. Welsh, *The Hero of the Waverley Novels*, 60–61.

33. Samuel Pickering, Jr., *The Moral Tradition in English Fiction, 1785–1850* (Hanover, New Hampshire: University Press of New England, 1976), 97. A similar point is implied by George Levine's chapter title, "Scott and the Death of the Hero," in *The Realistic Imagination*.

34. Lukacs, *The Historical Novel*, 35.

Chapter 4

1. George Levine, *The Realistic Imagination: English Fiction from Frankenstein to Lady Chatterley* (Chicago: University of Chicago Press, 1981), 4.

2. Ibid., 4.

3. See, for example, Kathleen Tillotson's important discussion of *Mary Barton* in *Novels of the Eighteen-Forties* (London: Oxford University Press, 1961): Edgar Wright's *Mrs. Gaskell: The Basis for Reassessment* (London: Oxford University Press, 1965); Arthur Pollard's classic appreciation, *Mrs. Gaskell: Novelist and Biographer* (Cambridge: Harvard University Press, 1966); and Margaret Ganz's *Elizabeth Gaskell: The Artist in Conflict* (New York: Twayne Publishers, 1969).

4. David Cecil commented that in a world of Victorian eagles "we have only to look at a portrait of Mrs. Gaskell, soft-eyed, beneath her charming veil, to see that she was a dove." *Early Victorian Novelists* (London: Constable and Co., 1935), 197–98. I too am arguing that Gaskell was a dove, but the implications are different. As Martin Dodsworth pointed out about *Cranford*, the "serious concerns of the book have been neglected for a belle-lettristic study of incidental detail." In "Women Without Men at Cranford," *Essays In Criticism* 8 (1963), 133.

5. Carolyn Heilbrun, *Toward a Recognition of Androgyny* (1973; reprint, New York: Harper and Row, 1974), 77.

6. Ibid., 57. Margaret Homans's *Bearing the Word* (Chicago: University of Chicago Press, 1986) investigates Gaskell among "women writers of realistic novels, who wrote about women's experiences on the assumption that they could do so" (xiii). Extending Heilbrun's perspective, Homans finds the voice of the mother in Gaskell, but argues that "Gaskell's stories affirm the dependence of any language shared by a mother and a daughter on its containment within patriarchal power" (276). I would agree that this is the situation of the daughters but go on to argue that they often set themselves free.

7. Coral Lansbury, *Elizabeth Gaskell: The Novel of Social Change* (New York: Harper and Row, 1975).

8. Cranford, in *The Works of Mrs. Gaskell* (London: Smith, Elder and Co., 1906), 2:174. All further references to Gaskell's novels will be from this, the Knutsford edition.

9. Nina Auerbach, *Communities of Women: An Idea in Fiction* (Cambridge: Harvard University Press, 1978), 87.

10. These are, respectively, the last three words of *Rhoda Fleming* and the last sentence of the "Preface" to *The Vicar of Bullhampton.*

11. For Elizabeth Gaskell's hopes for *Ruth* and attitude to readers' responses, see *The Letters of Mrs. Gaskell*, ed. J. A. V. Chapple and Arthur Pollard (Manchester: Manchester University Press, 1966), 220–27. All further references to the letters are to this edition.

12. Two helpful studies of the fallen woman in Victorian literature are George Watt. *The Fallen Woman in the Nineteenth-Century English Novel* (New Jersey: Barnes and Noble, 1984); and Sally Mitchell, *The Fallen Angel: Chastity, Class and Women's Reading, 1835–1880* (Bowling Green: Bowling Green University Popular Press, 1981).

13. Lord Byron, *The Complete Poetical Works*, ed. Jerome McGann (Oxford: Clarendon Press, 1981), 3:16.

14. Paul Smith, *Discerning the Subject* (Minneapolis: University of Minnesota Press, 1988), 130.

15. Avrom Fleishman, *The English Historical Novel: Walter Scott to Virginia Woolf* (Baltimore: Johns Hopkins University Press, 1971), 15. Arthur Melville Clark commented years ago that Gaskell "takes her place among those novelists who have by design so treated the life of their own period as to produce fiction that was historical from the outset." "The Historical Novel," *Studies in Literary Modes* (Edinburgh and London: Oliver and Boyd, 1946), 4.

16. We see this in John Lucas's claim in a generally excellent discussion of Gaskell in *The Literature of Change*, 2nd ed. (1977; reprint, Brighton, Sussex: The Harvester Press Ltd., 1980), 2, that Gaskell's "last work, *Wives and Daughters*, has far more in common with the early *Cranford* than it has with what comes between. . . . For they are both beautiful idylls."

17. The debate, ongoing since Gaskell first published her work, distinguishes the Manchester novels from the southern, country novels, choosing either that the country novels are too sentimental and the urban novels powerfully realistic or that the urban novels are forced propaganda whereas the southern works have the pace and beauty of nature lovingly recalled. The problem with either side is that both assume a divded canon and from that infer a divided author (or, perhaps, the other way around).

18. Lucas, *The Literature of Change*, 2.

19. See Samuel Pickering, Jr.'s excellent discussion of unitarianism in *The Moral Tradition in English Fiction, 1785–1850* (New Hampshire: University Press of New England, 1976).

20. Ellen Moers, *Literary Women: The Great Writers* (1974; reprint, New York: Anchor Books, 1977), 28.

21. "Mrs. Gaskell," *The Victorian Novel: Modern Essays in Criticism*, ed. Ian Watt (New York: Oxford University Press, 1971), 221: and *Mrs. Gaskell's Observation and Invention: A Study of Her Non-Biographic Works* (Fontwell, Sussex: Linden Press, 1970), 68.

22. U. C. Knoepflmacher. "Thoughts on the Aggression of Daughters." *The Endurance of Frankenstein: Essays on Mary Shelley's Novel*, eds. Geroge Levine and U. C. Knoepflmacher (Berkeley: University of California Press, 1979), 88–122.

23. W. A. Craik, *Elizabeth Gaskell and the English Provincial Novel* (London: Methuen and Co. Ltd., 1975), 237.

24. See Jacqueline Berke and Laura Berke, "Mothers and Daughters in *Wives and Daughters*: A Study of Elizabeth Gaskell's Last Novel," *The Lost Tradition: Mothers and Daughters in Literature* (New York: Frederick Ungar Publishing Co., 1980), 95–109.

25. Ibid., 105–6.

26. Yet in the case of *Frankenstein*, Ellen Moers's reading of the novel in *Literary Women* in terms of mothers and daughters is certainly as successful as Knoepflmacher's different view.

27. Patricia Meyer Spacks, discussing novels about women's relations to a world outside themselves, comments that the "values of society provide a screen behind which women can conduct their inner lives; they may, at best, actually supply a means for expressing the dimensions of inner reality." *The Female Imagination* (1972; reprint, New York: Avon books, 1975), 352.

28. Craik, *Elizabeth Gaskell and the English Provincial Novel*, 250.

29. *Mrs. Gaskell's Observation and Invention*, 166; Aina Rubenius, *The Woman Question in Mrs. Gaskell's Life and Works* (Cambridge: Harvard University Press, 1950), 100. We might also recall Gaskell's own knowledge of Branwell Brontë.

30. In the example of Gaskell's son, the psychological explanation is implicitly sexist, as if Gaskell's novels were substitute babies, here aesthetic commitment a sort of sidetracked mothering instinct. While she may have begun to write to distract her from her grief at her son's death, her novels were not her children. She had four daughters who satisfactorily filled that role.

31. Spacks, however, questions our traditional view that Molly's marrying Roger is a happy ending, *The Female Imagination*, 118–19.

32. Lansbury, *Elizabeth Gaskell: The Novel of Social Crisis*, 211.

33. Deirdre David, *Fictions of Resolution in Three Victorian Novels* (New York: Columbia University Press, 1981), 39. See also Elaine Showalter's mention of the same point made by Lorna Sage in 1974. *A Literature of Their Own: British Novelists from Brontë to Lessing* (Princeton: Princeton University Press, 1977), 84.

34. Winifred Gerin, *Elizabeth Gaskell: A Biography* (Oxford: Clarendon Press, 1976), 140.

35. Among those who find the ending positive, see the excellent study by Andrew Sanders, *The Victorian Historical Novel* (New York: St. Martin's Press, 1979).

36. *Tess of the D'Urbervilles*, ed. Scott Elledge (New York: W. W. Norton and Co., 1979), 2nd ed., 11. All further references to *Tess* are to this edition.

37. Both Arthur Pollard and John Lucas have already noted the link between Gaskell and Hardy. See *Novelist and Biographer* and *The Literature of Change.*

38. Sanders, *The Victorian Historical Novel*, 199.

39. Ibid., 223.

40. Smith, *Discerning the Subject*, 130.

Chapter 5

1. The development of Eliot's reputation is traced in David Carroll, ed., *George Eliot: The Critical Heritage* (New York: Barnes and Noble, 1971).

2. George Eliot, *Middlemarch*, ed. Gordon S. Haight (Cambridge: Houghton Mifflin, 1956), 107. All further references to the text are to this edition.

3. Compare Zelda Austen's "Why Feminist Critics Are Angry with George Eliot," *College English* 37, 6 (1976):549–61; and Elaine Showalter's "The Greening of Sister George," *Nineteenth-Century Fiction* 35, 3 (1980):292–311.

4. See Mary Jacobus, "The Question of Language: Men of Maxims and *The Mill on the Floss*," *Critical Inquiry* 8, 2 (1981):207–22; and Nina Auerbach, "The Power of Hunger; Demonism and Maggie Tulliver," *Nineteenth-Century Fiction* 30 (1972): 150–71.

5. Some of the by now classic studies are Sandra M. Gilbert and Susan Gubar, *The Madwoman in the Attic: The Woman Writer and the Nineteenth-Century Imagination* (New Haven: Yale University Press, 1979); Ellen Moers, *Literary Women: The Great Writers* (New York: Anchor, 1977); Elaine Showalter, *A Literature of Their Own: British Women Novelists from Brontë to Lessing* (Princeton: Princeton University Press, 1977); and Patricia Meyer Spacks, *The Female Imagination* (1972); reprint, New York: Avon, 1976).

6. For a compelling discussion of the ways the fiction of Charlotte and Emily Brontë "have played an important part in British history," including literary history, see Chapters 4 and 5 of Nancy Armstrong's *Desire and Domestic Fiction: A Political History of the Novel* (New York: Oxford University Press, 1987), 191.

7. Leon Edel, *The Life of Henry James*, 5 vols. (1953–72; reprint, New York: Avon Books, 1978), 11:294.

8. Northrop Frye, *Fearful Symmetry* (1947; reprint, Boston: Beacon Press, 1962), 41.

9. For an excellent discussion of the idea of paradise in eighteenth- and nineteenth-century England, though from a perspective somewhat different from mine, see Max F. Schulz, *Paradise Preserved: Recreations of Eden in Eighteenth- and Nineteenth-Century England* (Cambridge: Cambridge University Press, 1985).

10. *The George Eliot Letters*, ed. Gordon S. Haight (New Haven: Yale University Press, 1954–78), 2:387.

11. George Eliot, *Adam Bede* (New York: Holt, Rinehart and Winston, 1965), 216, 9. All further references to the novel are to this edition.

12. *Selected Letters of Samuel Richardson*, ed. John Carroll (Oxford: Oxford University Press, 1964), 108.

13. *The Letters of John Keats*, ed. Maurice Buxton Forman (London: Oxford University Press, 1931), 2:363.

14. Eliot, *Middlemarch*, 613.

15. Among many others, see criticisms of *The Heart of Midlothian*'s structure in V. S. Pritchett, *The Living Novel* (London: Reynal and Hitchcock, 1946), and Dorothy Van Ghent, *The English Novel: Form and Function* (1953; reprint, New York: Harper and Row, 1967).

16. For a full discussion, see Frank Kermode, *The Sense of an Ending: Studies in the Theory of Fiction* (New York: Oxford University Press, 1967).

17. "The Novels of George Eliot," *A Century of George Eliot Criticism*, ed. Gordon S. Haight (Boston: Houghton Mifflin, 1965), 47.

18. The doubleness of Hetty and Dinah is interestingly discussed by Gilbert and Gubar, *The Madwoman in the Attic*, 443–99, passim.

19. For the view of how Mr. Stelling represents false culture, see Jacobus, "The Question of Language," 207–22.

20. U. C. Knoepflmacher, *George Eliot's Early Novels: The Limits of Realism* (Berkeley: University of California Press, 1968), 122.

21. Carol Christ, "Aggression and Providential Death in George Eliot's Fiction," *Novel* 9, 2 (1976):130–140.

22. Roland Barthes, *Critical Essays*, trans. Richard Howard (Evanston: Northwestern University Press, 1972), xvii.

23. Laurence Lerner, "Daniel Deronda: George Eliot's Struggle with Realism," in *Daniel Deronda: A Centenary Symposium*, ed. Alice Shalvi (Jerusalem: Jerusalem Academic Press, 1976), 92.

24. These appreciations pervade Eliot criticism. Some examples are Bernard J. Paris, *Experiments in Life: George Eliot's Quest for Values* (Detroit: Wayne State University Press, 1965), or the essays by George R. Creeger and Thomas Pinney in *George Eliot: A Collection of Critical Essays*, ed. George R. Creeger (Englewood Cliffs: Prentice-Hall, 1970).

25. I would say that attaining, and thus becoming, that earthly reward is what happens to Esther Lyons in *Felix Holt*.

26. *The Mill on the Floss*, ed. Gordon S. Haight (Boston: Houghton Mifflin Company, 1961), 394. All further references to the novel are to this edition.

27. Judith Lowden Newton, *Women, Power, and Subversion: Social Strategies in British Fiction, 1778–1860* (Athens: The University of Georgia Press, 1981), 153.

28. That angel is probably what Gilbert and Gubar call Eliot's angel of destruction. See their fascinating discussion, *The Madwoman in the Attic*, 478–535, passim.

29. Teresa de Lauretis makes this point, referring to making the subject, in *Alice Doesn't: Feminism, Semiotics, Cinema* (Bloomington: Indiana University Press, 1984), 178.

30. *Daniel Deronda*, ed. Barbara Hardy (Baltimore: Penguin Books, 1967), 879. All further references to the novel are to this edition.

Chapter 6

1. *Letters of George Gissing to Members of His Family* (London: Constable and Company, 1927), 156. See also John Lucas, "Meredith's Reputation," *Meredith Now*, ed. Ian Fletcher (London: Routledge and Kegan Paul, 1971), 205–21.

2. *The Letters of Ezra Pound, 1907–1941*, ed. D. D. Paige (New York: Harcourt Brace, 1950), 137.

3. Meredith claims, in the opening chapter of *Diana of the Crossways*, that he is writing "Philosophy in fiction." *The Works of George Meredith* (New York: Charles Scribner's Sons, 1910), 16:19. All further quotations from Meredith's novels are from the volumes of this edition.

4. Some standard studies are Walter Wright, *Art and Substance in George Meredith* (Lincoln: University of Nebraska Press, 1953); Gillian Beer, *Meredith: A Change of Masks* (London: Athlone Press, 1970); and Judith Wilt, *The Readable People of George Meredith* (Princeton: Princeton University Press, 1975).

5. See, for example, the essay "George Meredith" by C. L. Cline in *Victorian Fiction: A Guide to Research*, ed. Lionel Stevenson (Cambridge: Harvard University Press, 1964), 324–48. See particularly 337–39.

6. Arabella Shore's "an early appreciation" first appeared in April 1879 in *British Quarterly Review* and is reprinted in *Meredith: The Critical Heritage*, ed. Ioan Williams (London: Routledge and Kegan Paul, 1971), 199.

7. Though books explicitly about women in nineteenth-century British fiction, such as Jenni Calder's *Women and Marriage in Victorian Fiction* (New York: Oxford University Press, 1976) or Lloyd Fernando's *"New Women" in the Late Victorian Novel* (University Park: Pennsylvania State University Press, 1977), do include discussions of Meredith's work, single-author studies of Meredith usually do not significantly discuss the issue of women in his work. An exception is Janet Horowitz Murray's recently published 1974 doctoral dissertation, *Courtship and the English Novel: Feminist Readings in the Fiction of George Meredith* (New York: Garland Publishing, Inc., 1987).

8. Carolyn Heilbrun very briefly offers the perspective that Meredith did write feminist novels, in *Toward a Recognition of Androgyny* (1973; reprint New York: Harper and Row, 1974), 70.

9. Kate Millett, *Sexual Politics* (New York: Avon, 1971), 135–36, 139.

10. Calder, *Women and Marriage in Victorian Fiction*, 188.

11. *Jane Austen's Letters*, 2nd ed., ed. R. W. Chapman (Oxford: Oxford University Press, 1952), 298.

12. Robert Louis Stevenson, "Books Which Have Influenced Me," in "Literary Papers," *The Works of Robert Louis Stevenson*, Vailima ed. (London: William Heinemann, 1922), 4:475.

13. Donald David Stone, *The Romantic Impulse in Victorian Fiction* (Cambridge: Harvard University Press, 1980), 315–16.

14. J. Hillis Miller argues somewhat differently that in *The Egoist* narrator and novelist have peered into the idea of the heroine to question the very notion of fixed character, in "The Clarification of Clara Middleton," *The Representation of Women in Fiction*, English Institute Papers (Baltimore: John's Hopkins University Press, 1981), 110.

15. Stone comments on the tension in Meredith's work between ideal and realities, but likens it to that between Shelley/Byron and Carlyle. *The Romantic Impulse*, 296–97.

16. George Gordon, Lord Byron, *Don Juan, The Complete Poetical Works*, ed. Jerome J. McGann (Oxford: Clarendon Press, 1986) 5:133.

17. See his interesting chapter, "Meredith: A Romantic in Spite of Himself," in Stone, *The Romantic Impulse*, 284–316.

18. Of Meredith's deep, general susceptibility to Shelley's, and Byron's, influence. Lionel Stevenson quotes his comment on visiting the actual spot on the Lido where Shelley had stood with Byron: "I love both those poets; and with my heart given to them

I felt as if I stood in a dead and useless time." In *The Ordeal of George Meredith* (New York: Charles Scribner's Sons, 1953), 94.

19. Williams, ed., *Meredith: The Critical Heritage*, 199, 200.

20. Gillian Beer, *Meredith: A Change of Masks* (London: Athlone Press, 1970), 70. See her whole discussion of the novel, 70–107.

21. Of many positive readings, see Jenni Calder's discussion in *Women and Marriage in Victorian Fiction* and Norman Kelvin's in *A Troubled Eden: Nature and Society in the Works of Meredith* (Stanford: Stanford University Press, 1961).

22. Percy Lubbock's "A Final Appreciation" first appeared in *Quarterly Review* (April 1910). It is reprinted in Williams, ed., *Meredith: The Critical Heritage*, 509.

23. Williams, ed., *Meredith: The Critical Heritage*, 505.

24. Barbara Hardy, "*Lord Ormont and His Aminta* and *The Amazing Marriage*," in *Meredith Now*, ed. Ian Fletcher (London: Routledge and Kegan Paul, 1971), 311–12.

25. Joseph Kruppa, "Meredith's Late Novels: Suggestions for a Critical Approach," *Nineteenth-Century Fiction* 19 (1964–65):271.

26. For a full discussion of the reception of the later novels, see Lionel Stevenson's *The Ordeal of George Meredith*.

27. Donald David Stone, *Novelists in a Changing World* (Cambridge: Harvard University Press, 1972), 145–46.

28. Jan Gordon, "*Diana of the Crossways*: Internal History and the Brainstuff of Fiction," in Fletcher, ed., *Meredith Now*, 250–51.

29. Beer, *A Change of Masks*, 150.

30. Stone, *Novelists in a Changing World*, 158.

31. Beer, *A Change of Masks*, 140.

32. Teresa de Lauretis, "Feminist Studies/Critical Studies: Issues, Terms, and Contexts," in *Feminist Studies/Critical Studies*, ed. Teresa de Lauretis (Bloomington: Indiana University Press, 1986), 9.

33. Wright, *Art and Substance in George Meredith*, 144. But see Beer's discussion in *A Change of Masks*, 160–63.

34. Stone, *Novelists in a Changing World*, 148.

35. Ibid., 152.

36. Ioan Williams, "Introduction," *Meredith: The Critical Heritage*, 2.

37. Yet Meredith's use of images was picked up by modernist poets, and in particular by that contemptuous commentator on Meredith's talents, Ezra Pound.

Chapter 7

1. Feminist critics have not focused intensely on James, in part, of course, because he was a man. But there are some excellent studies, three recent ones being Carren Kaston, *Imagination and Desire in the Novels of Henry James* (New Brunswick: Rutgers University Press, 1984); Susanne Kappeler, *Writing and Reading in Henry James* (New York: Columbia University Press, 1980); and Elizabeth Allen, *A Woman's Place in the Novels of Henry James* (New York: St. Martin's Press, 1984).

2. Leon Edel, *The Life of Henry James*, 5 vols. (1953–72); reprint, New York: Avon Books, 1978), 2:310. All further references to this classic biography will be to the volumes in this edition.

3. John Carlos Rowe, in an interesting discussion of James's "identification with women," *The Theoretical Dimensions of Henry James* (Madison: University of Wisconsin Press, 1984), comments that "the fundamental limitation of James's feminism is its subordination to a *literary* model, which fails to suggest any effective means of social transvaluation and seeks only the consolations of art," 91.

4. *The Portrait of a Lady*, Norton Critical Edition, ed. Robert D. Bamberg (New York: W. W. Norton and Company, 1975), 10, 11. All further references to the novel are to this edition.

5. Arnold Kettle, "Henry James: *The Portrait of a Lady*," *An Introduction to the English Novel* (1953; reprinted in *The Norton Critical Edition*, New York, 1975), 671–89. This remains one of the most brilliant and unsettling essays written on *The Portrait.*

6. From "The Lesson of Balzac," quoted by Edel, *The Life*, 5:282, 283.

7. Jamesian commentators, perhaps especially James himself, have seemed particularly taken with creating an Olympian group of influences on his fiction. I wonder if we are to conclude that his greatness is somehow increased by showing that he played his literary games with an international set of the big boys.

8. The lack of recognition of Austen's formal influence on James is seen even in such a sensitive commentator as William Veeder, *Henry James—The Lessons of the Master: Popular Fiction and Personal Style in the Nineteenth Century* (Chicago: University of Chicago Press, 1975).

9. For an excellent traditional discussion of the preface, see Laurence B. Holland, "The *Portrait*'s Preface," *The Expense of Vision: Essays on the Craft of Henry James* (Princeton: Princeton University Press, 1964), 3–16.

10. Richard Chase, *The American Novel and Its Tradition* (Garden City: Doubleday and Company, 1957), 129.

11. See Oscar Cargill's discussion of the gallery of "*limited* heroines," with Emma Woodhouse as the prototype, in *The Novels of Henry James* (New York: Macmillan Company, 1961), 82.

12. Apart from James himself, F. R. Leavis probably wrote the most well-known criticism linking these heroines, in *The Great Tradition* (1948; reprint Garden City: Doubleday and Company, 1954).

13. See, for example, George Levine, "Isabel, Gwendolen, and Dorothea," *ELH* 30 (1963):244–57.

14. For a discussion of the general subject, see Janet Todd, *Women's Friendship in Literature* (New York: Columbia University Press, 1980).

15. Her fallen heroes can, as when Willoughby marries the heiress he doesn't love, in *Sense and Sensibility*.

16. Neither, of course, does Hardy.

17. As Richard Chase phrases the question, "Is James himself subtly vindictive in his attitude toward Isabel?," *The American Novel and Its Tradition*, 128.

18. See Manfred Mackenzie's discussion of the novel's ending, in *Communities of Honor and Love in Henry James* (Cambridge: Harvard University Press, 1976), 99–106.

19. Kettle, "Henry James: *The Portrait of a Lady*," 687.

20. Ibid., 689; and Tony Tanner, "The Fearful Self: Henry James's *The Portrait of a Lady*," *Critical Quarterly* 7 (Autumn 1965):219.

21. Virginia C. Fowler, *Henry James's American Girl: The Embroidery on the Canvas* (Madison: University of Wisconsin Press, 1984), 82.

22. Ibid., 82.

23. Levine, "Isabel, Gwendolen, and Dorothea," 256.

24. Leon Edel, *The Life*, 5:70.

25. Henry James, *The Ambassadors* (New York: Charles Scribner's Sons, 1909) 1:83. All further references to the novel are to the two volumes of this edition. For ties between James and Strether, see Edel's discussion of *The Ambassadors* as James's second chance, *The Life*, 5:70–78.

26. Edel, *The Life*, 5:27–28, 68–79.

27. Ibid., 2:422, 426–28.

28. Ibid., 3:90.

29. See "The Art of Fiction," *The Art of Criticism: Henry James on the Theory and the Practice of Fiction*, eds. William Veeder and Susan M. Griffin (Chicago: University of Chicago Press, 1986), 165–96.

30. Ian Watt, "The First Paragraph of *The Ambassadors*: An Explication," *Essays in Criticism*, 10 (July 1960):250–74.

31. Holland, *The Expense of Vision*, 281.

32. F. W. Dupee, *Henry James* (New York: William Sloane Associates, 1951), 246.

33. F. O. Matthiessen, *Henry James: The Major Phase* (New York: Oxford University Press, 1944), 39.

34. Robert E. Garis, "The Two Lambert Strethers: A New Reading of *The Ambassadors*," *Modern Fiction Studies* 7 (Winter 1961–62):305–16; U. C. Knoepflmacher, "'O rare for Strether!' *Anthony and Cleopatra* and *The Ambassadors*," *Nineteenth-Century Fiction* 19 (March 1965):333–44.

35. Maxwell Geismer, *Henry James and the Jacobites* (Boston: Houghton Mifflin Company, 1963), 288.

36. Arabella Shore, "an early appreciation," first appeared in April 1879 in *British Quarterly Review*, and is reprinted in *Meredith: The Critical Heritage*, ed. Ioan Williams (London: Routledge and Kegan Paul, 1971), 199.

37. Of the many major book-length studies of James's work, many of which do treat the subject of heroines and some of which do mention the subject of gender in *The Ambassadors*, only the work of Sallie Sears marks as a theme and looks with some fullness at the subject of gender as it is explicitly discussed in the novel. Her conclusions, interesting as they are, are the opposite of mine. See *The Negative Imagination: Form and Perspective in the Novels of Henry James* (Ithaca: Cornell University Press, 1968), particularly 134–46.

38. Along with such standards as James's own 1905 lecture, "The Lesson of Balzac," and the constant offhand references by such classic critics as Edel or Richard Poirier or F. O. Matthiessen, see Peter Buitenhuis, "Literary Influences: All the Breezes of the West," *The Grasping Imagination: The American Writings of Henry James* (Toronto: University of Toronto Press, 1970), 17–37.

39. Edel, *The Life*, 5:23.

40. Ibid., 5:22.

41. Among many, see Sears's *The Negative Imagination* for the argument that Woollett is a matriarchy.

42. It seems to me finally too partial a truth to claim, as does Kaston in *Imagination and Desire*, that Mrs. Newsome is "ominously maternal" (93), or, as does Sears in *The Negative Imagination*, that Woollett is a matriarchy (134).

Index